1824

THE WORLD'S FIRST FOOT-BALL CLUB

1824

THE WORLD'S FIRST FOOT-BALL CLUB

John Hope and the Edinburgh footballers:
a story of sport, education and philanthropy

John Hutchinson and Andy Mitchell

1824: The World's First Foot-Ball Club

First published 2018 by Andy Mitchell Media, Dunblane, Scotland.
Contact: *andymitchellmedia@gmail.com*
Website: *www.scottishsporthistory.com*

ISBN: 978-1986612449

John Hutchinson has been researching the social history of football for nearly 50 years, and published his first book, the pioneering *The Football Industry*, in 1982. He has had an abiding interest in John Hope's Foot-Ball Club which has developed over two decades with a series of extended research articles and has culminated in this book.

Andy Mitchell runs a sports history website and has written numerous articles and several books on football history, including *First Elevens: The Birth of International Football*. He is lucky enough to work in the game as a media officer for UEFA, and previously was head of communications at the Scottish Football Association.

Front cover: a scene from an extraordinary 360-degree panorama of *Edinburgh and the Surrounding Countryside*, published around 1841 by William Macgill and the lithographer Friedrich Schenck. This view looking south from Calton Hill depicts young men playing football, showing that the game was already an accepted part of everyday life in the city (see page 62). Cover designed by Maureen Mitchell.

Title page: the cover of John Hope's first Football Book, in which he recorded the membership records and accounts from 1824-31.

CONTENTS

INTRODUCTION

The Game

ON A bright Saturday afternoon in early December, about thirty young men chatted excitedly as they walked out onto the rough parkland next to Dalry House, a mile or so west of the city of Edinburgh. They were all in their late teens or early twenties, well-off and full of the enthusiasm of youth. Eagerly anticipating two or three hours of vigorous rough-and-tumble, most wore ducks – light canvas trousers – boots and shirts. Some had short blue jackets, in the style of the time, a few wore military-style caps.

They had made their way from their lodgings or their parents' houses in the elegant New Town, coming westwards along Maitland Street, out of the city past the Hay Market, and south to Dalry, which still had the air of a country village. There were trees and fields surrounding the old mansion house, which had hothouses growing vines and peaches. Two of the boys carried long painted poles of wood, to make what they called the hails, and one, a stocky boy of about 17 with curly hair, had a heavy, round leather ball which he had had specially made by a glover in George Street.

His name was John Hope and this was his Foot-Ball Club. The year was 1824.

The Club

This book began as the simple story of one man and his football club, but it has evolved into a wider picture of sport and society in the city of Edinburgh, the people who lived in it, their social networks and their influences on the world around them.

Football was widespread in schools and villages throughout Britain from medieval times and took on many forms before the Victorians embarked on the process of codification. There were attempts in the 1840s to write down rules at Rugby School, Eton College and Cambridge University – where a short-lived club was set up by an Old Rugbeian, Albert Pell, as early as 1839. A club was founded at Trinity College, Dublin, in 1854, while Scotland's oldest is the Academical Football Club in Edinburgh, established in 1857. When footballers got together they formed organisations and Sheffield, also founded in 1857, makes a strong claim to be the oldest existing association football club.[1]

1

Yet to find the world's very first club dedicated to football, of any code, one has to go back to 1824, when John Hope established what he simply called The Foot-Ball Club in a field just outside Edinburgh. No other contemporary football clubs are known to have existed for at least another twenty years.

Those young men might have been expected to leave football behind when they left school. By persisting with their juvenile activities and continuing to play this vigorous contact sport into adulthood, the members were ahead of their time in a global context, but we show in this book that the Foot-Ball Club fitted perfectly into the vibrant sporting culture which existed among a particular social class in Edinburgh.

The city already had a wide range of thriving clubs and societies related to physical exercise. Edinburgh sportsmen had already formed the world's first archery club, first golf club and first gymnastic club; they had written the first rules for golf, bowls and curling, and presented the first trophies for golf and bowls.

The Foot-Ball Club continued in the same pioneering spirit, and the club's members played a key role in the ongoing development of football, in all its forms, far beyond their time and place. They had an impact on the game's future progress by passing on their enthusiasm and experiences to their sons, younger brothers and relatives.

Thanks to their influence, Edinburgh can lay claim to a number of football 'world firsts': the first club (1824), first written rules (1833), first medal (1851), first inter-school match (1858) and first organised games for girls (1861). There were Edinburgh-educated men at the founding meeting of the Football Association in 1863, and the city hosted the first rugby international match in 1871, in which the Scotland team was captained by the son of a Foot-Ball Club member.

These represent a sound basis for John Hope to be celebrated today. His Foot-Ball Club, which he ran almost single-handedly until 1841, attracted an extensive membership, for whom he wrote rules of play and managed a solid financial structure. The club should be his defining legacy, yet when John Wolffe wrote Hope's entry in the *Oxford Dictionary of National Biography*, he detailed only his religious and philanthropic side and never once mentioned the word 'football'. For decades his club was forgotten, its influence ignored when histories were written on the origins of football.

There are several reasons for this. For a start, the club kept a low profile, and not a single mention of its activities has been located in the press or publications during its existence. And although several of the club's members wrote memoirs or had biographies written about them, only one of these (that of Hope himself) referred, even obliquely, to the football club they joined in their youth. Perhaps Hope and his fellow members had no wish to seek publicity, or it may reflect social attitudes which tended to disapprove of sporting activities which some considered inappropriate, or to dismiss them as trivial.

While this absence is frustrating for historians and makes an investigation of this particular club challenging, it also raises the pertinent question as to what other football activities may have taken place in early nineteenth-century Britain, similarly unreported and therefore unknown.

Reverend David Jamie, one of Hope's trustees and a fervent apologist for his religious beliefs, deemed the club barely worthy of mention when he published Hope's life story.[2] According to Jamie, Hope's only recreations as a young man are a little archery and fishing. He writes not a word on football until he brings it up when referring to Hope's lifestyle and personal habits years later, describing him as 'a devoted lover of football' who 'when over thirty years of age still acted as secretary and treasurer for a very select club of young Edinburgh lawyers'.

Yet Jamie did reveal a glimpse of Hope's enthusiasm as he then quotes from a letter he sent to a friend in Paris in the late 1830s: 'The football club resumed in October; the fun first-rate. I played for three hours on Saturday. Had business not kept me from the field this winter, I would have been in splendid wind. As it was, I am pretty swift, and am still a good hand at rolling down my opponents. Mr Esplin is very keen, and the life of the club. He brings out the men. He plays first rate. He gives a splendid ground kick – so sure. We mutually respect each other, but we are daily approaching to a keener contest. He has had more practice than I, and carries six years less than I do. He is short, and there is no upsetting him; but I hope to roll him next Saturday. The club gave occasion to some very spirited caricatures by my brother Jamie, I being, of course, the principal butt. We got new caps, very neat, improved by Esplin, like jockey caps.'[3]

That one paragraph is virtually the only impression left by John Hope of his passion for football but it says a great deal. In this brief correspondence he embodies all the essentials of a sporting club: the playing, the physical contact, the organisation, the team uniform, the rivalry, the respect for fellow members, the hope that it will all be better next week, the futile attempts to regain lost youth, the regret for not training enough and the laughter and camaraderie of a group of healthy and energetic young men united for one specific athletic purpose.

It was a sports club in every sense of the phrase: an association of people, united in a common sporting purpose – in this case football – meeting periodically, with membership rules, fees and disciplinary procedures. Its rules were 'urban' in character, i.e. based on kicking rather than carrying the ball, and therefore pointed the way to the association game which emerged later in the century.

The majority of Foot-Ball Club members had solid Edinburgh origins, and would go on to professional careers in the Scottish capital, but the club clearly welcomed members who had different backgrounds, and who had learned football at other schools and locations. It differed from other sporting groups only in that the conviviality which the members all sought was achieved mostly on the pitch rather than in drinking and dining afterwards.

Hope wrote almost nothing else about football (at least, nothing that has survived), throughout his school and college years and his early working life. This is a great pity as it would be fascinating to hear more of what inspired and motivated him, why football was such an important component in his life. Yet, paradoxically, he devoted enormous time and energy to compiling – and preserved to his death – the minutest details of the finances and membership of his 'very select club'.

This book about the Foot-Ball Club is only possible due to Hope's obsession with recording and filing away the minutiae of his life.

The Man

Through all these wider considerations, the story keeps coming back to the same man, in all his guises. John Hope was not just a footballer, but a philanthropist, social reformer, educationist, town councillor, temperance campaigner and religious zealot.

He remained interested in football long after the Foot-Ball Club had runs its course, and his legacy can be seen in the promotion of the game throughout his life. In the 1850s, he encouraged the creation of parks and playing fields in the city of Edinburgh, with specific instructions that they were to be used for football. In the 1870s he encouraged the formation of a club which was a founder member of the Edinburgh Football Association, and which in turn became part of the national structure of the game in Scotland.

In doing so, Hope's laudable motivation was always to improve the lives of the poor, as he considered football to be a useful means of encouraging a healthy lifestyle. Yet in many respects his methods and ideas sit uncomfortably against modern standards.

He was not one for half measures. He was brought up in a wealthy but unostentatious household, but whereas his father favoured 'companionable temperance',[4] Hope was resolutely teetotal. Whereas his father offered 'restrained benevolence', the son spent thousands of pounds annually on charitable causes.

John Hope in 1865. He liked this photo so much that he had it printed up as a calling card.

He was determined to be rational in his decisions in an attempt to keep all aspects of his life, and the people around him, under control. His instructions were written in practical, no-nonsense language, which he expected to be carried out to the letter. He rarely backed down in an argument. He persevered in this single-minded manner right through his life, with a relentless logic that extended even to lighting his fire using English coal, because he had found through trial and error that it gave more heat and less trouble than Scottish coal.

This autocratic attitude conspired to bring him many devoted followers but he was anathema to others, a figure of derision. Many of his family would have nothing to do with him.

His frequent correspondence in the Edinburgh papers brought forth regular and often cruel rebuttals of his extreme views. His anti-alcohol stance in the Town Council, while having numerous sympathisers, was regularly rejected by the majority of the councillors who enjoyed their entertainment at the city's expense. In 1858, a policeman kept watch on his house after students opposed to his temperance views daubed paint several times on his front door and threw clay bullets through his windows.

His strident No-Popery views are abhorrent to us today and they clearly caused deep concern and offence to Roman Catholics in Scotland then and now, yet at the time this stance was widely supported and was even the policy of the Church of Scotland.

For whole sectors of Edinburgh society, Hope was an eccentric worthy of ridicule; his use of the practical Homburg hat (instead of the more formal silk top hat) incurred great scorn, as did his curious health regime.

Hope was undoubtedly a difficult man, who preferred to set up and control his own organisations rather than join with others and risk any compromise. Fortunately for him, he had the wealth and the personal drive to allow himself the luxury of running these organisations as he wished them to be run, to the extent of funding a trust which would carry on his work after his death.

The Archive

Of all Hope's legacies, the most useful to modern historians is his unique and slightly overwhelming archive of papers and documents of all kinds. When he died in 1893, this amounted to over 200 boxes of personal papers and the sheer volume of Hope's papers reflects his meticulous attention to detail: each letter copied, sometimes more than once, then cross-referenced; every penny spent is accounted for.

The Hope archive, now residing in the National Records of Scotland in Edinburgh, is a treasure trove which opens a door into his world. It includes account books from the Abstainers' Company to the Cadets' Boots Fund; bursaries he gave to educate boys; attendance records, rule books, letters, certificates, photos, receipts. He kept lists of books he had lent to people, with the dates out and the dates back in again.[5] Who but a pedantic hoarder would keep his packing list for clothes to be taken with him on holiday? Yet there it is, a unique insight into what a conservatively-minded, respectable lawyer from Edinburgh needed on a trip away.

The football element represents just a tiny proportion of the archive, but the passing mention of the Foot-Ball Club in Jamie's book prompted their rediscovery by Dr Neil Tranter. He became the first sports historian to study Hope's club, the results of which he published in a pioneering article in 1993.[6] Then in 2007 and 2008, John Hutchinson went much deeper into the details of Hope, his club and its place in the history of football.[7]

These papers were in the traditional style of narrative history, detailing the footballing activities and Hope's connections with life in Victorian Edinburgh: the law, the church, national and local politics, the teetotal movement, workers' half holidays, public playing fields, education and philanthropy. This was sufficient material in itself to tell the story, but the digital age has introduced new ways of pursuing historical research which have opened many more doors, revealing a web of influence far wider than Jamie and his contemporaries could have realised. That has made a good story into an extraordinary story.

This book reflects the development of social and sports history over the last three decades. When Tranter was researching his first article, the boxes of uncatalogued papers, some of which had not been touched for a hundred years, were accessed through a reading room into which one could take only a pad of paper and a pencil, and every word had to be laboriously transcribed. By the time the second series of articles were written, many of the boxes had been catalogued and others discovered, and researchers were allowed to transcribe John Hope's lengthy Victorian writings straight to their laptops.

Today, the material has been rigorously catalogued and all the Foot-Ball Club records have been digitised by the National Records of Scotland.[8] Furthermore, with the huge expansion of digital source material in other fields ranging from genealogy to newspapers, related records whose very existence was unknown twenty years ago, or whose remote location made them inaccessible, can be cross-referenced.

Lytton Strachey, in his *Eminent Victorians*, noted that historical research was a little like tossing a bucket into the sea to find out what comes up. Now, through the internet, we are discovering not only new areas of sea into which we can toss our bucket, but whole new oceans. Who knows what evidence will emerge in future, but for the moment we can at last look in much closer detail at the people in this story, and tie together a lot of previously loose threads.

This book takes already familiar material about John Hope's Foot-Ball Club and adds an analysis of who the club members were, and how they interlinked through a close-knit web of interests and relationships. We show that this was not just a quirky, historically-isolated sports club for gentlemen in one particular city, but that it impacted upon Edinburgh society and beyond, and had an indelible influence on the early and long-term development of football.

Acknowledgements

The authors would like to thank a number of individuals and institutions which have helped to provide information, illustrations, guidance and suggestions. In particular we acknowledge the ground-breaking research by Dr Neil Tranter, without whom the world would possibly still be unaware of the existence of the Foot-Ball Club.

Much of our research has been done over a period of years in the National Records of Scotland, and we are grateful for permission from Drummond Miller LLP to reproduce images from the John Hope archive, held in the papers of Messrs D and JH Campbell WS. The staff at the National Records of Scotland have been unfailingly helpful and supportive, and even invited us to deliver a talk in the magnificent Dome in New Register House.

At Edinburgh University's Old College Library, staff unearthed the portrait of John Hope on our back cover, and the University Library's Centre for Research Collections provided fresh images of Archibald Flint's fascinating drawings. The National Library of Scotland's digitised maps and photographs were invaluable. Alec Hope's research into John Hope's connections with Telford was useful, as was Mary Davidson's article on her forebear Scipio Mactaggart, a club member. By a happy coincidence, Andy Mitchell's mother Ann had published a comprehensive historical account of the residents of the Moray Estate, including Moray Place and its neighbouring streets. We also welcomed encouragement, information and suggestions from Guy Oliver, Richard McBrearty, Graham Curry, David Swinfen, Tom Langton and Chris Lee.

Much of our research, however, has been conducted online in ways which were not possible just a few years ago: we gleaned a wealth of detail from the British Newspaper Archive, ScotlandsPeople, subscription genealogy sites and the large (and growing) range of digitised books and periodicals.

We must also thank our wives, Sue Hutchinson and Maureen Mitchell, for their support and tolerance over the long months and years of research and writing, and we are indebted to Maureen for her design of the front cover.

We have made every effort to check facts, dates and references, but we recognise that research sources and methods will continue to develop and further information may yet come to light. We would be delighted to hear from anyone who can provide additional insight into the club and its players. In the meantime, if there are any errors they are entirely our own.

John Hutchinson and Andy Mitchell

---

[1] Sheffield FC actually claim to be the world's *first* football club, and have incorporated the wording into the club crest, but this is demonstrably untrue.

[2] Rev David Jamie BD, *John Hope, Philanthropist and Reformer* (1900). The biography was published seven years after Hope's death, having had to wait until the legal disputes about his will were settled.

[3] Jamie, p99.

[4] According to a flattering article in the *Fife Herald*, 4 January 1855.

[5] GD 253/18/9

[6] Tranter, *The First Football Club?*

[7] Hutchinson, *Sport, Education and Philanthropy* and *Football in Edinburgh*.

[8] Hope Papers, National Records of Scotland, GD253. The Foot-Ball Club papers within GD253/183/1 to GD253/187/7 have been digitised and can be viewed on screen in the Search Room in Edinburgh; see the Appendix for a description of their contents. Most of the remaining Hope archive can be consulted in the Search Room in paper form.

Chapter 1

HERITAGE AND HOME

JOHN HOPE was born on 12 May 1807 into a wealthy family which was synonymous with the Edinburgh establishment.

The Hopes had been influential in the city since at least the 16th century, when a merchant called John Hope was listed in the Edinburgh Burgess Rolls of 1516-17. His descendants prospered, acquired land, married well and accumulated titles, and the new-born boy could trace his roots to Sir Thomas Hope of Craighall (1573-1646), who was Lord Advocate.

He was related to a long line of Scottish public figures including the Earls of Hopetoun and Marquises of Linlithgow, the Hopes of Hopetoun, the Hopes of Pinkie, the Hopes of Rankeillor and the Hopes of Craighall. Their names became part of the fabric of Edinburgh, as land which was owned or developed by the various branches of the family gave their names to numerous streets: Hope Street and Hope Terrace; Hope Park, Hope Park Terrace and Hope Park Crescent; Hopetoun Crescent and Hopetoun Street; and Rankeillor Street.

Hope's grandfather was a world-famous botanist, Dr John Hope (1725-1786), Professor of Medicine and Botany at Edinburgh University and King's Botanist in Scotland. He introduced the Linnaean System of botanical classification to Scotland and erected a monument to Carl Linnaeus, still to be seen today in the Royal Botanic Garden. As Regius Keeper of the Garden, he was the driving force behind its establishment at a site on Leith Walk, and is pictured (*left*) in one of Kay's famous Edinburgh Portraits.[1] Dr Hope began the regime of research, development and collaboration with other scientists and plant collectors

11

which made the Garden a world leader in its field and his contribution is recognised by the principal entrance to the Garden's present site in Inverleith being named after him, the John Hope Gateway.

His father James (1769-1842) ensured that the family remained at the forefront of society. He was at the High School with Sir Walter Scott and is mentioned in Lockhart's biography of Scott as one of the brightest scholars of his year. He trained as a lawyer, was apprenticed to James Walker WS of Dalry, became a Writer to the Signet[2] himself in 1799, prospered greatly and married his old boss's 19-year-old daughter Jane in 1805. That union sealed the link between the families, as James Walker had already married James's sister Marion after his first wife died (hence John Hope's maternal grandfather was also his uncle).

At the time of the Napoleonic Wars, James Hope was made Lieutenant Colonel of the 2nd Battalion, 2nd Regiment of the Royal Edinburgh Volunteers in 1803, having been commissioned with the rank of Major in 1798. John Hope recalled in later life the memory of standing at the window of their house in Queen Street watching his father ride by in uniform at the head of his men. It clearly made a strong impression on the boy, who would be active in the next wave of the Volunteer movement in the 1860s.

The wider family contributed to a sense of greatness. James Hope's brothers included John (1765-1840), a Major in the 18th Royal Irish Regiment of Foot, and Thomas Charles (1766-1844), Professor of Chemistry at the University. Neither of these uncles married, and John inherited considerable property from them when they died.

Thomas Charles – he was generally referred to by both names – was part of the family household and had a strong influence on the young boy. A respected academic who is credited with the discovery of strontium, his spectacular public lectures attracted large crowds, especially of ladies. No less a figure than Charles Darwin, whose time as student at Edinburgh in 1825-27 was otherwise pretty miserable, spoke very highly of him, commenting that the lectures he had attended 'were intolerably dull, with the exception of those on Chemistry by Hope'. In 1830, Thomas Charles inaugurated the Hope Scholarship, awarded annually to the best four students sitting the physiology and chemistry exams for the first time.[3]

It all added up to quite a formidable legacy for young John, who was the eldest of nine children. He had seven sisters and just one brother, James, eleven years younger, who for some years practised law with him, and with whom he frequently quarrelled.

John Hope was born at Dalry House, his maternal grandparents' home, a 17th century mansion on the western outskirts of Edinburgh.

Although he never lived there for any length of time, it was a place to which he would return when he selected a neighbouring field as the Foot-Ball Club's first home.

John Hope's birthplace Dalry House, as it is today

Dalry House was then firmly in the countryside, surrounded by fields. It was sold after James Walker's death in 1817, changed hands several times, and remarkably is still standing today in Orwell Place, having survived the growth of the city round about it. Now hemmed in by streets of tenements, it languished for a while as a local authority day centre before it was recently brought back to life as upmarket private housing.

From 1808, the Hope family home was 65 Queen Street, a large elegant townhouse at the western end of this main thoroughfare at the heart of Edinburgh's New Town. It doubled as his father's legal office. John Hope's life during his formative years, as the eldest son of a well-off Edinburgh legal family, one of the city's social elite, was comfortable and well connected, if probably rather plain and unostentatious.

According to his biographer's descriptions, the boy – sometimes called Johnny by his family – was stocky, curly-haired, careless about his dress, and always active, fond of walking, running, wrestling, archery and fishing. Reverend Jamie devotes only a few pages to Hope's youth, in which he refers to social events in Edinburgh, being invited to friends and relatives and houses in the country, and enjoying the cultural side of New

13

Town life. He was taken to concerts and the theatre, and expressed an interest in architecture, particularly in the great building work going on all around him as the city expanded. He attended the High School, learned languages ancient and modern, and was taught to ride. His letters to friends, cousins and particularly to his sisters and aunts, were usually of a light, social nature.

The Hope family homes in Edinburgh at 65 Queen Street (left) and 31 Moray Place

When Hope was 14, he caught a serious fever, apparently the only serious illness in his whole life, and recalled that his hair grew 'quite curly' from having been shaved as part of the cure. It was during this illness, on 6 April 1822, that his mother died, from giving birth to his sister, Frances. Although it must have been a traumatic time for him, he left no impressions of her death; indeed, he wrote very few references to his mother, just one pencilled note which mentions her weeping on the death of one of his friends earlier the same year.

Frances (known as Fanny) was the youngest of his seven sisters. The loss of their mother gave John considerable responsibility in later years to look after his sisters, three of whom, like him, never married. Although he clearly loved them, they also quarrelled and would spend a great deal of time and money in litigation against each other.

Towards the end of 1824, shortly after John left the High School to enrol at the University and at exactly the time he formed his Foot-Ball Club, the family of nine children and widowed father moved to 31 Moray

Place. Here they joined their uncle Thomas Charles who owned the property, set in a classical octagon arranged around a communal pleasure garden. This newly-built three-storey town house was deceptively large, being twice as wide at the back as its frontage, and could accommodate them all comfortably.

James Hope also moved his business to Moray Place and wrote early in 1825 of the new home's attractions: 'I have changed my quarters, driven from my former by want of room, approach of buildings, shops, etc. I am now 500 yards to the north-west of my former house, a new place formed in the fields to which we used to look with admiration, but now studded with houses. We are on the top of a bank above a ravine.'

That short distance took the family away from the congestion of the city centre, to what was then the very edge of the city's northern limit. It was an enclave of calm, high above the Dean Valley, close enough to maintain a city lifestyle but far enough to escape its ills, such as the cholera epidemic of 1832, when he observed: 'We are still in this place, free from the pestilence which surrounds us – a circumstance almost miraculous considering that it has raged for a fortnight within five miles of us.'[4]

That house would be John Hope's home for the rest of his life, and even after his death it remained in use for over a century as legal offices. It was the home of the Hope Trust until quite recently, in 2015, but now 31 Moray Place has gone full circle and is converted back to housing, like many of the neighbouring properties.

Walking round Edinburgh today, it is easy to soak up some of John Hope's environment. As well as Moray Place, all the key buildings in his life are still standing: Dalry House, Queen Street, the High School, the University Old College.

In the quadrangle of the last of these, John Hope added to the family's imprint on the city with his own permanent memorial to his prestigious forebears. In 1866, in appreciation of what his grandfather and uncle had done for Edinburgh, he paid for two fine granite fountains, intended to symbolise the flow of learning but also to provide a supply of clean water.

The architectural stability of Hope's surroundings is echoed by the careful preservation of the extensive family archives, not least his own personal papers that include the Foot-Ball Club records.

One of the granite fountains in Edinburgh University's Old College which John Hope installed in 1866 in memory of his grandfather and uncle

---

[1] Dr Hope's portrait was drawn by Kay in 1786, but not published in book form until 1837.
[2] The Society of Writers to His/Her Majesty's Signet is Scotland's oldest and largest body of solicitors. It has medieval origins, when trusted writers (lawyers) signetted (certified) documents destined for the civil courts.
[3] The Hope Scholarship caused a scandal in 1870 when the top four students were all women, from the first women undergraduates in Britain, known collectively as the Edinburgh Seven. Professor Robert Christison and other members of the University establishment refused to award the scholarship to female students, and instead it went to the highest placed male students. The outcry at this discrimination would eventually lead to women being admitted as students on equal terms, but not until 1892. The scholarship fund survived the scandal and indeed the fund has been augmented, with five Hope Prize Scholarships now awarded annually by the University of Edinburgh.
[4] Quoted in Ann Mitchell, *No More Corncraiks*, p34

Chapter 2

AN EDINBURGH EDUCATION: TALENT, PERSEVERANCE AND INDUSTRY

TOGETHER WITH most of the sons of Edinburgh society, John Hope attended the city's High School where he was taught in the same buildings as his father and his uncles before him.

Each day, he left the family home in elegant neo-classical Queen Street, one of the main thoroughfares in the ever-growing New Town which was described by a later resident, RL Stevenson, as the 'draughty parallelograms'. He crossed George Street and Princes Street and passed the ancient Nor' Loch,[1] walked over the North Bridge to the medieval Old Town with its dark wynds and closes. Then he descended from the High Street to the Cowgate where, close by the old city walls, he reached High School Wynd. Above him stood the High School of Edinburgh.

In all, it was a walk of just over a mile, but it was a journey from light to dark, from Enlightenment to Medieval Romanticism, a stark contrast developed by Stevenson in the story of *Jekyll and Hyde* and by Scott in his *Waverley* novels.

Hope's educational diet as a senior pupil included Latin and Greek, covering the Roman greats such as Ovid, Virgil, Horace and Tacitus, as well as Greek texts ranging from Aesop's *Fables* to Homer's *Iliad*. He studied Geography and French and undertook exercises in grammar, recitation, translation and verse.[2] He must have felt some pride in his efforts, as he preserved examples of Latin homework.

Hope had tutors to help him with his school studies, as well as an instructor in horse-riding. His classics tutor was Alexander Gentle,[3] son of a lawyer, who, when he left in 1823 to become a minister in Morayshire, commended Hope for his 'perseverance in study'.

Reverend Jamie makes little mention of the boy's time at the High School and in fact is quite disparaging about his mental abilities. He notes that Hope 'was not in any way distinguished above his fellows. His mind was not of the sparkling order. He was a steady, plodding worker, but did not dazzle with meteoric brilliance.'[4]

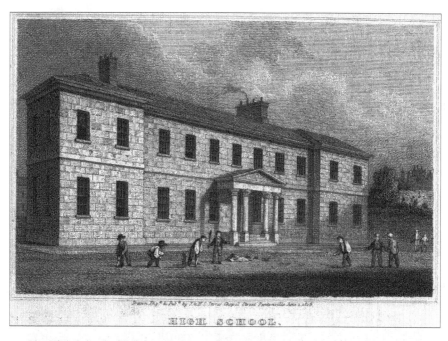

HIGH SCHOOL.

The High School of Edinburgh, then and now, barely changed in 200 years. Above, illustrated by James Storer in 1819, with boys playing cricket in the Yards. Below, how it looks today as the Edinburgh Centre far Carbon Innovation, part of Edinburgh University.

That summed up John Hope's school years, at least as far as Jamie saw it; he does not record that sport was an essential component of High School life, only commenting that 'as an athlete, he made no great show, but he rather prided himself upon his running and his wrestling.'[5]

There is no written record as to whether Hope played football at school, but the answer must surely be 'yes', and not just because he subsequently formed a club with fellow former pupils. There is plenty of evidence that football was an integral part of the High School boys' daily diet over two hundred years ago.

A brief history of the High School

The High School of Edinburgh started out in early medieval times as a religious educational establishment under the auspices of the Abbey of Holyrood. For many years, it led a peripatetic existence within the city walls, housed in various buildings, suitable and unsuitable, all between the Netherbow and the Cowgate.

After the Reformation, the school took on the Protestant faith and was transferred from the Church to the care of the Town Council. It became the city's main school and in 1578 moved to a purpose-built building in the gardens of the former Blackfriars monastery. The school had two circular towers with crow-stepped gables (another tower and spire were added later), surrounded by a large open area where the boys were encouraged to take exercise. About 1590, the school was officially designated the *Schola Regia Edinensis* (The King's School of Edinburgh) although generally referred to as the 'Tounis Scule' (town's school). It was the first in Britain to be called a High School and as its fortunes ebbed and flowed it remained a constant presence in the life of young Edinburgh men.

The boys were noted for their scholarship in Latin, Greek and English but were also known for their 'bickering' (brawling) with other boys not at the school and with students from the nearby 'Tounis College' (the town's college), properly the University of Edinburgh, founded a few hundred yards to the west in 1582.[6] This unruly behaviour came to a head in the riot of 1595 which resulted in the killing of Bailie John Macmoran, shot by a High School boy, William Sinclair, when the school was under siege. Sir Walter Scott immortalised another riotous incident involving High School boys in the Green-Breeks episode of his novel *Waverley*.[7]

As demand for education grew, the cramped buildings struggled to cope and there was clearly a need for a more spacious and fitting environment. In 1777, the Blackfriars site was replaced by a fine two-

19

storey classical building further up the hill. This was where John Hope and his male relatives studied, and two hundred years on, the school building and its surroundings have changed little: entered through pillared gates on Infirmary Street, it is now part of Edinburgh University, housing the Edinburgh Centre for Carbon Innovation.

However, although great men such as Walter Scott passed through its portals, the High School was not the educational utopia they might have relished, if one accepts the reminiscences of the judge and author, Lord Cockburn (1779-1854): 'Having never been at a public school before, and this one being notorious for its severity and riotousness, I approached its walls with trembling, and felt dizzy when I sat down amidst above 100 new faces. The general tone of the school was vulgar and harsh. Among the boys coarseness of language and manners was the only fashion... No lady could be seen within its walls. Nothing evidently civilised was safe. Two of the masters, in particular, were so savage that any master doing now what they did every hour would certainly be transported.'[8]

A typical High School boy of the period

Cockburn also described what a High School boy was likely to wear, a uniform which had changed little by John Hope's day if contemporary engravings are anything to go by. He wore a round black hat, a shirt fastened at the neck with a black ribbon, and a large waistcoat with two rows of buttons and buttonholes so that it could be swiftly changed when one side got dirty. Brown corduroy breeches were tied at the knee above long socks, and clumsy shoes with brass or copper buckles were designed to be worn on alternate feet daily.

In common with most schools in Scotland, the High School was a day school, but its reach extended far beyond Edinburgh. Pupils from elsewhere in the country and children of Scots serving in the Empire were sent to board with schoolmasters, with relatives or in lodging houses. The school's great tradition was to take boys of intellectual potential, of whatever social background, and train them for the next generation of ministers and school teachers.

However, demands for education in Scotland, and particularly in Edinburgh, were changing. There were those who believed that the tradition of producing classically-educated men for the clergy and teaching was a constraint on the growing need to produce scientifically and practically educated men for the burgeoning professions of the middle class: the doctors, businessmen and particularly lawyers. Lord Cockburn was one of many leading citizens who felt that a classical education was, for a large number of boys, 'foreseen to be useless'. In 1824, he was one of the founders of the new and privately-run Edinburgh Academy, which opened its doors with the promise of a liberal and modern curriculum. It immediately attracted a large proportion of the High School's traditional clientele, ending its effective monopoly on the education of Edinburgh's elite.

The Town Council's response was quickly forthcoming, and within a year work had begun on a school complex on Calton Hill in an attempt to meet the Academy's attractions head on. In 1829, having adopted a prefix to become the Royal High School, it decanted in its entirety to its dramatic new site. 'The High School was a great object of civic pride,' wrote RD Anderson, the great historian of Scottish education, and he quoted the words of the Solicitor General, John Hope (a distant relation), at the laying of the foundation stone: 'It was there where the proud characteristic of Britons was fully exemplified – its classes were open to boys of all ranks and circumstances. It proved what was the use of a school in a free state – it was not birth, rank, or fortune, that in this country could reach the highest place, but talent, perseverance, and industry'.[9]

That sentiment was echoed more widely in the success of Scottish schools at creating opportunity - which became apparent when the ability to write could be measured: following the introduction of civil registration in 1855, 89% of men and 77% of women in Scotland signed their marriage certificates, compared with just 70% and 59% in England and Wales.[10]

The outlooks of the liberal Edinburgh Academy and the more traditional Royal High School may have diverged in curriculum, but they had one major element in common: the recognition that energetic young boys needed space and encouragement to take part in games if they were to reach their full potential. One of the marked effects of this emphasis on physical activity was that both of these leading Edinburgh institutions supplied a steady stream of members to the Foot-Ball Club.

Curiously, in his entire history of school and university education in Scotland in the 19th century, RD Anderson never once mentions sport, let alone football. Yet the culture of activity would have an important impact on the personal development of the boys, and hence on the development of modern sport.

The High School, in fact, had developed a tradition for sports and games from medieval times.[11] As early as 1610, the school set up archery butts for its pupils, and not for defensive or military purposes. The Treasurer was instructed: *'to cause big (to be built) ane pair of Butts to the scholaris of Hie School beside the same at the tounis wall'*.[12]

The school continued to emphasise the need for a balance between learning and play. A committee of the Presbytery of Edinburgh, appointed to visit the school in 1709, noted 'that the scholars, every fortnight, be allowed to play and refresh themselves one whole afternoon'. Dr Alexander Adam, Rector for 43 years until his death in 1809, wrote in 1797 that 'play days' were Saturday in winter and Wednesday and Saturday in summer. By the early nineteenth century, the roll of up to 800 energetic boys had a spacious yard in which to play, so it is little surprise that John Hope and his classmates enjoyed sport and reaped its benefits.

This encouragement for boys to participate in sport for their moral well-being is a concept which put the High School many years ahead of other Scottish schools, reflecting the importance that play had in the daily life of the boys. The premise continued to be promoted by the school authorities after Hope moved on: an 1827 report on teaching at the High School recommended 'proper intervals being allowed for air and exercise'; and in 1846, four of the twenty-two *Regulations for Discipline at the High School* specifically referred to play and games of ball.

The alliance between a healthy mind and a healthy body was further detailed by Benjamin Mackay, a master from 1820-43 who may well have taught John Hope. Caithness-born Mackay, known for his flamboyant dress, was a major influence in the lives of generations of High School boys and their families, teaching classics in both its old and New Town locations and endowing the school with academic prizes; in 1829 the *Edinburgh Literary Journal* called him 'an enlightened wielder of the ferrule'. His thoughts on the benefits of exercise might just as well have been written with Hope in mind: in his *System of Education practised in the High School of Edinburgh*, published in 1834, he quoted words which Plato had written over two thousand years earlier: 'The best education is that which gives to the mind and to the body all the force, all the beauty, and all the perfection of which they are capable.'

He went on to explain: 'In that opinion of the great philosopher I cheerfully concur. It must be admitted that vigour of mind is intimately connected with health and strength of body. In youth particularly, much exercise is necessary for the full development of the bodily organs. For this reason, I have always been delighted to see boys take a great deal of exercise in the open air. Up to the age of sixteen, they ought not to be confined to study more than five or six hours a day, and I think they ought always to have Saturday to themselves. The boys of the High School have a fine run in their own playground, and they ought to show that they appreciate it. The more exercise young people take, the healthier and more vigorous they become. Hard protracted study in early youth cramps the mind as well as the body. Exercise cannot be neglected with impunity in manhood or old age any more than youth.

'All young people should act upon the maxim 'early to bed, early to rise'. But at whatever hour boys may be required to get up, I would have them to consider walking, running, leaping, hand-ball, foot-ball, cricket, shinty, bathing, fishing etc, as the appropriate amusements and recreations of their vacant hours; and, if they take my advice, they will, up to the age I have mentioned, devote to these exercises nearly as much of their time as to their daily lessons.'[13]

As a curious aside, Mackay was also a man of property and one of the tenements he owned, in Gabriel's Road near the present Café Royal, housed Ambrose's Tavern. This was made famous in *Noctes Ambrosianae* (Nights at Ambrose's), a series of lively and comic conversations on the events and characters of the day, published in Blackwood's *Edinburgh Magazine* from 1822-35.[14] Those tenements were sold in 1854 and demolished four years later to build New Register House – where the Foot-Ball Club records are now housed.

Football in the High School Yards and beyond

The boys played and ran about relentlessly at the site which the High School occupied from 1777 to 1829, developing a game of football with its own rules to fit the location. In the confined spaces of the High School Yards, a hard surface bounded by stone walls, theirs was an urban game, a game of the built environment. It evolved on a similar pattern to that enjoyed by boys at Charterhouse and Westminster in London, where full body tackling, or 'collaring', was likely to cause injury and damage to clothing. Right from the start of football history, players from these urban schools tended to favour the non-carrying game and hence became early advocates of association-type football.[15]

23

The essential features included a ball with an inflated bladder which was contested between two groups of any number of players, who kicked or hustled the ball towards a goal or 'hail'. Clean catching, like a present-day rugby 'mark', was allowed and was rewarded by an unimpeded kick; but passing, carrying and running with the ball were not allowed. Hacking, which became the great dividing issue in England, was never mentioned.

This culture of enthusiastic football playing at the High School has been alluded to by several former pupils. Sir Walter Scott had a lifelong limp from polio, yet he made no secret of his love of football. He organised the contest on 4 December 1815 at Carterhaugh between intense Border rivals which can be considered a turning point in the game's development, the first flickering of a new attitude that would transform football from an undignified local rabble to a codified international pastime.

FOOT BALL.

A romanticised imagining of the Carterhaugh Ba' game, published in *Popular Pastimes* in 1816

Scott wrote a song about that game, which contained the immortal line: 'And life is itself but a game at football'. His biographer (and son-in-law) John Gibson Lockhart wrote that Sir Walter 'would rather have seen his heir carry the Banner of Bellenden gallantly at a football match on Carterhaugh, than he would have heard that the boy had attained the highest honours in the first university in Europe'. That sentiment was later echoed by 'Old Brooke' in *Tom Brown's Schooldays,* who said he would sooner 'win two School-house matches running than get the Balliol scholarship any day'.

A few years on, Sir Robert Christison, an eminent Victorian doctor[16] who was at the High School from 1805-11 before going to Edinburgh University, recalled the importance of play in his schooldays: 'During my High School days I stuck to my lessons pretty well, as may appear from the places which I held in the classes. But I confess I was at least equally faithful to play. Shinty (hockey), clacken,[17] football, races, leaping, wrestling, tops, peeries (peg-tops), bools (marbles), and papes (cherry-stones), each in its season, had a fair share of my time and attention at school.' Christison looked back nostalgically to a period before the organisation and codification of games in schools: 'The games which had been handed down to us unchanged from one generation to another of High School boys, have not been spared by ruthless tooth of reform. Football was then a first-rate game, though there was neither 'hacking', nor 'mauls', nor 'touching down', to put life and limb in danger.'[18]

A poem describing football as it was played in the Yards in the 1820s is quoted by Trotter, in his history of the High School:

What sound was that which thundered in mine ear?
I heard, and boyhood rushed through every vein;
I saw the football flying to the sphere,
I hear it bounding on the yards again:
Now comes the rush, the shouting, and the strain,
The shin's disaster, and the answering wail.
Blest he who caught the ball from all the muddy train,
Led off the van, pursued its muddy trail,
And, victor, drove the bladder thundering to the Hale! [19]

A number of other comments about High School football can be added to these references. 'A Plain Man' reminisced in the *Scots Magazine* in 1824: 'In due time I escaped from such nurture and came to play ball in the College, instead of the High School Yards; yet I neglected not my studies.'[20] Another anonymous correspondent wrote in 1835: 'We all belonged to the High School indeed, and here was its play-ground. Cricket we had never heard of but there was ample room and verge enough for foot-ball.'[21]

And most curiously, in 1923 a great Scottish sportsman, rugby and cricket international Harry Stevenson[22] told his hosts at the Rugby School centenary event – to their apparent discomfort – that he had evidence that High School boys had played a carrying game of football in about 1810, long before William Webb Ellis 'picked up the ball and ran'.[23] Unfortunately he did not reveal his source, but perhaps he had inside knowledge as it turns out that Stevenson's wife Mary was youngest daughter of William Scott Kerr, who was ex-High School, one of John Hope's closest friends and a founding member of the Foot-Ball Club.

Stevenson was one of many who benefitted from the Edinburgh Academy's equally positive attitude towards sport, and specifically football. From its very beginning the Academy placed great importance on having adequate provision for playground space, and the Directors' earliest Minute Books recorded a discussion on the desirability of making provision for an unidentified game called 'Ball'.[24] To this day the front of

25

the school is a large open yard which is still played on as energetically as in 1824, the year it opened. One of the Academy's earliest pupils, James Macaulay[25] described games during his six year stay (1824-30): 'The usual boys' games were played in the grounds, called the yards, the walls of which formed the goals (i.e. 'hailes') for hockey or for football, played in primitive Scottish fashion, before Rugby or Association rules were known.'[26]

A generation later, Alexander Fergusson recalled his time in the 1840s: 'As for the Foot-ball of those days, it was a game of the most primitive kind; crude, and devoid of regulation or rule; hardly recognisable in the complicated manly Rugby game now played at the Academy. In those days the most cruel 'hacking' with iron-toed and heeled boots was allowed, and suffered, in what was called a 'muddle' – the modern maul.'[27]

That all changed in 1854, when the Academy acquired a dedicated sports ground at Raeburn Place and shortly afterwards became the first Scottish school to formalise its rules for football. By an accident of history those rules were based on Rugby School's handling code rather than Hope's preference for a non-handling game.[28] However, the Academy continued to call the sport 'football', and still does so today.

Overall, football was clearly an integral part of schoolboy life in Edinburgh in the early nineteenth century. Hope's visionary achievement was to take the game beyond the schoolyard.

Sport for students

Despite the enthusiasm of Edinburgh's schoolboys for football, there is scant evidence of adult or student football before this time, although one mid-18th century student, Henry Mackenzie (1745-1831), recalled there was a park in which to play: 'We, the lads of the College, used to play at football on the grounds now covered by buildings.'[29] This refers to Lady Nicolson's Park, which later became the site of Nicolson Square, Nicolson Street and South College Street.

It appears the game was considered a juvenile activity, to be discarded once the boys went up to study at the University, where the 'rush and shouting' was frowned upon. The authorities actively discouraged sport, not just to keep students busy studying and out of the taverns, but as a means of preventing riot and disorder amongst students and townsfolk. The young men were encouraged to move on, metaphorically and physically, to a less energetic life in adulthood.

That was certainly the case in the autumn of 1824 when 17-year-old John Hope and his contemporaries left the High School to enrol at the

'Tounis College'. Scottish universities were staunchly academic and Hope was expected to work hard and study – no more, no less. He duly took courses in a variety of subjects for two full sessions, but as was common at the time, did not graduate (nor did his contemporary at Edinburgh, Charles Darwin) and left in 1826. Jamie notes that Hope distinguished himself by winning a prize in the Logic class but says little else about the time he spent there. Having been freed from the strictures of university study, Hope travelled widely, staying with friends in various parts of England (London, Bath, Manchester and Liverpool) and making his first visits to France and Switzerland.

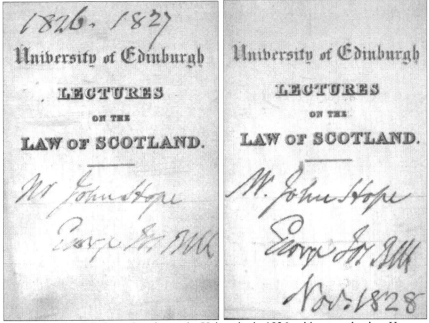

After leaving full-time education at the University in 1826, without graduating, Hope continued to attend Law lectures to prepare for the entrance examination to the Society of Writers to the Signet.

At home, he settled down 'to regular and hard reading of law' in the practice of his father, rising at six for his studies under the guidance of a legal tutor, John Bayne, who reported favourably to his father: 'I receive both much profit and pleasure from the enquiring disposition of Mr John Hope'. Indeed, Bayne seems to have taken quite a shine to Hope, writing that 'without flattery I have met with no pupil yet who enters so much 'con amore' into the study as you did.'[30]

The hard work paid off and in November 1829 'Mr Hope passed his legal examination and was admitted to the Society of Writers to the Signet'[31] whereupon his sycophantic biographer Jamie moved on to record page after page of details of Hope's views, correspondence and actions on matters religious, political and teetotal.

It would have been perfectly normal at that time for the young man to have given up playing football. For example, Sir Robert Christison, mentioned earlier, described in great detail in his autobiography the minutiae of his classes at the University of Edinburgh, his professors, his fellow students and the societies he attended, but made no mention at all of student football, the game in which he had been so active when at the High School just a year or so earlier.

That omission was echoed later by Hely Hutchinson Almond, the famous Headmaster of Loretto who became so important a figure in the development of Scottish rugby football in the latter half of the nineteenth century. He had 'enjoyed very much' a form of football at Glasgow Collegiate School: 'It was not a bad game we had there; the great beauty of it was that there were no rules.'[32] Yet he wrote sadly of the dearth of active recreation in his student days at the University of Glasgow in the late 1840s: 'A few enthusiasts took to rowing on the Clyde. One of them was capsized and, as if an immersion in that mixture of fluids was not punishment enough, the poor fellow was pilloried in a Glasgow paper for amusing himself when he ought to have been at his studies. I went from Glasgow a pale-faced student, having nothing to do with my afternoons but roam aimlessly about streets and roads.'[33]

Clearly there was no organised opportunity or encouragement for Scottish students in the opening decades of the nineteenth century to continue playing their high octane, rowdy school football. There were a few reports of kickabouts in and around Edinburgh's Nicolson Square but, in general, the wider trend in the city in the early 1820s was towards rational, non-contact sports such as golf and curling, and those were mostly for older men.

Yet, in spite of all this negativity, Hope persuaded his erstwhile schoolfriends that it would be fun to keep on playing the game they enjoyed so much. Under his leadership, the young students formed the world's first club dedicated to football and it not only survived, it thrived. By tapping into a latent demand for vigorous sporting activity, John Hope broke the mould.

---

[1] The Nor' Loch was being drained at the time and would later become the site of the railway line to Waverley.

[2] According to the *Course of Study in the Rector's Class*, GD 118/11/5

[3] Rev Alexander Gentle (1798-1969) became Minister in Alves, Morayshire.

[4] Jamie, p7

[5] Jamie, p8

[6] The University of Edinburgh is the youngest of the four ancient universities of Scotland, founded at a time when England, a far larger and richer country, had only two. Unlike St Andrews, Glasgow and Aberdeen, all of which were founded before the Reformation, Edinburgh did not have a religious origin, and from its beginnings was purely secular as the Town's College, under the aegis of the Town Council.

[7] Sir Walter Scott, *Waverley*, Appendix III (1814)

[8] Henry Cockburn, *Memorials of His Time* (1856), p11-18.

[9] *RD Anderson, Education and Opportunity in Victorian Scotland. Schools and Universities* (1983), p20. The ceremony took place on 29 July 1825.

[10] Anderson, p8

[11] The High School was not the only one. In the 17th century, Aberdeen Grammar School master David Wedderburn attempted to capitalise on his pupils' love of football by using football language and illustrations to get their attention in his Latin grammar, *Vocabula* published in 1636.

[12] Ross, *The Royal High School* (1934), p64

[13] Quoted in Steven (1849), appendix X, p197-8

[14] The dialogues were written largely by Professor John Wilson ('Christopher North') with notable contributions by James Hogg the Ettrick Shepherd, John Gibson Lockhart (Walter Scott's son-in-law and biographer) and William Maginn, a Dublin journalist.

[15] See Montague Shearman, *Athletics and Football* (1887) for more on this.

[16] See footnote in Chapter One on the Hope Scholarship.

[17] A clacken was a light wooden single-handed bat, with small, round flat head, used for hitting a ball in the playground game of hailes.

[18] Christison, *The Life of Sir Robert Christison, Bart.* (1885), p32

[19] Trotter, *The Royal High School,* p121.

[20] *Scots Magazine*, 1 September 1824; also the *Edinburgh Magazine and Literary Miscellany*, September 1824. Vol 94, p336

[21] 'Anglimania' in *Blackwood's Edinburgh Magazine*, August 1835 – later used in *The Recreations of Christopher North*, Vol 2, p403, (1842). NB 'ample room and verge enough' was a phrase used in relation to the construction of the new High School on Calton Hill. It originally came from a poem by Thomas Gray, *The Bard, a Pindaric Ode* (1757).

[22] Henry James Stevenson (1867-1945) was educated at Edinburgh Academy and was capped 15 times at rugby for Scotland from 1888 to 1893.

[23] Letter to *The Scotsman*, 26 November 1937.

[24] *The Edinburgh Academical FC Centenary History*, p9.

[25] Dr James Macaulay (1817-1902) attended the Academy from 1824 to 1830. He was a surgeon in Edinburgh until 1850 when he abandoned medicine for the literary world. He was editor in chief of the Religious Tract Society's publications including *Leisure Hour* and *Sunday at Home*, and was later the founder of the *Boy's Own Paper* and *Girl's Own Paper*.

[26] *The Edinburgh Academical FC Centenary History*, p10.

[27] Alexander Fergusson, *Chronicles of the Cumming Club* (1887), p53.

[28] In 1854 Francis Crombie, who had spent two years at Durham School, returned to Edinburgh and brought with him the rules of Rugby football, which were eagerly taken up his fellow pupils at the Academy.

[29] *Anecdotes and Egotisms of Henry Mackenzie* (1927), p40; quoted in *Book of the Old Edinburgh Club*, Vol 22, 1938, p82.

[30] Jamie, p18

[31] Jamie, p15

[32] HH Almond, *Rugby Football in Scottish Schools*, in Rev F Marshall, *Football the Rugby Union Game* (1892), p51.

[33] RJ Mackenzie, *Almond of Loretto* (1905), p13.

Chapter 3

THE EVOLUTION OF SPORT IN EDINBURGH

WHILE THE establishment of a football club was something entirely new in 1824, John Hope was following in a fine tradition of sporting innovation in Edinburgh.

The evolution of sport in the city, and in particular of ball games, has a lengthy historical background. In this chapter, we examine this history in some detail, albeit our knowledge of the ebbs and flows of sporting activity depends largely on the serendipity of what records were written down at the time, what survived and what we have rediscovered.

What is clear is that, from medieval times onwards, taking part in sport was a normal part of everyday life for Edinburgh's middle and upper classes. The capital offered a wide range of sporting opportunities for vigorous young gentlemen (some were also available to women) who could afford the time and the money. To preserve their social exclusivity they formed clubs, and the city gave birth to the world's first archery club (1676), first golf club (1735) and first gymnastic club (1785); later it saw the first national association of clubs, for curling (1838).

Where there are clubs, there are rules to permit competitions, cups and trophies. Again, Edinburgh sportsmen wrote the world's first known rules for golf (1744), bowls (1769) and curling (1811); they competed for the first trophies in golf (also 1744) and bowls (1771).

The template of sports club membership was therefore well established in early 19th century Edinburgh when the old 'healthful recreations' evolved into 'athletic sports', in the sense of competitive activity involving physical exertion. Into this exciting environment the Foot-Ball Club was born, a product of its time, and joined a long list of socially exclusive clubs, competing for members with sports old and new.

Sport from medieval times

Over the centuries, Edinburgh's city fathers and the university authorities had a fluctuating attitude towards games, ranging from positive encouragement to downright disapproval.

Some sports enjoyed royal patronage in the medieval period. The Lord High Treasurer recorded several lost wagers by King James IV on tennis matches, while the reign of James VI, before he left for London in 1603 (taking his golf clubs with him), appears to have been a period when sports flourished in the city. The royal court led the way, with the king playing golf and likewise encouraged his elder son, Prince Henry, a father-to-son theme which recurs throughout the examination of sport in Edinburgh.

Students benefitted from this approval and in the 16th century, after the Reformation, lawful games for bodily exercise were actually promoted by the university, the Town Council and the General Assembly of the Church of Scotland – always provided they did not give an excuse to students to miss lectures, nor lead to drinking, gambling or disorder in the streets.[1] That is probably why there was no tradition of folk football in the tightly enclosed spaces of Edinburgh's medieval streets and closes, where damage to property and disruption to daily life would have been inevitable.

Apprentices occasionally used a ball as an excuse for a riot and one particular tradition involved kicking a flaming ball around the Grassmarket,[2] but the traditional Scottish ba' games of Old Handsel Monday (January), Candlemas (February) and Fastern's E'en (Shrove Tuesday) were largely restricted to the smaller towns and villages of the Borders, the Lothians and up to Stirlingshire and Perthshire. It was a curious distribution, sometimes linked to the areas of the Roman occupation of the country, where *harpastum* had been played by the occupying soldiers, the theory being that the vestiges of this ancient ball game lived on in rural areas, modified by local legend and tradition.

In 1591, the university was allotted its own playing field on the Burgh Muir and there were official 'play days' when the students were taken to the field by one of the regents (lecturers) for supervised games. This 'College Pitch' was on Gallowgreen, the area now occupied by the buildings of Preston Street Primary School.[3] In the same decade, the Town Council built a *caitchpule* court (for handball, rackets or real tennis) near the university, paying a workman '*half-a-crown for half ane day to the college in helping up the catchpul*',[4] and established archery butts '*for the colleginers recreation*' on land to the south of the university already used by the students for recreation.[5]

During the years of unrest in the Civil Wars of the 17th century, sport sank into the shadows. When attitudes relaxed again after the Restoration of the monarchy in 1660, sport emerged from the negativity of the Kirk and the civic authorities: golfers started to knock balls around Bruntsfield and Leith Links, horse racing began again on Leith Shore, Musselburgh and elsewhere, and bowling greens were laid out in the city by landowners on their estates. Archery was strengthened by the founding in Edinburgh of the Royal Company of Archers in 1676, the nation's first sporting society, and was given a competitive edge by the Silver Arrow competitions sponsored by burgh authorities.

Edinburgh Town Council felt it necessary in 1695 to limit the time that students were allowed to play games,[6] and we know that they were active in sports thanks to a remarkable set of drawings by Archibald Flint, who graduated with an MA in 1673.

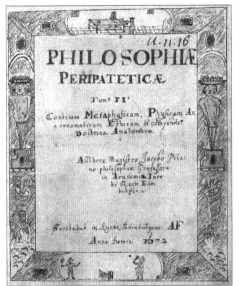
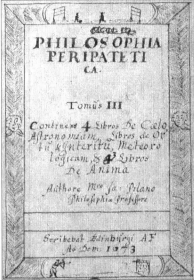

The remarkable sporting doodles in the margins of his student lecture notes, made by Alexander Flint in the 1670s, include the oldest known illustration of football in Scotland (Centre for Research Collections, Edinburgh University Library)

Adorning the margins of Flint's dictates (lecture notes) are small pen sketches of men – presumably students – playing billiards, tennis, football and archery; he also drew a caricature of his regent, probably James Pillans, looking slightly over-dressed for a university lecturer. These sketches, surviving in the University Library, include probably the oldest illustration of football in Scotland yet discovered.

Two men in hats are kicking a ball about the size of a present-day football between a curious set of three-barred goal posts. Finlayson speculates that this may be associated with some kind of scoring differential depending on which bit of the goal the ball crosses; alternatively, he says they might relate to the location, Gallowgreen, reflecting the shape of the gallows themselves. He raises the question of whether the old Scots term 'hail' developed into the word 'goal' as a corruption of 'gallow'.[7]

These are fanciful ideas awaiting positive proof, but the illustration of the Burgh Muir gibbet on the Timothy Pont map of the city, engraved around 1610, looks remarkably similar.[8] Finlayson also notes that the Latin translation of one of James VI's works calls football *'pila Scotica quae pede propellitur'* (a Scottish ball which is propelled by the foot).[9]

Around the same time, there is a lovely account in the National Records of Scotland of the money spent by Alexander Heriot, who was perhaps a factor for the Gilmour household, on behalf of Alexander Gilmour of Craigmillar (just south of Edinburgh), reflecting what the young man about town needed in 1671-3: *'A great comb to his periwig, half a dozen golf balls, a football at fastern's even'*.[10]

Golf was clearly considered a suitable game for a student of that era, as Thomas Kincaid, an Edinburgh surgeon's son, reveals in his diary for 1687-88, when he was about 26 years old, that he played on Bruntsfield Links, 'near the Tounis College', and on Leith Links.[11] Kincaid goes on to describe *'the only way of playing at the Golve'*, giving instruction on how to adopt the correct stance and hit the ball, while elsewhere in his diary he outlined how golf clubs were made.

Kincaid studied medicine and Dutch at the university but was not admitted to the Incorporation of Surgeons of Edinburgh by examination; it was only when he presented his father's extensive library of medical books to the surgeons that he achieved membership. He also developed a talent for archery and went on to be an active member of the Royal Company of Archers, becoming just the third winner of the Edinburgh Arrow in 1711.

Sport was again considered an essential part of a young gentleman's life, drawing on the Renaissance ideals which had been briefly resurrected by James VI. As James Somerville (1632-90), a minor laird wrote: *'The having of bowlling-greenes, buttes for archerie, tines-courts, and bulliart tables, in and about noblemen and gentlemen's houses, is better farre ffor manly exercize, then to pass the tyme in drinking, smocking tobacco, ffingering of cards and tables.'*[12]

Bowling greens, archery butts, tennis courts and billiard tables became an accepted part of the landscape for Edinburgh gentlemen, but the enthusiasm of the university authorities for some of these sports appears to have waned in the 18th century. There is little evidence for specific student recreational activities of any kind at this time.

Symptomatic of this was the decline in tennis, formerly a popular student recreation. The medieval tennis court next to Holyroodhouse fell into disuse and was sold by public roup in 1750, suffering the ignominy of being converted into a cloth factory before being destroyed by fire in 1775. Racket sports of some kind appear to have struggled on in the city, as John Hallion's Tennis or Fives Court was advertised in the early 1800s adjacent to his tavern in Rose Street, although the only contemporary reports of matches taking place there are for cock fights.[13]

Cock fighting, by then, was a fading survivor of the old, sometimes brutal, sports of the Middle Ages. It is a reflection of the changes in society in general that the Puritans, the Sabbatarianists, the Rationalists and a whole host of others conspired together to kill them off.

Sport enters the modern era

In the Age of Enlightenment, some of the older sports of a more peaceful and rational nature did continue to prosper and develop. There were also new sports in Edinburgh in a time of innovation, and we make no apology for pointing out that several of these sporting initiatives are considered 'world firsts', including the formation of clubs, the creation of competitions and prizes, and the publication of rules.

The most ancient sport was archery which had evolved from military use to a competitive gentlemanly recreation, encouraged through the contests organized by the Royal Company of Archers. Founded in 1676, this encompassed a particularly elite and exclusive group of citizens, one of great relevance to John Hope. He and his family were Archers and one of his ancestors, Thomas Hope, had given the land of Hope Park to the Company to build Archers' Hall.[14] The Hopes dominated the prestigious Edinburgh Silver Arrow competition in the early years of the 19th century: his father James and his uncle Thomas Charles between them won it no less than eight times between 1800 and 1812.[15] Among their kinsmen Charles Hope, an advocate, won it in 1789 while John, 4th Earl of Hopetoun, was Captain General from 1819 to 1823.[16]

Following in the family tradition, in the summer of 1825 John Hope hired Dalry Park to practise his archery – the same field where he had launched the Foot-Ball Club a few months earlier – and was duly accepted as a member of the Royal Company of Archers in 1827. He was fortunate, as opportunities for students to take up archery were few and far between.

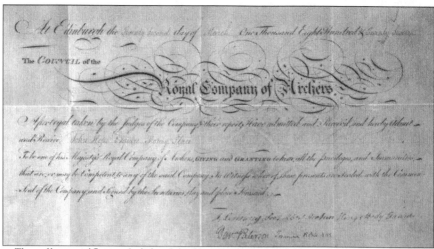

The vellum certificate admitting John Hope to the Royal Company of Archers in 1827

The archers had strong links to golf, the most prominent of the 'peaceful' sports. In the 18th century the earliest clubs and competitions emerged in the city, and golf soon developed into a popular recreation for gentlemen, whose desire for membership, competition and exclusivity became apparent as the game's rules and rituals developed. Golfhall, the first clubhouse, was built in 1717 at Bruntsfield Links, where the first club, the Edinburgh (later Royal) Burgess Golfing Society, was founded in 1735. Their games were given added spice in 1744 when the Edinburgh Silver Club was made on the instructions of the Town Council.

The setting up of this, the world's first golf competition, prompted the founding of the Company of Gentlemen Golfers (later the Honourable Company of Edinburgh Golfers) who printed the first rules in 1744, which became the blueprint for golf clubs all over Scotland and beyond. As numbers of players grew, two more city clubs followed before the end of the century, Bruntsfield Links in 1761 and Royal Musselburgh in 1774. Edinburgh is therefore home to four of the world's six oldest golf clubs.[17]

Then, as now, golfers took their sport very seriously and in 1768 a number of them each subscribed £30 – a massive sum beyond the reach of most citizens – to build a clubhouse on the south-west corner of Leith Links.[18] Leith Links, like Bruntsfield, was annotated as 'a Common for Playing at the Golf' in John Ainslie's city map of 1804, which identified the Golf House and its attached bowling green.

This enterprise and the associated competitions emphasised golf's status as socially exclusive, which was reflected in the *Sporting Magazine* of 1795 describing the members of The Honourable Company as 'lawyers, tradesmen and gentlemen'.[19] The Burgess Society at this time was also mostly made up of professional men, but as befitting a club with links to the traditional Edinburgh guilds, it had also a number of city tradesmen, including shoemakers, dyers, slaters and even a soap boiler.[20]

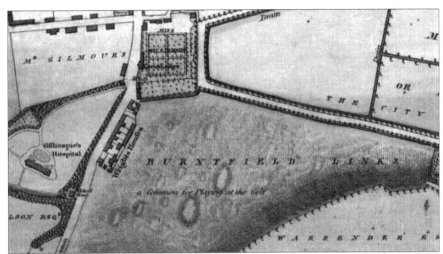

Ainslie's 1804 map clearly marks Bruntsfield Links (above, spelled as Burntfield) and Leith Links as areas for sport, with golf and bowling to the fore (National Library of Scotland)

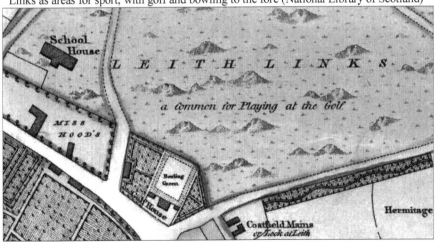

There are few records of students playing the game in this period, and playing numbers generally declined during the French Revolutionary and Napoleonic Wars. Then, in the early 19th century, golf resumed its inexorable rise to universal popularity. In fact, it became so well embedded in the establishment that in 1817 the *Scots Magazine* reported on civic works being carried out in Edinburgh to give work to unemployed men, one of the projects being to level and enlarge the golf grounds at Bruntsfield. Nobody complained at public money being spent on such a scheme.

Bowling also expanded from its medieval origins in the 18th century, encouraged, organised and enjoyed by much the same sort of demographic as golf. Contemporary maps of Edinburgh provide some interesting evidence, notably Edgar's map of 1742 which shows at least five bowling greens in the city, four of them near the university,[21] in addition to private bowling greens in gentlemen's country houses in the suburbs.

In 1768, the Edinburgh Society of Bowlers, the world's first bowling club, acquired the lease of a green near Heriot's Hospital. The following year, in order to get a Seal of Cause from the city magistrates (to establish their status as an organization similar to a guild), they were obliged to write down their rules.[22] These were the first laws of bowling in the world and similarly their trophy the Edinburgh Silver Jack, which dates from 1771, is the oldest bowling trophy; it was given by William Tod, a merchant, and the winner each year would attach a silver medal. The trophy is now in the National Museum of Scotland.

A little later, bowling was emulated by quoiting. The Edinburgh Bruntsfield Quoiting Club played annually for a silver quoit from 1823 when it was won by John Black Gracie WS, and in 1827 the Six Feet High Club (see below) followed suit. Generally, however, bowling and quoiting were tavern recreations and kept a low profile, so there are few reports of matches, which are almost entirely intra-club.

The other great summer pastime, cricket, was a later arrival on the scene and did not become established as a club game in Scotland until the 1820s. Nonetheless, it was clearly played by English troops garrisoned in Scotland after Culloden, as around 1750 the 'scarlet vermin of hell' were rebuked for playing cricket in Perth on the Sabbath.[23] The first recorded cricket match in Scotland was in 1785 in the unlikely setting of Alloa.[24]

When Lord Palmerston, an Old Harrovian and the future Prime Minister, came to Edinburgh University in 1800 he could not find enough people to 'muster up' to play cricket and turned reluctantly to golf, which he considered 'a poor game compared to cricket, but better than nothing.'[25]

However, if he had waited just a few more years he might have found solace: the *Caledonian Mercury* reported a match in 1806 between 'the gentlemen who play cricket on the Calton Hill' and the Edinburgh University club, which the latter won comfortably in front of 'a number of amateurs and spectators' at Leith Links. The players then withdrew to the Golf House for an elegant dinner which broke up at a 'late hour'.[26] In

1814, at an unspecified location in Edinburgh, eleven young gentlemen of the Thistle Club played against 'an equal number of gentlemen attached to the Herculean and Caledonian Clubs, assisted by professed players from the public seminaries in England'. Despite the cricketing experience of the English, the two-innings match was won easily by Thistle by 11 wickets.[27]

Club cricket clearly took place, but press reports are few and far between until the resurgence in cricket from the late 1820s, when the first recorded clubs were formed in Edinburgh and Leith. Cricket suffered initially from a lack of suitable fields on which to play as the golfers had got there first, as was made amply clear in the report of an 1828 match on Bruntsfield Links between the Aurora Club and the officers of the (English) 4th Regiment. The writer glibly suggested that 'probably the best plan would be for the gentlemen of the golfing clubs to leave the union hole out of their round while the cricket tent is pitched, by playing straight from the mid hole to the muir hole.'[28] This sacrilege drew a furious response from 'A Keen Golfer' in defence of the 'ancient and national game of golf'. He claimed that golfers had privileges and rights on Bruntsfield Links which are 'specially mentioned in the original grant of the Boroughmuir to the inhabitants of Edinburgh, and which have on many other occasions been since confirmed and recognised'. In effect, he said, the cricketers can go and play someplace else.[29]

Undaunted, cricket found a niche. In July 1831 Brunswick (founded in 1830) hosted Western, the first Glaswegian team to visit the capital, on a field in Newington. Then in 1832 Grange was founded, with some Foot-Ball Club members among its players, and their great gift to sport was the creation four years later of Grove Park,[30] the city's first dedicated enclosed sports ground, which later hosted the Foot-Ball Club.

There was also a thriving sporting culture in winter, when gentlemen adapted to the environment and established a whole new playground on the city's frozen ponds. The Skating Club at Duddingston Loch was active from the late 17th century, and the first curling clubs were constituted in the same era, by the same sort of people as the summer activities of golf and bowling. Duddingston Curling Society was formed in 1795 in the midst of a mini ice age, and, because the men who curled at Duddingston liked law and order, the first set of rules for the sport were printed in 1811. This was a couple of years after the foundation of the Edinburgh Curling Club, then Merchiston was next in 1818 (their membership in 1825 included some of the Foot-Ball Club players) and Lochend soon followed.

Curling was dependent on severe weather until the invention of artificial rinks in 1827, which gradually replaced the ponds and small lochs, many of which were drained for agricultural improvements. The final tier of the sport's organization was achieved in 1838 when the Grand Caledonian Curling Club (from 1842 the Royal) was founded in Edinburgh, the first national association of clubs, and the blueprint for sporting associations around the world.

Gentlemen who wanted to enjoy horseback activity could aspire to join the highly aristocratic Royal Caledonian Hunt Club, founded in 1777, which patronized several major Scottish race meetings, which the members combined with a week of wining, dining and dancing. Several of John Hope's relatives were active in the club, although he himself did not join.

For the masses in the city, their participation in sport was essentially limited to spectating at occasional holiday events or taking part in activities in the taverns. The Caledonian Hunt's meetings attracted large number of spectators from this end of society, and the holiday races on the sands at Leith were renowned for their associations with drinking, gambling and disreputable elements. The sands were hard going for horses and a proposal was mooted to create a grass course on the Meadows and part of Bruntsfield. The golfers were strong enough to resist this expansion of horse racing into the city[31] and instead, a new racecourse opened at Musselburgh in 1809. The Edinburgh Races transferred there in 1816, in conjunction with the annual fair, neatly removing the drinkers and gamblers from the city precincts.

Another popular sport which drew a number of middle class 'fancy' looking for excitement and gambling was boxing. A prominent Edinburgh pugilist named George Cooper was based at the Britannia Tavern in Leith and in 1821 he lost a high-profile bout to Thomas Hickman of London, known as 'the Gas Light Man'.[32] The Britannia Tavern remained a sporting house until Cooper, one of Scotland's earliest sporting professionals, departed to seek his fortune down south in 1824.

Attempts to play football or other sports in public places were actively discouraged, as the Edinburgh Police Regulations of 1814 made clear: 'No snow balls or squibs shall be thrown, nor foot-ball, shinty, or other game shall be played on any of the streets, squares, lanes or passages, under the like penalty, as aforesaid.'[33] That 'like penalty as aforesaid' was up to twenty shillings, not to be taken lightly. There are no records of any prosecutions for playing football in Edinburgh, so the regulations helped to ensure that sport remained largely for the privileged few.

Sport becomes vigorous

All the above pastimes were popular, but they did not necessarily involve a great deal of exertion, at least not from the gentlemen participants.

40

Vigorous exercise appears to have been rare in Edinburgh up to this point, although there had been occasional pedestrianism and foot races held on Musselburgh Links, generally as individual challenges for a bet.

That changed in the 1820s, a decade when the concept of taking vigorous exercise for pleasure and self-improvement started to take a firm hold, as *The Scotsman* noted in June 1823 with its comment that 'gymnastic exercises seem to be growing into credit here', in a report of a foot race in Holyrood Park. Coinciding with the early stages of the Foot-Ball Club, the movement towards rational sports for fresh air and exercise took off and a number of organisations began catering for athletic sport.

The Gymnastic Club trophy of 1775, in the National Museum of Scotland

There had been sporadic attempts before then, notably in the 1770s when three Edinburgh doctors, Andrew Duncan,[34] William Inglis[35] and 'Lang Sandy' Wood[36] founded a Gymnastic Club. Although little is known of its activities, its silver trophy, with 11 attached medals, has survived and is in the National Museum of Scotland. The Gymnastic Club was a drinking and dining club for doctors, one of many such for the amusement of the wealthier men of the city, but it also worked on the principle that exercise and conviviality were good for the body, the mind and perhaps even the soul. The members played sport and wagered, sang songs and were sociable, appreciating the beneficial effect of healthy exercise and the thrill of competing for medals and cups, but only as part of a social life which they all enjoyed.[37] The Gymnastic Club declined as its prominent members grew too old for gymnastics, or simply died, but their club was well ahead of its time – the London Gymnastic Society was not founded until 1826 – and its core philosophy lived on.

One of the earliest indications of the sporting revival can be found in the curriculum of a Military Academy established in Edinburgh in 1823 by Captain George Scott, a Waterloo veteran. Preparing boys for entry to the Army, Navy and East India Company, Scott offered instruction in 'fencing, single stick and other gymnastic exercises', which were described in his prospectus as 'agreeable, useful and healthy recreations to young gentlemen of any profession, as they may most materially tend to develop and increase the physical powers, improve the carriage, and create manly confidence'. The *Scots Magazine* praised Scott for his approach to physical well-being: 'The object proposed by Mr Scott is to introduce a system of bodily exercise which, while it affords considerable amusement and total relaxation of the mental faculties, brings into full and healthy action all the muscles of the body. It is astonishing that the benefits of physical education should have been so entirely overlooked or neglected in this country. We would have boys well planted on their legs, their chests thrown forward, and their muscular powers called into almost constant exercise by fencing, running, wrestling, climbing and other tasks recommended by approved writers. Four-fifths of our young men are educated as if they were never to pass beyond the precincts of the library or the drawing room.'[38]

The young men who learned these athletic skills carried them into adulthood and although George Scott died within two years[39], his ideas had taken root; the week after his death a public meeting was held to set up a new Scottish Military and Naval Academy in Edinburgh, which continued to emphasise physical fitness.

Other city schools took a similar line. The High School already had its long-established yards where John Hope and his classmates played football, the directors planning the new Edinburgh Academy were at pains to ensure it had space for the boys to play, and Heriot's Hospital enthusiastically adopted gymnastic exercises.

There is evidence that the military were also adopting more vigorous activities. When the 92nd Regiment, later the Gordon Highlanders, was garrisoned at the Castle in 1828, the *Edinburgh Evening Courant* reported on their 'Military Gymnastics': 'For three Saturdays past the public have been highly amused by the 92d regiment practising athletic exercises. They have been marched to Bruntsfield Links without arms or accoutrements, in their drill dress. A large oblong square being formed, leaping, running, football, not forgetting the dance, then took place, free from all interruption, to the gratification of the spectators. The young officers mix in these healthy exercises and, under proper caution, it will no doubt tend to gain the esteem of the men. Besides the above games, they have races blindfold and in sacks, which afford infinite diversion. We understand these amusements will continue weekly.'[40]

Among the wider adult population, as athletic sports started to become fashionable, the movement was led by the Highland Club, which had been founded in Edinburgh in 1820 to promote the interests of the north of the country. It held its first sports meeting at Leith Links in January 1826, their trials of strength, foot races and a game of shinty attracting an enormous crowd of up to 20,000 spectators, which caused great confusion. The following year, having learned from the experience, their sports were moved to a private field beside Bruntsfield Links, admission by ticket only for 'respectable individuals'. Also in 1826, the Breadalbane Oak Club, for Perthshire residents in Edinburgh, held the first of their annual games of shinty in the city.

These initiatives were closely followed by the Six Feet High Club (with a rather obvious height restriction for members), established in 1826 by David Birrell 'for the express encouragement, practice, and promotion of all national and manly games'.[41] The idea had begun with Birrell, club captain, wanting to provide a squad of fine, upstanding men, all as tall as he was, to act as the sovereign's bodyguard in Scotland. He had attended George IV's visit to Scotland in 1822, and, together with Sir Walter Scott, that great champion of sport and pageantry, saw the benefits of a group of men who were fit, active and athletically competitive.

This thinking man's fitness club contained, like the Gymnastic Club before it, a lively mixture of Edinburgh's sporting and literary characters, particularly the Tory set. Its membership was capped at 135 and each member had to be six feet 'in his stocking soles' but there were exceptions: Sir Walter (who did not meet the height requirement) was an honorary member, taking the ceremonial title of 'Umpire for Life'. There were also honorary memberships for 'Christopher North', otherwise known as Professor John Wilson, Professor of Moral Philosophy at the University, great sportsman and Royal Archer, and James Hogg, the 'Ettrick Shepherd', who was a great runner but also a little short. Henry Glassford Bell, the lawyer and poet, was a 'full' member as was George Roland (sometimes spelled Rowland) the gymnast, writer and fencing instructor to Edinburgh schools. One Foot-Ball Club member who has been identified as a member of the Six Feet High Club is Robert Oliphant.

The club's motto was *scientia viribus juncta*, loosely translated as 'the alliance of skill and strength', and their badge was a quoit, which featured on their elaborate dress uniform, which Radford describes as: 'A double breasted coat of the finest dark green cloth, with a velvet collar, and the club buttons carrying the club motto. When competing, they wore dark green freize jackets, though this might have been confined to fencing and some other 'gymnastic' exercises.'[42] The adoption of an expensive uniform was designed to maintain the exclusivity of the membership.[43]

It had an exercise room in Thistle Street East in the New Town, and used a field at Canonmills, the members meeting three times a week. However, the most keenly anticipated events were the outdoor general meetings held twice a year, the first taking place in May 1827 in a field near the Hunter's Tryst (a pub in Oxgangs Road which is still there). This may have been Scotland's first amateur athletics meeting devoted entirely to running and throwing and organised by an athletic club (clan and Highland Games devotees may argue). Initially there were three events: quoits, putting the stone and a steeplechase, although by 1835 it had added rifle shooting and golf to its list of sporting events. Throughout, it maintained its gentlemanly amateur status, mixed with a particularly Scottish flavour and a good dinner afterwards.

Like many of the clubs of its time, its days were numbered and in the late 1830s, after Scott and Hogg had died, the club ceased. However, its members, as individuals, had gone on to influence the development of athletic events elsewhere in Scotland, such as laying down the rules governing hammer throwing and the shot put - rules which, nearly 200 years later, are still accepted as the standard throughout the world.[44]

The club had already prompted the creation and progress of the St Ronan's Border Games. After Sir Walter Scott used St Ronan's Well as the title of a novel published in 1823, the townsfolk of Innerleithen were anxious to cash in on the emerging tourist trade from thousands of his readers. Thus Sir Walter, James Hogg and several members of the Six Feet High Club including Adam Wilson, its star athlete, got together to produce an athletics meeting along the lines of their General Meetings, but much larger. John Gibson Lockhart and his publisher William Blackwood were also soon involved. These Games took the athletics of the Six Feet High Club and mixed them with Border legend and romanticism which only Scott and Hogg could provide, to create an extraordinary mixture of gentleman's sporting gala, rather dubious pageantry and pre-Victorian tartan tourist attraction. It is still going strong to this day and claims to be Scotland's oldest organised sports meeting.

The Games were part of the tide of romanticism which swept through Scotland after the upheavals of the industrial and agricultural revolutions, the Napoleonic Wars and the unrest which followed. Sport became very much part of this attempt to re-establish some of the certainties of the older, safer world. Sir Walter had started the movement by recalling some of the atmosphere of medieval Border warfare in promoting the Carterhaugh Ba' Game in 1815, and when he found the ancient Selkirk Arrow he invited the Royal Archers to Selkirk to shoot for it in 1818. The romantic revival continued elsewhere with the Kilwinning Papingo (an archery target) from 1828, the Marchmont Arrow from 1830, and the whole movement culminated in the Eglinton Tournament, organised by the Earl of Eglinton in 1839.

44

Conclusions: sport's integral role in Edinburgh life

In the thirty or so years either side of 1800, there was a growing desire on the part of a number of men in Edinburgh and the Scottish Lowlands to enjoy sports in the company of like-minded others, in clubs and societies. Whether they be golfers, curlers, archers, athletes, cricketers, bowlers, quoiters, skaters or footballers, more and more professionals such as lawyers, doctors, ministers, businessmen and small landowners enjoyed rational sports for fresh air and exercise, coupled with the social benefit of camaraderie, which they enjoyed in organised clubs with membership criteria and rules.

These clubs were all mindful of the need to restrict access, effectively summing up the principle that these recreations were aimed at the middle and upper classes, and the masses were to be excluded from participating and spectating. As the clubs grew in popularity they took on a particularly Scottish dimension, establishing the basis of the whole structure of sport in the 19th century. To this day, many clubs owe a great deal to the close links many of these men had to each other through school, university, occupation, family or place of residence. Conversely, Scottish clubs owe very little to the well-documented development of sport at the schools and universities of England.

The cumulative evidence of all this activity demonstrates that sport was an integral part of life for middle class men in Edinburgh. There was considerable experience in the city – probably more than anywhere else in Britain – of forming clubs, setting up competitions, managing membership, and writing rules.

In this environment, John Hope's decision to create the world's first football club is understandable, as he was following in the well-trodden footsteps of his peers. His initiative in establishing the Foot-Ball Club added a new dimension to the choices open to young gentlemen, and immediately proved to be popular.

---

[1] For a detailed review of medieval student sport in Edinburgh, see CP Finlayson, *Illustrations of Games by a Seventeenth Century Edinburgh Student,* in *Scottish Historical Review XXXVII,* No 123, April 1958.

[2] Charles J Smith, *Historic South Edinburgh* (1978), p161

[3] Finlayson, p6

[4] Finlayson, p4

[5] Finlayson, p7

[6] Burnett, p40

[7] Finlayson, p8

[8] Timothy Pont (c1565-1614) produced the first detailed maps of Scotland. His map of Lothian and Linlithgow was engraved in Amsterdam between 1603 and 1612.

[9] Quoted by Finlayson, p6, footnote 2.

[10] National Records of Scotland, GD 122/3/2

[11] Kincaid's diary has been transcribed by the National Library of Scotland. Link: http://digital.nls.uk/golf-in-scotland/serious/kincaids-diary/index.html

[12] Quoted in Burnett, p28

[13] The court was at the western end of Rose Street and remained in use until the late nineteenth century, long enough to see a resurgence in racket sports. By the 1840s it was 'kept exclusively for rackets', a professional was employed, and in 1864 Prince Alfred played rackets there.

[14] Archers' Hall, which opened in 1777, still stands in Buccleuch Street, Edinburgh.

[15] James Hope WS won the Edinburgh Arrow a record six times in 1801, 1803-05, 1808 and 1812, while Thomas Charles Hope won it in 1800 and 1807.

[16] Paul, *The History of the Royal Company of Archers* (1875).

[17] They do not play in central Edinburgh any more: the Royal Burgess is at Barnton, the Honourable Company at Muirfield, Bruntsfield Links at Musselburgh.

[18] Arnot, p210-11.

[19] Quoted in Harvey, *Playing by the Rules, Sport in History* Vol 31 No 3 Sept 2011, p330.

[20] J Cameron Robbie, *The Chronicle of the Royal Burgess Golfing Society of Edinburgh* (1936), Vol 1, p20.

[21] Burnett, *Riot, Revelry and Rout,* p43.

[22] A Seal of Cause (or Burgess Charter or Incorporation) was also granted in 1800, on the same day, to the Burgess Golfing Society and the Honourable Company of Edinburgh Golfers, which helped them keep a hold on their playing area on Bruntsfield Links. Incorporation enabled clubs to purchase property, which was more important for golfers and bowlers who needed the infrastructure of a well-prepared and laid-out course and clubhouse, than it was to footballers, who only needed a rough field and some poles for goals. See also J Cameron Robbie, p36-37 and 56.

[23] Noted by the historian Andrew Lang in 1909, quoting 'a violent Cameronian pamphlet'.

[24] It was played between two select teams at Schaw Park, Alloa, for a thousand guineas a side.

[25] Kenneth Bourne, *Palmerston: The Early Years 1784-1841* (1982), p15.

[26] *Caledonian Mercury*, 10 July 1806.

[27] *Caledonian Mercury*, 30 July 1814.

[28] *Edinburgh Evening Courant*, 23 June 1828

[29] Others who claimed to be able to use Bruntsfield Links include drilling soldiers, exercising horses, shinty players, animal grazing, cattle fairs, students and local residents.

[30] It was in Grove Street, later built over.

[31] *Caledonian Mercury,* 1 Dec 1810 and *Scots Magazine*, January 1811

[32] *Caledonian Mercury,* 16 July 1821, describes attempts to stage a rematch; see also *Boxiana* and Pierce Egan

[33] *Caledonian Mercury,* 18 April 1814. The New Police Act was first published in Edinburgh in 1805, and this revision added a number of new details.

[34] Andrew Duncan (1744-1828) was a pioneer in the study of mental health who was instrumental in setting up a humane asylum in 1807. He is remembered today by The Andrew Duncan Clinic. Duncan also went on to found the Aesculapian Club, another medical dining club with exercise at its core, which still exists.

[35] William Inglis (1713-92), a surgeon, was an important early sporting figure in Edinburgh. He was captain of the Honourable Company of Edinburgh Golfers, and a famous portrait by David Allan shows him in full golfing garb.

[36] Alexander Wood (1725-1807) was a well-known surgeon and socialite, a friend of Robert Burns. At least one of his descendants was a member of the Foot-Ball Club.

[37] Burnett, *Riot, Revelry and Rout*, p215

[38] *Scots Magazine*, August 1824.

[39] He was buried with military honours at Inveresk in July 1825.

[40] *Edinburgh Evening Courant*, 3 April 1828

[41] See Peter Radford's excellent study, *Six-Feet Club*, Athlos (2015). Birrell was also a member of the Burgess Golfing Society and was its captain in 1830.

[42] Freize is a coarsely-woven woollen cloth. See Radford, p10

[43] The Burgess and other golfing societies had similarly elaborate uniforms, partly to maintain club spirit and social exclusivity but also for safety reasons when playing on open public spaces.

[44] Radford, p12

These four pages in John Hope's first football notebook record the 61 founding members of the Foot-Ball Club in its opening season, 1824-25.

Chapter 4

THE WORLD'S FIRST FOOT-BALL CLUB

IN DECEMBER 1824, a 17-year-old newly-enrolled student at the University of Edinburgh carried a leather ball to a field on the western outskirts of the city and, accompanied by an eager group of his fellow students, founded the Foot-Ball Club.

John Hope's initiative is now considered so momentous that in the University's sports history timeline, the first entry is the acquisition of the Burgh Muir playing area in 1591, and the second is the setting up of Hope's club in 1824.[1] It was a remarkable achievement for someone who was still almost a boy, and few students could find such an exalted place.

Hope recorded an enormous amount of detail about the club, and his extensive archive reveals all the intrigues of the exclusive club he ran for seventeen years. He followed the template which had been established by the golfers, the curlers and the archers in setting up and managing a membership organisation for recreational activity, keeping a register of members, what they paid and where the money went. He preserved negotiations for pitches, letters of engagement and wrote a tentative set of playing rules.

Some of the 300 members were loyal to the club for a number of years, others joined fleetingly for a single season or less, but their names did not enter the book until they paid their subscription which started at 1s 6d in 1824 and rose to 8 shillings by 1836, the last recorded season.

The rise in cost was perhaps one of the reasons why the club ultimately folded but Hope was determined to keep the club on a sound financial footing, and managed to ensure it made a surplus in most years. He noted meticulously how the subscriptions were spent: on rental of a playing field, purchasing footballs and bladders, providing hailsticks (goalposts) and other paraphernalia, and paying wages for local helpers.

Hope gave the club added authority by printing an annual guide for club members, giving details of playing dates and times (Wednesday 3pm and Saturday 4pm), and perhaps information on club rules. A hundred copies each season cost an average of 5 shillings, except in 1834 when a more elaborate publication called 'Notes of Days' cost 13s 6d to produce. Sadly, although the receipts from the printers are in the archive, none of these guides are known to have survived, which is unfortunate as they may have contained additional information on the conduct of the club.

Hope's organisational drive made him a natural leader, and his pride in his creation was reflected in a chatty social letter which his old school friend and fellow footballer Henry (Harry) Logan wrote to him from London on 4 June 1825. It was typical teenage correspondence, talking of all the girls at the balls, and who had kissed whom (both Hope and Logan were then 18), but the main thrust of the letter was football: 'I am very much delighted to hear from you so famous an account of the Foot-Ball Club, but how could I expect to hear otherwise as long as it has so active a member to direct it, and how I envy you the pleasure you must have had the day there were thirty nine players out, such kicking of shins & such tumbling. I am glad Nathan has improved so wonderfully.'[2]

Unfortunately we do not have the 'famous account of the Foot-Ball Club' which prompted Logan's letter. In fact, there is little of Hope's own impressions of how the club was doing, but we can deduce a great deal of information from the archive.

How they played

We know from membership records that football games involved up to 40 men playing at the same time, wearing caps to distinguish sides. Their football was of a robust and healthy nature, in which Hope enjoyed 'rolling down my opponent', as he called it. They played on rough grass fields, in the city suburbs, both in summer and winter, and they called their goal by the old Scots word, a 'hail'. All games were played within the club membership as there simply was no other club with which to play competitive matches.

Their football was clearly a competitive game with a code of behaviour, including a ban on tripping, and a defined playing area. Their game had progressed from the schoolboy pastime of the High School Yards, and Hope's club appears to mark a step on football's evolutionary path from the high-contact, often violent, origins in the folk football of a less sophisticated age to the more sanitized, codified form which emerged in the 1850s.

The most pertinent evidence for this is written, somewhat incongruously, on the back of a club budget statement for summer 1833. Here, Hope jotted down what appear to be the world's first ever rules for football, of any code. At that time the club was buoyant and attracting new recruits, many of whom who may not have had the implicit understanding of how to play and how to behave that former High School boys would have had, so he probably felt he needed to establish some guidelines.

Whether the rules were then printed and circulated is not known, but Hope was well ahead of his time in writing them down. This was over a decade before the first English public schools and Cambridge University thought it worthwhile to print their own rules,[3] and fully thirty years before the Football Association took on board the task of codifying the non-handling game.

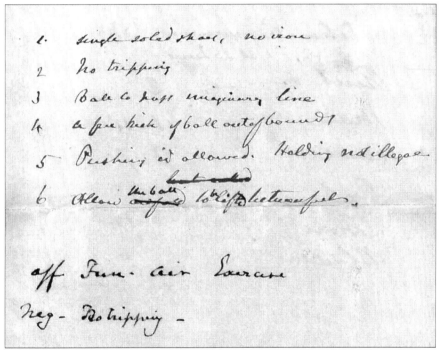

The world's first known set of rules for playing football, written by John Hope in 1833

Hope wrote in his own hand:

1. *Single soled shoes, no iron*
2. *No tripping*
3. *Ball to pass imaginary line*
4. *A free kick if ball out of bounds*
5. *Pushing is allowed. Holding not illegal*
6. *Allow the ball to be lifted between fields*

Underneath, he noted the attributes of the game:

Aff [affirmative] Fun, air, exercise
Neg [negative] No tripping[4]

These rules are brief, and leave much to the imagination, but they are highly significant not just in what they say, but what they do not say. In many respects this is similar to the early editions of Rugby School's laws in the 1840s, which stated they were to be regarded 'rather as a set of decisions on certain disputed points in football, than as containing all the Laws of the Game, which are too well known to render any explanation necessary.'[5]

Hope's first two rules indicate a concern for safety and a desire to avoid injury. After all, the members were young men who needed to be able to walk to work or study the next morning. Therefore the players could be robust (Logan mentioned 'such kicking of shins' so there was clearly a risk of being kicked) but they were expected to avoid hurting their opponents unnecessarily. It seems to have worked, as there are no mentions anywhere in the correspondence or club records of serious injury.

Rules three and four introduce the concept of a method of scoring. The game needed winners and losers so a goal was scored when the ball passed over the 'imaginary line' – and we know from the financial records that there were painted 'hail sticks' which operated as goalposts. Similarly, to stop the play wandering off into the distance, this 'imaginary line' extended right round the pitch; so, if the ball went beyond the agreed boundary it would be retrieved and kicked back into play.

Rule five is interesting as it introduces an element of physical aggression, allowing players to push and hold their opponents (as rugby allows to this day within defined circumstances such as tackling and scrums). However, pushing and holding are a long way from the 'no holds barred' approach in traditional folk football.

The final rule is harder to analyse, particularly as this is the only rule that Hope redrafted. There are words crossed out, so perhaps he had difficulty in condensing accepted practice into a short sentence. It appears to mean that the only time the ball could be lifted, i.e. picked up or handled, was when it was out of play 'between fields'. If that is correct it confirms that this was a forerunner to the non-handling code that became association football, in line with the game played at the High School, and as was also the case with Hope's 1854 Rules (see Chapter 8).

What is more, this practice of no handling, carrying or running with the ball accords with the conclusions of the sub-committee of Old Rugbeians set up in 1895 'to enquire into the Origins of Rugby Football'.[6]

They stated that 'In 1820, the form of football in vogue at Rugby was something approximating more closely to Association than what is known as Rugby Football to-day'. That, of course, was before William Webb Ellis 'picked up the ball and ran with it' in 1823, an apocryphal story but one which nonetheless marks the start of the division between association and rugby football.

Where they played

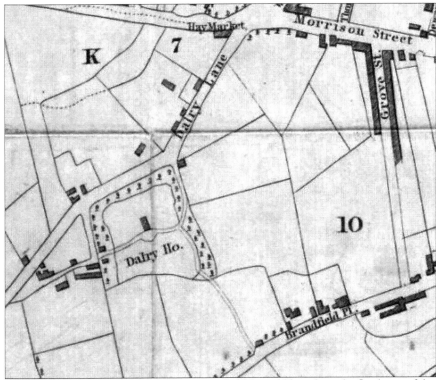

Dalry House and surrounding fields, any one of which could have been the first home of the Foot-Ball Club (Lizar's map of Edinburgh, 1835; National Library of Scotland)

The Foot-Ball Club had several grounds, curiously all of them beyond the suburbs in the south and west of the city, quite a distance from the New Town where most of the members lived. It may have been that sporty types were used to the area close to Bruntsfield Links and it was not until the 1850s that John Hope latched on to the possibilities of the Stockbridge area in the north of the city.

Some of the paperwork relating to the Foot-Ball Club's grounds. From the top: a receipt from George Spence for the rental of Dalry Park in 1826; a receipt for damage to Dalry Park in 1831; and a receipt from John Girdwood for the summer season in Greenhill Park.

The club's first home in 1824 was Dalry Park on the western fringes of the city and they remained there until 1831. At first sight this park appears to have been chosen as it was near to Hope's birthplace, Dalry House, but he had never lived there for any length of time and his Walker relations had vacated the property in 1817.[7] Dalry Park was essentially an enclosed farm field of grass, and the ground rental would have compensated the owners for refraining from its alternative use as grazing for cattle.

It was leased from a cowfeeder called George Spence for 5s 3d (a quarter guinea) per month, and there is a series of rental receipts in the archive, which make it clear that Hope also leased the park to practise archery in the summer. One of them, signed by Spence, covers both sports: 'Received from Mr John Hope one pound one shilling Sterling as rent for shooting in Dalry Park last summer with bow and arrow, and also received one pound one shilling Sterling for playing foot ball in said park from 12 Nov 1825 to 12 March 1826.'[8] After Spence died in 1827, the arrangement was continued with his widow, Janet.

Although Dalry Park's exact location is uncertain as this was open countryside at the time – several fields are potential candidates on contemporary maps – it may be the same area of ground that was used in the previous decade for the annual fair. From 1814-16 the annual All Hallow Fair was held 'in a park at the west end of Fountain Bridge, opposite to Dalry, and marking with Gilmore Place'.[9] The area is now covered by the late 19th century tenements of Dalry Road and Caledonian Crescent, a few hundred yards from where Heart of Midlothian's ground, Tynecastle, is today.

The lease came to an abrupt end after the players managed to damage the ground, although quite what they did is not specified. A badly spelled note dated 25 June 1831 from a George McGill, perhaps a neighbouring cowfeeder, confirmed 'Received from John Hope Esq, 15 shillings Sterling as payment for damidges dun to Dilray Parks'.[10]

The footballers were clearly no longer welcome in Dalry and reconvened at Greenhill Park, just to the south of Bruntsfield Links. The land belonged to Sir John Forbes of Pitsligo and a signed memorandum of agreement was drawn up between his agent John Girdwood and Hope in December 1831, leasing the park for the football club to play in summer and winter on Wednesdays and Saturdays: 'When the club meets and plays in the months of May, June and July, it is to pay at the rate of two pounds a month, and when it plays at any other period of the year, it is to pay at the rate of ten shillings a month. The club has commenced this season on the 26th November, and from that date payment runs.'[11] The enhanced rental for the summer season was due to the grass having to be cut, and this was reflected in higher subscription rates for members.

Greenhill Park, like Dalry, was then open countryside and the precise location of the playing area is uncertain as it was covered by upmarket housing from the 1850s and is now approximately the area around Greenhill Gardens. The park was also used for sports in the 1830s by the Breadalbane Oak Society (see Chapter 3).

The club's third and final home was Grove Park, the city's first dedicated enclosed sports ground. It was opened in Grove Street in 1836 as a home for Grange Cricket Club, and was managed by their English professional, John Sparks (1778-1854) who lived in a cottage on the grounds. Although he ran it primarily for cricketers – even the schoolboys of Edinburgh Academy paid him twopence each for the privilege of playing cricket on his ground – he also let it out to diverse sportsmen including footballers, pedestrians and pigeon shooters. Grove Park hosted the first international cricket match in Edinburgh in 1849 and remained the home of Grange CC until 1862 when the land was needed for development, and the Fountain Brewery was built on the site.

In 1840, in the twilight of the club, Hope wrote to the trustees of John Watson's School to ask if the school field would be available for playing football. He might reasonably have expected them to agree, as his brother James was a director of the school, and so they did, but with reservations: 'The directors do not at present see any reason to object to it provided you satisfy the tenant as to injury done to the pasture, or disturbance to his cattle. The directors retain the power of withdrawing this permission at any time they please on giving a fortnight's notice as stated in your letter.'[12] In the event, the request was not followed up, and within a year the club had ceased.

Playing equipment

Football has been played since medieval times with an inflated pig's bladder inside a stitched leather casing. The world's oldest known football, discovered in Stirling Castle, dates from around 1540 and follows this model which was simple to make but notoriously prone to bursting.

The imperfect technology had hardly improved by the 19th century and footballs were a major ongoing item of expenditure for the Foot-Ball Club, as the accounts reveal. Leather cases cost 2s 6d or 3s each and a total of £8 was spent on cases over the period recorded, mostly bought from John Christie & Son, breeches makers and glovers in George Street, or more expensively from a Mr Ainslie.

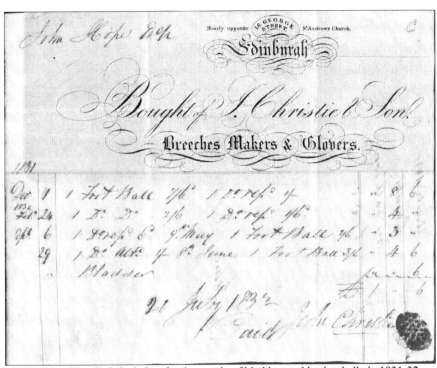

A receipt from Christie & Son for the supply of bladders and leather balls in 1831-32

Twice a week in the summer of 1834, John Hope carefully recorded how many bladders had burst and remained in stock, and noted the number of players who turned out.

57

At least the leather was fairly durable, which was more than could be said for the contents. No doubt the city's butchers were more than happy to supply pig bladders, for which they charged between 3d and 6d each, and it was just as well they were cheap as a constant supply was needed. Hope carefully recorded the stock levels each week, and although sometimes the balls would survive unscathed, on other days up to five bladders burst in a single session. Overall, the purchase of 274 bladders is recorded in the accounts for a total of £6 10s 11d.

In addition, there was all the paraphernalia of ball maintenance, such as little tin pipes for blowing them up, wire for lacing up the seams, and oil to soften the cases which were then stretched over a wooden last to achieve a 22-inch circumference.

It is a surprise to find a bottle of whisky in the accounts, but it was designated for soaking and cleansing the bladders, an indication that keeping the players supplied with match-worthy balls was not just expensive and time-consuming, it was also rather disgusting. The perils of inflating a bladder were neatly described by Colonel Alexander Fergusson from his time as a boy at the Edinburgh Academy in the 1840s: 'The ball was composed of a raw bladder, fresh, but that is hardly the word, from the butcher's hands, enclosed in a leather case. The 'blowing' of this contrivance was a disgusting operation in which a quill was used as a mouth-piece. The process was taken in turns as a necessary, but repulsive, duty - one not without risks. Consequently, it was considered prudent to perform the operation of orally inflating the bag at home because, as certainly as anyone attempted to do so at school, somebody would watch his opportunity and, when the bag was three-quarters filled, squash the whole thing flat. The effect of the foul blast from the unsavoury interior of the ball, thus forced down the throat of the unhappy blower, is not to be described.'[13]

David Murray had similar memories from the following decade: 'The ball in use in my younger days was an ox-bladder enclosed in a leather cover, but latterly a bag of india-rubber similarly enclosed came into use. The former was lighter and more resilient, the latter was more convenient; it was perfectly round while the bladder was somewhat elongated. Both were filled by blowing from the lungs.'[14]

Hope took the sensible measure of employing a man, sometimes assisted by a boy, to be in attendance on match days to blow up the balls and ensure there was a steady supply for the players. The same man would look after the equipment, prepare the pitch by putting up and taking down the hailsticks and undertake odd jobs such as painting. At a shilling a week, it was a lucrative little part-time job, and wages amounted to £12 8s over the whole period.

What the players wore

Hope and his playing colleagues never recorded precisely what clothes they wore to play football, except for references to 'distinguishing caps', and one comment in a late 1830s letter: 'We got new caps, very neat, improved by Esplin, like jockey caps.'[15]

There is, however, a clue in one letter written to Hope in 1831 by Walter McCulloch, his school and university friend who was a member throughout the club's existence. In a piece of good natured banter expected of high-spirited young men in a sports club (they were 24 at the time), McCulloch wrote in mock-heroic style: 'My dear John, nought daunted by the past I will venture again into the field tomorrow provided you can assure me my armour awaits its lord'. Hope, as ever, filed the letter with a brief synopsis on the back, noting '16 Dec 1831, Walter McCulloch wants his football jacket'.

This raises the question as to the nature of a 'football jacket'. Was it an ordinary outer garment which Hope knew that McCulloch always wore to play football, or was it some kind of special identifiable sporting garment, which would later develop into a football strip? We will perhaps never know.

On the whole, it appears that normal outdoors clothes and boots generally sufficed for playing football in this era, effectively limiting participation to the well-off due to the cost of cleaning or repairing them. Some contemporary accounts appear to confirm this. One well known contemporary image is Cruikshank's satirical cartoon dated 1827, simply titled *Foot Ball*, of uniformed soldiers playing a riotous game on the parade ground, wearing short military jackets, light trousers, shoes and various caps and military head gear.[16] The historian Matthew Bloxam recalled Rugby School around 1820: 'As to costume, there were neither flannels nor caps, the players simply doffed their hats and coats or jackets, which were heaped together on either side near the goals until the game was over.'[17]

The image then, is a familiar one of 'jackets for goalposts', of boys going up to Bruntsfield Links or to Dalry Park, throwing their short blue jackets into a pile in time-honoured fashion.

Fergusson says much the same about Edinburgh Academy boys playing cricket in the 1840s: 'The Elevens doffed their jackets, laid them in a heap, and the game went on. There were no flannels, fielding jackets, cricketing caps, pretty ties, nor newspaper paragraphs in those remote ages. Pads were rarely used, and hardly necessary, seeing that the bowler's hand was strictly kept down by law. Much of the bowling was 'under hand.'[18] Schoolboys of the time normally wore, he continued: 'what is now called an Eton jacket, of blue cloth – unmistakable broad cloth – a fair expanse of linen collar, gloves, and trousers of spotless 'Russia duck' – a product as rarely heard of now as the Great Auk – that came from the iron with a surface like that of white satin.'

They played largely in all white (or at least light colours) which is perhaps the most unsuitable colour considering the way grass and mud stains the material, but it seems that until the 1870s, when the far more suitably coloured tweed became fashionable, most footballers (and cricketers) played in their everyday trousers and shirts, and these happened to be white or neutral in colour.

The white Russia duck, a strong hemp flax linen or canvas,[19] evolved into the white cricket flannels and also into the white rugby and soccer knickerbockers (again the most unsuitable colour for a muddy pitch). Perhaps the last of the footballers to wear 'long whites' was Lord Kinnaird, who won five FA Cups in his trademark trousers.

There seems little doubt that the use of so illogical a fabric reflected an element of conspicuous consumption by middle class men and boys who had servants at home to wash and press the muddy results of an afternoon on the playing fields.

Not all of them were so heartless. Lord Kingsburgh said that as late as the end of the 1850s Edinburgh Academy boys played in old clothes of any sort, without having clean clothes to change into and no showers to wash in. He described the changing facilities at Raeburn Place at that time: 'A small loft over an outhouse in the garden of a villa in the corner of the field, approached by a wooden ladder ... no basins, no lockers... The only thing we could do after we had played our match (we came out quite as dirty as you do now) was to go up into that loft and smoke until it was sufficiently dark and we could go through the streets without being mobbed.'[20]

For civilians in Edinburgh at the same period, however, we have to look to Thomas Shepherd. In 1829, he published his series of views of Edinburgh, called *Modern Athens*.[21] His aim was to record, in all their splendour, the proud monuments which gave the city its classical name. Shepherd could not resist also including something of the life of the city and its people through strategically placed figures, going about their business, wearing their everyday clothes.

Here, exquisitely drawn and engraved, are the men, women, children

60

and animals of Modern Athens: the Newhaven fishwives with their enormous creels; the tall decorative Highland soldiers in full military dress; the carters and carriers, the beggars, the street-sweepers, men and women on foot and in carriages; hundreds of spritely dogs; and the children, sometimes walking demurely with their parents, sometimes scampering about the streets with their toys, and in two engravings, as a bonus, playing with a large, round football.

Thomas Shepherd's 1829 engravings show balls in everyday Edinburgh life

In the scene on the left, in front of Holyrood Palace, a group of boys and a girl are playing with two football-sized balls, as soldiers, a man and his dog and a family walk by. In the other, of the Lawnmarket, a little boy walks alongside his elegantly dressed mother with what is undoubtedly a football at his feet, the ball also being chased by two dogs.

In these snapshots of life in the streets of Edinburgh, boys and girls with footballs appear to be common enough sights in 1829 for Shepherd to include them in what was, for him, a commercial operation. Perhaps these children were included to appeal to his potential market of respectable and middle-class citizens, but the message is that kicking a ball about the streets or in a park was perfectly acceptable and normal.

Further evidence is on this book's front cover, the nearest thing we have to an image of a game of football in progress in the city in this period. It comes from a set of six lithographs called *Edinburgh and the Surrounding Countryside*, published around 1841 by William Macgill and the lithographer Friedrich Schenck. Together the six views show the 360-degree panorama from Calton Hill, and one of them looks south, over the Royal Mile to Arthur's Seat and the distant Pentland Hills. In the centre ground is the roof of the 'New High School', and on the grass foreground, two groups of young men are playing football.

Macgill and Schenck's panorama of Edinburgh in the 1840s, looking south from Calton Hill, where several young men are playing football

The ball they are playing with is round and clearly of the air-filled bladder variety, designed to be kicked. One is kicking it, left footed, and the artist and engraver have captured well the leg movement, head position and arm balancing of a footballer. Two others jostle with each other to receive the ball, while a couple more hover around looking suspiciously off-side. Two more young men to the right appear to be throwing a ball amongst themselves in another game.

Detail of the young Edinburgh football players in Macgill and Schenck's 1841 lithograph

The players are smartly dressed in caps or hats, short blue jackets (blue was then the fashionable colour), white shirts, waistcoats and long light-coloured trousers - all typical of the period.[22] The men nearby are wearing longer coats with military style caps, and the weather is clearly fine and summery because the ladies have light coloured dresses and some have parasols.

In the broader picture, the medieval buildings of the Old Town are plain to see, so too the classical shapes of Georgian Edinburgh, but intruding into this ancient world is the belching smoke from the 'Edinburgh Coal Gass works' (*sic*) and the distant chimney of the 'Railway Station, St. Leonard's hill'. This is perhaps the first illustration of a railway station in the city, terminus of the coal and passenger line from Dalkeith, known as The Innocent Railway.

It is fitting that a game of football should be part of this vision for the future.

Declining years of the Club

From 1836 the Foot-Ball Club stumbled on but it was a shadow of its former vibrant self. Hope was about to turn 30, he had a busy life and was heavily involved in work and politics. The detailed records of membership and finance dry up, and the limited papers in the archive show that while Hope was still interested, and probably still active, he tried very hard to pass on the management to somebody else.

He failed to find any takers, and it is perhaps ironic that the club's greatest strength, his leadership and organisational abilities, may also have provoked its demise. Hope kept such a firm personal grip on the club's affairs that it would have taken a brave man to step into his shoes, and the Foot-Ball Club did not emulate other sporting clubs in the city in creating a formal committee structure.

For example, amongst the golfers, bowlers and curlers, dining together was an important part of the club structure, so they needed a dining secretary to organise events. Nor did football offer wagering, which needed a committee member to regulate it, or organise competitive matches, on the outcome of which bets could be placed and which required a team captain. And so long as the footballers could simply turn up and play on any old field, there was never any move to acquire property, which would have provided a permanent base, as well as requiring members to administer and finance it.

However, Hope's efforts to recruit a successor do reveal some more about the way the club was run. In June 1836 he drew up a list of 26 'football names', accompanied by a note which read 'The apparatus is with John Hope. The field could be easily got and a chairman to do the needful.' He also compiled a 'Football Memoranda' which outlined the costs of running the club and the equipment required:

Summer rent £1 per month, commencing with June
Winter rent, i.e. before the grass, 10s per month
Wooden ball
Football cases, neat leather cases 3/6 each
Bladders 3d each
Spare laces
Tin pipe for blowing 2d
Wire 1d
Cloth brush 2d
Moreen bag 3/6 and making 6d = 4s
Keep the bladder in whisky
Gow got 1/6 a day for blowing
Hail sticks painted

It appears he may have persuaded a man called James Gow[23] to help him, then attempt to take over running the club. His name first appears in a letter from Hope to all members in May 1834, giving details of playing times (Saturday at ½ past 2 and Wednesday at 3), and notifying that the subscription of five shillings was to be collected by Gow.

Then five years later, for season 1839/40 there is a subscription sheet, neatly drawn up: *James Gow, chairman, 10 Forres Street, will call upon the Old Members of the Foot Ball Club to receive their subscription for the present season. The club meets at present each Saturday at two o'clock in Grove Park, west of Gardener's Crescent. The subscription is five shillings.*[24]

James Gow - chairman No 10 Forres Street, will call upon the Old Members of The Foot-ball-Club to receive their subscription for the present season - The Club meets at present each Saturday at two o'clock in Grove Park west of Gardeners Crescent. The subscription is Five Shillings
1839 - 1840 John Hope W.S.

Date	Name of Member	Sum	That it is paid

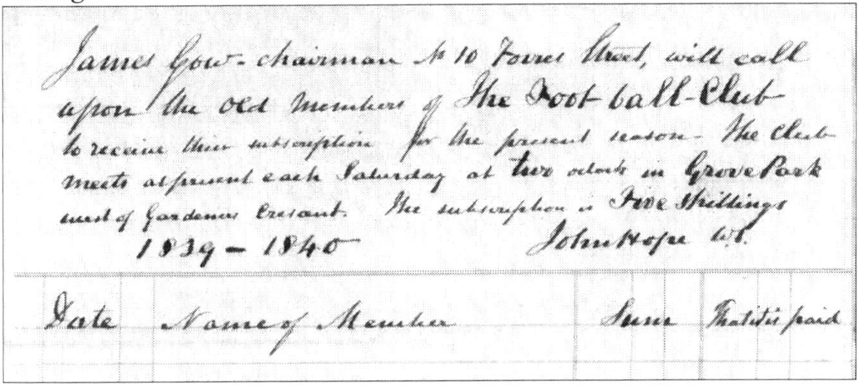

The subscription sheet, pictured above, has columns headed: 'Date', 'Name of Member', 'Sum' and 'That it is paid'. Tellingly, all four columns are entirely blank.

It was not quite the end and there are indications of activity after that. As we have already seen, in March 1840 Hope asked if John Watson's School north park would be available for playing football. The directors gave their approval, 'provided you satisfy the tenant as to injury done to the pasture or disturbance to his cattle'.[25]

In December 1840, Hope received a letter from his cousin, John Forbes Walker-Drummond: 'Mr Drummond begs to acknowledge receipt of an intimation from the Foot-Ball Club, for which he is much indebted to its worthy representative. Mr D has not the least intention of becoming a member at present, as he imagines the subscription and entry money would not be a good investment in the present apparent circumstances of the club, at least if one may judge from the miserable pittance of paper upon which the intimation is written.'[26] It may not have been a serious attempt to invite him to join, as Hope has noted 'impudence to the football club' on the

back, adding 'a trick of Jamie's, JD humbugged' which infers the invitation was a practical joke by his younger brother James.

There might still have been a demand for the club as there is a letter dated 25 February 1841, from John G Campbell of 7 Great King Street, who had been a member ten years earlier. He wrote: 'Dear Sir, I intended some days since to have called regarding the Football Club. Will you let me know what is the amount of subscription? There are three or four who would wish to attend, but as their stay in Edinburgh will be only be for about two months, they would like to know if they might do so paying a smaller amount than the regular charge for the year. Do you meet on Saturday?' Campbell was in his 30s so his football days were probably behind him, and no doubt he was asking on behalf of some young friends, but he either received a negative response, or no response at all.

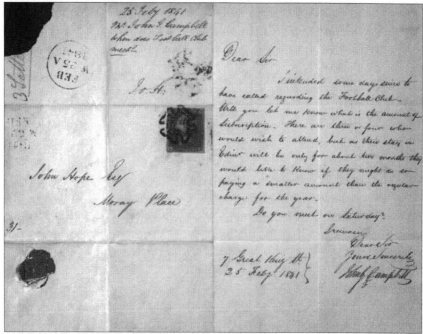

John Campbell's letter of February 1841 is the final item of correspondence in the club files

It is clear that, as numbers had dwindled, the club's activities had been increasingly subsidised by Hope, a position he could not sustain and he must have decided to draw a line. The very last sheet of paper in the club archive is a note from his accountant, dated 14 April 1841: 'I acknowledge to have now and formerly received from you the sum of £4 13s 1d to make up the football deficiency, 1839, 1840 and Book. George Esplin'. It was time to call it a day. The Foot-Ball Club was no more.

Ahead of its time

While much of the foregoing analysis provides a general overview of the club membership and their background, it is hard to escape the conclusion that Hope's Foot-Ball Club was ahead of its time. It operated with no opponents and no rivalry, and there were no similar clubs elsewhere in the UK. In the end, it ran out of air.

This was probably the conclusion drawn by founding member William Scott Kerr when he went on to Cambridge University, and wrote to Hope in 1827 of his disappointment that he could not continue playing the game there: 'I think it very unlikely that football would be favourably received. The favourite sports are cricket, tennis, billiards, fives, boating and some others which I shall not mention.'[27]

He was wrong. Football did come to Cambridge but it was not until 1839 that the first known attempt to form a club and devise an acceptable compromise of school football rules was made. It was followed by other attempts at codification, notably in 1846, 1848 and 1856, which all had fleeting success but it was not until 1863 that the game we now recognise as association football took shape.

In Edinburgh, there is no trace of organised adult football in the 1840s, but the following decade saw a resurgence. In the 1850s the city hosted the first match for a medal, then the leading schools and their former pupils started to play each other to a fixed set of rules. Before the end of the decade the Academical Club and the University played their first competitive match.

That gap between the demise of the Foot-Ball Club and the birth of modern football, of all codes, covers an entire generation, and one might be tempted to dismiss the club as a historical quirk. But, as we reveal in subsequent chapters, the opposite appears to be true: there are a number of tangible links which clearly demonstrate the club's impact on the future development of football.

There are many individual stories which indicate that knowledge and enthusiasm for football were passed on through the generations. Most pertinently, John Hope himself remained interested in promoting football long after his Foot-Ball Club had been wound up, and he retained a strong preference for the kicking rather than carrying game.

---

[1] University of Edinburgh, Academy of Sport, Our History: www.ed.ac.uk/education/institutes/spehs/academy-of-sport/about/history. Website accessed 9 March 2018

[2] Hope Papers, GD253/183/14/12.

[3] The first publication of *Laws of Football at Rugby School* was in 1845, then in 1847 the Eton College field game rules were first printed. The 'Cambridge Rules' of football were first devised in 1846, then printed in 1848 and stuck to a tree at Parker's Piece, although no copies are known to have survived.

[4] GD253/183/7/3

[5] *Laws of Football as played at Rugby School* (1851).

[6] *The Origin of Rugby Football; report (with appendices) of the sub-committee of the Old Rugbeian Society appointed in July 1895* (1897).

[7] Dalry House was advertised to let in the summer of 1817, and the household furniture was sold at auction in November 1818.

[8] GD253/183/5a

[9] *Caledonian Mercury*, 19 October 1815

[10] GD253/183/5d

[11] GD253/183/5b

[12] GD253/26/5/33

[13] Alexander Fergusson, *Chronicles of the Cumming Club* (1887), p53.

[14] David Murray, *Memories of the Old College of Edinburgh* (1927), p445.

[15] Jamie, p99. The name refers to George Esplin, club accountant in its later days.

[16] Robert Cruikshank, *Foot Ball* (1827); engraved by George Hunt, published by Thomas McLean, Haymarket, London.

[17] Matthew Holbeche Bloxam, *Personal Reminiscences of Rugby School as it was in 1813*; paper read at a meeting of the Rugby School Natural History Society, 17 November 1883.

[18] Fergusson, p55

[19] Russia duck came in various weights and levels of finish. The coarser varieties were used for tents, canvas bags, gaiters, sails and covers, with finer varieties for trousers and waistcoats, and the finest, what we would call linen, for shirts. The familiar white Hanoverian soldiers' gaiters used duck, as did most of the armies and navies of the world, either in its white or natural hemp coloured finish. It is still readily available in various forms from suppliers to the military re-enactment societies.

[20] *Edinburgh Academical Club Centenary History* (1957), p18

[21] Thomas H Shepherd, *Modern Athens, displayed in a series of views; or, Edinburgh in the nineteenth century* (1829)

[22] John Hope was sensitive as to who wore jackets and who wore coats. In 1842, he sent money to one of his acolytes called Murdoch to buy clothes, advising him to get a jacket: *(1) because it is 8s or 10s cheaper; (2) I prefer to keep lads in jackets, as keeping them out of mischief and men's society, for men will not so much associate with jacketed lads as with coated lads.* Jamie, p72

[23] James Gow is described as 'chairman' in the subscription sheet, but this appears to be his occupation as sedan chair operator rather than his position within the club. Apart from his New Town address in Forres Street, he does not fit the usual demographic of Foot-Ball Club members, and later in life worked as a railway porter.

[24] GD253/183/6

[25] GD253/26/5/46

[26] Letter dated 4 December 1840, GD253/26/5/89

[27] Letter dated 14 May 1827, GD 253/183/15/4

Chapter 5

THE FOOT-BALL PLAYERS

THE CHARACTER of the Foot-Ball Club is defined by its members, and one of the major elements of our research has been to find out more about the players. The names of just under 300[1] young men went into John Hope's lined notebooks, which cover nine of the club's 17 years in existence, as he recorded meticulously each payment of a subscription to the Foot-Ball Club. It is likely that many more members joined during the years for which there are no records, but even so, the amount of information available is far greater than for almost any other contemporary sporting organisation.

We have been able to identify the majority of the football players with reasonable confidence and the complete known membership is detailed in Chapter 11. For the first four seasons, most of the players were recorded by name only, sometimes only by a surname or even as 'Hamilton's friend'. From 1831, Hope was more expansive and generally noted an address beside each name, adding an occupation in some cases, although in one case he simply wrote 'forgot name'. Hope's handwriting is, on the whole, easy to read but he did have a little trouble with consistency or accuracy in spelling.

Even from a superficial glance at the names, it is clear they were gentlemen or the sons of gentlemen. One was noted as 'gone to the country', another was called Scipio[2] after a Roman general, and John Rolland is described in schoolboy fashion as *minimus*. The surnames are predominantly Lowland Scots, with a smattering of Highland, only a few English and no obviously continental European – a reflection that, even in the latter days of the Enlightenment, Edinburgh was still a parochial Lowland Scottish city.

A detailed analysis has been a laborious process. Several of them wrote memoirs or had detailed obituaries written about their lives, but not a single one (apart from Hope himself) mentioned their youthful enthusiasm for football or their participation in this club. Despite this, we have uncovered many of their stories through a close study of contemporary records (including city directories, news reports, obituaries, censuses, university and school registers, and membership lists of local and national organisations). We have conducted a thorough examination of the membership in several fields including addresses, origins, education and professions. The results are fascinating, revealing a great deal about who these early footballers were and their wider links to the development of football in Scotland.

The Foot-Ball Club membership and subscription records for season 1831-32

Membership numbers

1824/25	61	1831 summer	70
1825/26	77	1831/32	60
1826/27	84	1832/33	30
1827/28	72	1834 summer	27
		1836 summer	26

The Foot-Ball Club appears to have been an immediate success as there are 61 names in the membership roll for its opening season of 1824-25, which clearly represents a much wider group of young men than simply Hope's former classmates. They met weekly, although not everyone played every

70

week; Henry Logan's letter of June 1825 revealed he was impressed by a turn-out of 39 players.[3]

In the following years the club expanded a little and held strong at 77 (1825-26), 84 (1826-27) and 72 (1827-28). Over these first four years of existence, this amounts to 180 individual members, of whom 15 retained their membership throughout that period, and a further 17 for three of those seasons, so there was an enthusiastic core group.

From 1828 there is a three-year gap in the records, in the course of which Hope went on a year-long Grand Tour in 1829-30. It seems likely the club continued to operate during this period, though as there are no records for these years we do not know under whose control.

When records resumed in 1831, membership remained steady at 70, the first time the club is known to have had a summer season, and most of these men continued through the winter as there were 60 in 1831-32. However, for no obvious reason the membership then declined sharply, with just 30 in 1832-33 and 27 in summer 1834. By this time, it appears the club had started to stagnate as in 1836, the last surviving list of members, only two of the 26 names were new and both of them were brothers of existing members.

It was around this time that Hope, coming up to his 30th birthday, discovered religion, abstentionism and other causes, while his legal business was developing rapidly. His attention was, understandably, diverted from the club. There are no lists for subsequent years and the only identifiable members are a few whose names appear on correspondence and club papers before the club faded away in 1841.

Apart from Hope, only two men featured on all the membership rolls from 1824 right through to 1836. These were Robert Hamilton and Walter McCulloch, both his direct contemporaries at the High School and Edinburgh University and both of whom, like him, became Writers to the Signet. Overall, 52 men were members for three or more seasons. However, over half of all recorded members (181) joined the club for just one season before losing interest or moving on, a scenario which many sports clubs today will recognise.

Addresses and connections

When John Amyatt, an English chemist, visited Edinburgh in the 1770s at the height of the Scottish Enlightenment, he remarked to William Smellie, editor of the first edition of the *Encyclopaedia Britannica,* an observation which epitomises all that the city must have meant at that time: 'Here I stand at what is called the Cross of Edinburgh[4] and can, in a few minutes, take fifty men of genius and learning by the hand'.[5]

Fifty years later, by which time Edinburgh's population had grown rapidly from around 50,000 to three times that size, most of the well-to-do professionals, lawyers, professors, writers, architects, businessmen, gentlemen and minor landed gentry had migrated north from the overcrowded Old Town across the valley to the elegant New Town. But although the venue had changed, Amyatt could probably have said something very similar had he then stood in George Street or Charlotte Square as the professional classes of the city in the 1820s lived and worked in a very small area, the bright and breezy New Town. The later Victorian sprawl of suburbs towards the Grange, Morningside and Newington had barely started.

Edinburgh's was a close-knit community, socially and physically. Middle class children grew up in their parents' houses, then, when they married, typically moved only a street or so away, returning to buy or rent their own houses in the same streets as their parents when they could afford to. Just as it had been in the Old Town, so it was in the New: many men and women spent their entire lives, through childhood, school, marriage, work, socialising and old age, within the same two or three streets, and naturally met their relatives, friends and colleagues every time they opened their six-panelled Georgian front doors.

This can be confirmed by Ann Mitchell's painstaking analysis of who lived where and when for all the houses of the Moray Feu in the west end of the New Town.[6] It bears useful comparison to the members of the Foot-Ball Club, many of whom gave addresses in Moray Place, Ainslie Place, Forres Street and Albyn Place, all neighbouring streets.

In Moray Place, which had 50 or so residences in 1831, not all the householders gave an occupation, but of those that did, ten were listed as working in the legal profession, six were soldiers or their families, two bankers, one dentist and 22 were landowners or gentlemen, assumed from their titles or designations.

The residents included the Hope family at 31 Moray Place, where John and his brother James lived. Their aunt, Mrs Walker, was next door in 32. Other Hopes lived in 44, and at 12 was Charles Hope, Lord President of the Court of Session (whose step-grandson was Lord Kingsburgh, an important name in the history of rugby, shooting and other sports later in the century). Next door to him at 13 were three sons of James Hunt of Pittencrieff – James, John and William – all members of the Foot-Ball Club. On the other side at 47 lived Sir James Moncreiff Bt, whose five sons included another James, not just a member of the Foot-Ball Club but one of the founders of the Grange Cricket Club, and later an important legal and political figure as Lord Advocate and an MP.

Around the corner in Ainslie Place, there were 25 addresses with eight lawyers, three doctors, one soldier, eight landowners and the influential Tory publisher, William Blackwood at number 3. His son, James was a member, as were Charles Buchanan and his brother at 8. Next door to Blackwood at number 2 was the Horsman family, whose son, Edward, joined with James Moncreiff in 1832 in founding the Grange Cricket Club while the third of the founding trio, David Mure, came to live in Ainslie Place in 1843.

A similar pattern follows in surrounding streets with three Wardlaw brothers – Gerard, James and Robert – all Foot-Ball Club members who lived at 9 Albyn Place. In Forres Street, which was full of teachers of music, painting and foreign languages, perhaps because some of the houses were built as flats and therefore cheaper to buy or rent, we find John Omond, whose brother was a surgeon, at number 4. Close by in number 8, Peter Ogilvy and George Semple lived in property registered to Robert Mitchell, the first classics teacher at the Edinburgh Academy,[7] so they were probably home boarders. Walter McCulloch, a club member throughout its existence, was at number 10.

Many of these brothers and close residents are listed, one after the other, as club members, suggesting that word of mouth had a large part to play in publicising the club and that they came along to sign up at the same time. This pattern of proximity and companionship is reflected throughout the New Town.

Another of these was George Wedderburn, son of the Solicitor General who lived in 31 Heriot Row, one of Edinburgh's most prestigious streets. Born in 1817, he attended the Edinburgh Academy from 1825-31 before embarking on a legal career. When he joined the Foot-Ball Club in 1834 he wrote a letter to Hope in the jocular style of the period: 'Dear Sir, Requesting you to hold my former epistle *pro non scripto* [ie, as if I had not written it], I send you the subscription and reckon myself a member of the Royal Corps of Mid-Lothian Football Players. If my legs recover by Saturday I will endeavour to be present at the meeting on that day. Hoping that the mutton chops I sent gave you no queasiness.' Hope has annotated the letter 'Geo Wedderburn joins football'.[8]

Wedderburn played at least from 1834-36, when club records ended, and his elder brother James also joined in 1836. George went on to become a WS, moved round the corner to Ainslie Place and, like many other members of the club, died unmarried in 1865. It is intriguing that a student of only 17 should write to Hope, ten years older and already a WS, on such equal terms, and only serves to emphasise what a close-knit community there was among New Town residents.

This closeness was summed up neatly by Sir Charles Bell, Professor of Surgery at Edinburgh University, who wrote when he and his wife moved into 6 Ainslie Place in 1837: 'This is a capital house, with two spare rooms, and all your old friends within a gunshot, and all living in harmony and kindness.'[9]

From 1831-36, the addresses listed in the membership rolls include virtually every major street in Edinburgh's New Town: Melville Street (9), Heriot Row (7), Moray Place (6), Albyn Place (4), Drummond Place (4), Forres Street (4), Great King Street (4), Royal Terrace (4), Ainslie Place (3), Albany Street (3), George Street (3), Northumberland Street (3), Queen Street (3), Royal Circus (3), Walker Street (3), two each for Castle Street, Cumberland Street, Carlton Street, Dublin Street, Hope Street, Howe Street, London Street, Manor Place, Nelson Street, Raeburn Place, Randolph Crescent, Royal Crescent, St Andrew Square, and one each for Abercrombie Place, Broughton Street, Charlotte Square, Forth Street, Gloucester Place, North Northumberland Place, Rutland Square and Saxe Coburg Place.[10]

These represented the vast majority of members, and less than ten per cent lived outside the New Town area: one each in Canaan Park, Comely Green, Craiglockhart, Howard Place, Inverleith Row, Liberton Cottage, Marchmont, South College Street, Wharton Place and Windmill Street. Apart from the last three, which were in the vicinity of the University and therefore likely to be student lodgings, not one member lived in the historic Old Town.

All the addresses are principal thoroughfares and not the lanes or servants' streets, which reinforces the gentlemanly origins of the members, even allowing for the possibility that a few may have listed a business address.

Curiously, the club played exclusively in the south and west suburbs of Edinburgh, a distance of one or two miles from the members' homes. It is surprising that there were not more players from the fledgling middle-class developments of Marchmont, Newington and Morningside.[11]

Educational background

As well as living in close proximity, many of the founding members had learned their football in the High School Yards and it is clear that attendance at the High School greatly influenced club membership, particularly in its early years.

However, although Hope was a High School boy who enrolled as a student at Edinburgh University in 1824 and subsequently became a lawyer in the city, the club was clearly not a former pupils' club for the High School, nor just for university students, nor was it 'a very select club of Edinburgh lawyers' as Jamie described it. Players were educated both in Edinburgh and further afield, and while many emulated Hope by embarking on a legal career, others entered a range of professions such as business, medicine, the church and the armed forces.

Unfortunately, the High School has virtually no records of its pupils at that time (they were apparently destroyed when the school moved to its present site in the late 1960s), and so far it has only been possible to confirm 19 club members as former pupils, largely from prize lists and obituaries. However, given the High School's status as the city's leading school in the early 19th century, and its ability to attract boarders from elsewhere in Scotland, the actual number is likely to have been considerably higher.

Another important source of members which can be quantified was the fledgling Edinburgh Academy, which was established in 1824 as a direct challenge to the dominance of the High School and attracted many of its former clientele. The Academy has maintained a comprehensive register of all its pupils since its foundation and we have confirmed 56 of them as Foot-Ball Club members, some of them while still at the school. One of those was James Hope, John's younger brother, who exemplified the change in tradition by going to the Academy in 1826, aged 8. He spent seven years there, including the season he joined the Foot-Ball Club.

The Academy's burgeoning culture of ball-playing allowed it to take over from the High School in the vanguard of Edinburgh school sport. As we shall see in Chapter 8, this led to the Academy opening a dedicated sports ground at Raeburn Place in 1854 (with former Foot-Ball Club member Kenneth Mackenzie on the organizing committee). It founded a cricket club for former pupils, then adopted Rugby rules for the footballers who went on to establish the Academical Football Club in 1857, which printed rules of play early in 1858.

Another example of this progression between the schools and in sport was that of George Todd Chiene (1809-82) who was educated at Crail in Fife before coming to the High School. He was a Foot-Ball Club member in 1826/27 as he trained for a career in accountancy in the city. His sent his sons John and George to the Edinburgh Academy where they both played for the school football team, and later John was the first President of the Scottish Rugby Union in 1873, while George was captain of the Academical Rugby Club in 1867.

Beyond the High School and the Edinburgh Academy, there is little evidence of the other principal city schools – such as Loretto (founded 1827), Merchiston Castle (1833) and the former hospital schools of George Watson's, John Watson's and George Heriot's – being a source of young footballers.

A proportion of the club members were educated further afield before making their way to Edinburgh to finish their instruction at school or enroll at the University. It appears that many boys were educated privately or at small schools, although some are recorded at 'academies' which were effectively crammers for entry to the armed forces and the civil service, particularly in India. They came from all round the country, from the Scottish Borders (eg George Ainslie of Roxburghshire) to the Hebrides (eg Ewen Macneill of Barra) and the Northern Isles (eg Henry Cheyne and James Irvine from Shetland). Some remained in Edinburgh after their studies to embark on a professional career, others returned to their family homes and may well have taken their enthusiasm for football with them.

Also of interest is the English element. At that time Oxford and Cambridge universities only accepted Church of England conformists, so non-conformists and Roman Catholics were obliged to seek their higher education in Scotland or abroad, and Edinburgh University, in particular, was a popular choice. When these boys came to Edinburgh to study, the fact that they chose to join the Foot-Ball Club infers that they may have already played a form of football.

One of these was George Witham, a member of the club in its first two years while a medical student. Born in 1805 into a prominent Roman Catholic family in County Durham, he had been educated at Stonyhurst, a Jesuit school in Lancashire, which had a tradition of playing a form of folk football, known as The Grand Match, with a pancake as a prize for the winners. Witham attended classes at Edinburgh University alongside Hope at the same time as he played football (while his father, a reckless gambler and scientist, mixed with the scientific set in the New Town). He then bought a commission in the 68th Regiment of Foot, later the Durham Light Infantry, where he raced horses and ran as a pedestrian (professional foot racer), until he inherited his family estates and retired to be a country gentleman. His religion is particularly significant given the virulent anti-Catholic views expressed by Hope in years to come.[12]

Among other English-schooled members was John Bigge of Ripon, who had a year at Edinburgh Academy before private study which took him to Durham University and a career in the church. Sir John Ogilvy had spent four years at Harrow, where he probably played football. There were several medical students including Evan Cameron (Jersey), Henry Chaplin

76

(Suffolk), Edward George (Ramsgate) and Charles Underwood (Herefordshire). And Joshua Hewitson, a Quaker from Northumberland, appears to have studied painting during his three seasons of club membership from 1825-28.[13]

Expenses sheet of the Foot-Ball Club for 1831-32, detailing the purchases of bladders, leather cases and sundry paraphernalia, as well as payments to James Stewart for blowing up balls, and rental for Greenhill Park.

A spread of age

The founders were largely of similar age and over half of the identified members in 1824 were born in 1806 or 1807.[14] The oldest was Archibald Inglis, born 1801 and in his final year as a medical student, while four (Balfour, Cameron, Hogarth and Keir) were born in 1810, which reflects the fact that it was not uncommon at that time for 14-year-olds to matriculate at the University.

As time went on, the spread of ages became wider as the 'old hands' continued playing and a steady flow of young recruits entered the fray. The date (or at least the year) of birth of over a hundred members reveals that around half of the members signed up when they were aged 17 to 19.

77

Youth was no barrier, and John Hope's little brother James was only 13 during his one season of play. Overall, the youngest was 12-year-old John Rolland *minimus*, who came along with his 24-year-old brother James for two seasons, starting in 1826. That also marked the upper age limit as none of the members appears to have been older than 24 on joining.

With the length of membership ranging from less than a season to 12 years, the age of ceasing to play was of course higher, and as the records stopped in 1836 it is likely they were higher still. Of those we know about, the vast majority had hung up their boots by 24 and only small numbers beyond that age. The three who lasted throughout the club – Hope, McCulloch and Hamilton – were all about 29 in 1836, and six others stopped aged 25-27.

The spread of ages indicates that the club was largely aimed at students and young professionals, but schoolboys were also welcomed. The latter is surprising as they might have been expected to struggle with the physicality of older youths, and indicates they wanted to play in a more organised football scenario than with their peer group in the schoolyards.

Professions

Given the relative youth of the football players, few of them were in employment at the time they joined and most were still in higher education. However, the members were almost all destined for a career and virtually every one of them entered a profession, in law, medicine, the army and the church. There is little evidence of landowning aristocrats or of lower middle-class occupations such as shopkeepers, clerks or schoolteachers, and no involvement at all of manual workers (except as employees).

Given Hope's family and professional connections, it is little surprise that over half of his fellow football players went into the legal profession. Of 156 members whose careers have been identified, 90 became lawyers and the majority of those (57) were Writers to the Signet. The comprehensive directory of the Society of Writers to the Signet, published in 1890, has simplified the task of identifying these members but even allowing for that, there is no escaping the powerful influence of the legal profession. There is an additional factor in that some members were sons of lawyers but chose a different profession.

Edinburgh, then as now, was a city of lawyers, and many lawyers had the time, the affluence and the social status to influence a great deal of business and social life in the city and to indulge in recreations of all kinds.

In the 18th and the early part of the 19th century, these would have tended to be the traditional rural sports of shooting, fishing, hunting, archery and long-distance walking, some of which Hope himself enjoyed on friends' estates, but this range of activities expanded to include 'modern' sports such as golf, curling, cricket and football.

The next most important contingent was medicine, thanks to Edinburgh University's position as an important centre of medical teaching. Eighteen members studied medicine and the majority of those became doctors or surgeons. For example, among six members of the Spens family whose names appear on the register were four sons of Dr Thomas Spens, the President of the Royal College of Physicians. Thomas, who was four years older than Hope and had already graduated in medicine in 1824 when he became a founding member, was in the Indian Medical Service and died in Calcutta in 1836 (his son Thomas Hope Spens died in the Indian Mutiny in 1857). William Spens was in the same year as Hope at the High School and became an accountant; James was at Edinburgh Academy and entered the Army; and the youngest brother John was also at the Academy, studying medicine while a Foot-Ball Club member from 1831-34. For good measure their cousin Nathanael Spens, Hope's great friend and fellow Royal Archer, was also a founding member. He became a lawyer and his sons were in the Army: Colin who died in Cherat in 1867, and Nathaniel James, the last of the line, who was killed in Kabul in 1879.

Another extended family link saw four sons of another President of the Royal College of Physicians, Sir William Newbigging, playing for the club, three of them as founders. William and George studied medicine, Robert and John were lawyers, and sadly all four of them died before their father.

Other medical students of note include two future Presidents of the Royal College of Surgeons, James Dunsmure and Andrew Wood, while Alexander Wood (no relation) was elected President of the Royal College of Physicians in 1858. James Wedderburn straddled both the medical world and the army, as a surgeon with the Coldstream Guards and later the Scots Greys.

A great number of Edinburgh families had strong military connections, particularly with the army; there was also the quasi-military connection with the Royal Archers. James Spens, already mentioned, was a Captain in the Royal Engineers, one of 12 members who had a military career. Craufurd Tait played football in 1824-25 before he joined the Bengal Native Infantry as an Ensign but fell ill shortly after arriving in India and died on the ship home, aged just 21.

Other soldier footballers were empire builders, notably Charles Staveley, who joined the club while studying at the Scottish Naval and Military Academy, was commissioned in 1835 and had a long and distinguished career around the world, retiring as General Sir Charles Staveley GCB. Along the way, he fought in the Crimean War, as did Robert Wardlaw of the 7th Dragoon Guards, one of three military brothers in the Foot-Ball Club, and James Ker, who was killed at Sebastopol. The inclusion of Lt Joseph Maitland RN in 1826/27 is interesting as he was the only member listed as a serving officer, and although he has not yet been identified, clearly he was not an active sailor during the football season.

There are also connections with the volunteer militia. John Hope alludes to his service as a yeoman on Portobello Sands around 1828[15] and went on in later life to be Colonel of a Volunteer battalion in the city (following in the footsteps of his uncle, a major in the Royal Irish Regiment, and his father, Colonel of the Royal Edinburgh Volunteers in the Napoleonic Wars). Thomas Goldie Dickson, footballer in 1836, was a Lieutenant in the City of Edinburgh Volunteers on its foundation in 1859.

When footballers obtained commissions and pursued a military career, quite likely they took their football enthusiasm with them and the army was active in the game in this period. In 1836, the Edinburgh papers reported: 'A match at foot-ball was played in one of Sir T[homas] D[ick] Lauder's fields at the Grange, between the troops of Captain C Stewart and Captain W Stewart of the gallant 71st (later the Highland Light Infantry). Colonel Grey and several of the officers, besides a select party of ladies and gentlemen, were on the ground, and appeared highly delighted at the scene. Sir Hew Dalrymple, who was among the officers who played, exerted himself most manfully on the winning side. The match was played 20-a-side, £5 a-side, and for the best of three games. Sir Hew Dalrymple goaling the ball in good style.'[16] The previous year Sir Hew (1814-1887) had succeeded his father, who was made a Royal Archer in 1825.

Five members entered the church. George Knight became a minister in the Free Church, while Thomas Marjoribanks took on a Church of Scotland charge in East Lothian. James Connell progressed from Edinburgh University to Glasgow and was then a Snell Exhibitioner[17] at Balliol College in Oxford before being ordained in the Church of England; he was later the author of many tracts and sermons against popery.

Connell was not the only Snell Exhibitioner who was associated, directly or indirectly, with the Foot-Ball Club. His brother Arthur, later Professor of Chemistry at St Andrews, went to Balliol in 1812; Sir James Wellwood Moncreiff, father of club member James, matriculated there in 1793; and John Gibson Lockhart, Walter Scott's biographer, in 1809.

In the next generation three great Scottish educationists all won Snell Exhibitions: Archibald Campbell Tait in 1829, Thomas Harvey (1842) and Hely Hutchinson Almond (1850). While at Balliol they came under the influence of the charismatic tutor (and later Master) Benjamin Jowett who was a great advocate of 'a healthy mind in a healthy body' and duly sent his 'Balliol Men', imbued with his philosophies, to schools and universities the length and breadth of Britain.[18]

Tait, whose elder brother Craufurd was a member of the Foot-Ball Club, was appointed Headmaster of Rugby School in 1842 at a time when football there was taking shape, and whose tenure coincided with the school's publication of the first rules of rugby football in 1845. Later the first Scottish Archbishop of Canterbury, Tait was not a player himself as he suffered from a club foot, but was brought up in a football family and almost certainly saw his brother play the game; poignantly, he named his eldest son Craufurd in his memory.

Harvey and Almond, both Glaswegians, put Jowett's ideas into practice by encouraging football at Edinburgh's leading schools. Harvey was head of Merchiston and then the Academy, while Almond developed his own distinctive brand of Muscular Christianity at Loretto. The outcome was the world's earliest inter-school football games in the late 1850s[19] and this led to the subsequent dominance of Rugby rules in Scottish adult football for many years.

Some club members went into the world of finance, notably the accountants George Chiene, Kenneth Mackenzie and William Spens who all set up accountancy firms in Edinburgh. Archibald Inglis was a banker who became Provost of Cupar, while Robert Allan was a stockbroker, albeit better known for writing a Manual of Mineralogy.[20]

Three members went on to be elected to Parliament: Thomas Balfour for Orkney and Shetland, James Moncreiff for Leith and Edinburgh, and Sir John Ogilvy for Dundee.

For the remainder, it is striking the number of different careers which they followed, not just in Scotland but around the empire. A few became landed proprietors, having inherited family estates or farms. Robert Dennistoun went to Demerara and Trinidad to run estates which he inherited from his father; Thomas Lyon was an indigo planter in India, Thomas Wood grew coffee in Ceylon.

Henry Logan, whose enthusiastic letter to John Hope (see page 50) revealed a passion for football, went to London to work for his elder brother William (later Sir William Logan, father of Canadian geology). Alexander and Archibald Cockburn were part of the famous family of Port wine merchants and opened the company's first office in London. William Bruce and James Dymock were also wine merchants.

Members also crop up in other contexts and four of them may well be the first footballers ever to have had their photographs taken. Allan Maconochie, Robert Dundas Cay, James Rannie Swinton and John Omond all posed around 1843 for the calotype pioneers David Octavius Hill and Robert Adamson.[21] Cay was subsequently a member of the Edinburgh Calotype Club and his portrait can be found in the biographical section.

Father to son

By comparing John Hope's footballing colleagues with the players of the following generation, a number of notable family links stand out, indicating that club members passed on their enthusiasm for the game to their sons.

Remarkably, for example, the captains of Scotland's first teams in association football and rugby football were both the sons of Foot-Ball Club members.

James Kirkpatrick (1841-99) captained Scotland in the first (unofficial) association international of 1870[22] and was an FA Cup winner with Wanderers in 1878.[23] His father was Charles Sharpe Kirkpatrick, a club member in 1831-32.

The following year Francis Moncreiff (1849-1900) led Scotland to victory over England in the first international rugby match, played at Raeburn Place in 1871.[24] He was the son of James Moncreiff, a club member in 1832-33.

Further close family connections in early codified football are not hard to find. In the first recorded Edinburgh Academy team of 1858, playing to rugby rules against Merchiston in one of the earliest inter-school matches, five of the nine known players were sons: two (Arthur and Harry) of Henry Cheyne, a member in 1827-28 and two sons (John and George) of George Todd Chiene, a member in 1826-27, together with Francis Moncreiff's elder brother James.

As well as many other father-to-son links in the early Academy football teams, a number crop up at other schools, such as Fettes where Hugh, son of William Allardice (member in 1831/32) and Thomas, son of Thomas Torrie (member in 1827/28) both played for the school; the younger Torrie also played for Scotland.

Taken individually, any of these associations could be a coincidence, but collectively they build up a picture of continuity between generations. It seems likely there are other, as yet undiscovered, links. This leaves no doubt that the football knowledge and enthusiasm of 1820s and 1830s players in Edinburgh was passed on and their sons made a contribution to the development of the game as Association and Rugby football.

Wider sporting connections

Although club members came together to play football, it will come as no surprise that was far from being their only sporting interest.

In the course of the 19th century a range of sports including golf, bowling, curling, target archery and tennis became popular in Edinburgh. One attraction was that they could be slotted into the busy schedule of the city law courts. As sport became more urbanized and regulated, clubs sprang up throughout the city, and as these clubs needed to be structured and managed, it is easy to see how these lawyers, as part of 'the great and the good' of Edinburgh society, put their skills into practice and went on to influence the course of sports development in the city and elsewhere.

One particular area of interest and influence is archery, which was practised for centuries as a means of defence, strongly encouraged by generations of Scottish kings, anxious that their subjects desist from playing golf and football when the English were threatening. In Edinburgh, there was one further reason for the practice of archery.

The Royal Company of Archers, founded in 1676, was designated in 1822 with a ceremonial role as the Sovereign's Bodyguard in Scotland, reflecting its membership drawn from the upper echelons of Scottish society: the nobility, landed gentry, the military and the respected professions. Being able to shoot an arrow was clearly an asset in certain sectors of Edinburgh society and to this day, in addition to their ceremonial duties, each year they shoot for (amongst other trophies) the Edinburgh Arrow, first presented in 1709.

It was not only a cause close to the hearts of the Hope family (see page 35), the family names of Cay, Cunningham and Spens appear both in the Foot-Ball Club's records and in those of the Archers' medal winners; others including Logan, Newbigging, Maitland and Maconachie are in the lists of those admitted to the Royal Company of Archers. Hope himself was admitted on 22 March 1827, on the same day as his footballing friend Nathanael Spens, a fellow legal apprentice with Hope's father. They were presented with the traditional vellum membership certificate, weighed down by the heavy red seal of the Company.

The wider Hope family were regular prize winners, as were several footballers: James Dunsmure won the Musselburgh Silver Arrow in 1866,

Charles Reid won the Kilwinning Papingo in 1844, while Archibald Swinton became Brigadier General of the Royal Archers.

There also those who participated in other sports. After James Moncreiff helped set up the Grange Cricket Club in 1832, its earliest opposition was the Brunswick Club, founded two years earlier and captained by Charles Nash who was also a Foot-Ball Club member.

There were keen golfers, notably Robert Oliphant who won the Royal and Ancient Golf Club's gold medal in 1834 and 1835, and he would likely have played against other footballers such as Patrick Keir, John and Henry Cook, who were all members of the R&A.

Walter McCulloch, club founder and close friend of Hope, was a noted all-round athlete, according to his obituary: 'He was considered the best middle-weight boxer in Scotland, in the uneducated days when pugilism was reckoned one of the noblest arts of man; and as a pedestrian few men in Scotland, if any, could beat him.'[25]

George Witham also tried pedestrianism, once taking on a wager of 50 guineas to walk 30 miles a day for six consecutive days, but ultimately failing because his feet became swollen.[26]

More sporting links are surely waiting for discovery.

Conclusions

The Foot-Ball Club was a vibrant organisation which catered for a wide variety of young men whose common link was that they sought fun and exercise by playing football in a civilised manner, with agreed rules. It was as much a social gathering as an athletic enterprise for this cross-section of upper and middle class male Edinburgh society.

Its members were part of a number of informal social networks which spread throughout many aspects of the city's life, through which they communicated with and influenced each other. The membership was dominated by future lawyers, yet at this stage of their lives their future career paths mattered little – their motivation was sport. Some networks related to school or university, some to work, some to family, some to where they lived, some to the games they played; or indeed several of these diverse networks. The members went on, through these networks, to greatly shape the city's future in many ways.

---

[1] The precise figure we have recorded is 290.
[2] Scipio Mactaggart, later Sheriff Clerk of Argyll and Provost of Inveraray.
[3] GD253/183/14/12
[4] The Mercat Cross in the High Street was the focus of Edinburgh life in the 18th century.

[5] William Smellie, *Literary and Characteristical Lives of Gregory, Kames, Hume and Smith* (1800), p161-2.

[6] Mitchell, *No More Corncraiks* (1998)

[7] He is remembered through his donation which set up a classics award at the school, the Mitchell Prize.

[8] GD253/25/2/3

[9] Charles Bell, *Letters of Sir Charles Bell, Selected from His Correspondence* (1870), p351 (quoted in Mitchell, p76)

[10] From an analysis of the Hope Papers, GD253/183/4.

[11] By comparison, one hundred years later, the addresses of members of the Royal Burgess Golfing Society in 1935, a group of men of not dissimilar socio-economic status, show that while about 20 per cent are in the New Town, by far the largest group are spread across these southern suburbs, reflecting very clearly the demographic shift in the city in the intervening years. See J Cameron Robbie, *op cit*, p89.

[12] John Hutchinson, *Revealed: town man kicked off world's first football club*, article in *Teesdale Mercury*, February 2016

[13] Joshua Hewitson exhibited a painting in 1828 at the Royal Institution (later the Royal Scottish Academy).

[14] Of the 36 founding members from 1824-25 who have been identified, 20 were born in 1806 or 1807.

[15] Jamie, p388

[16] *Caledonian Mercury*, 21 April 1836 and *The Scotsman*, 23 April 1836

[17] The Snell Exhibition was an annual scholarship awarded to students of Glasgow University to enable them to do postgraduate studies at Balliol College. It was endowed by Sir John Snell in the late 1600s and many of its scholars went on to positions in the Anglican community. Students from the east of Scotland who had attended Edinburgh University also took classes at Glasgow, which made them eligible.

[18] Almond was more than just a follower of Jowett: their families were connected. Jowett's mother was related to John Langhorne, the poet from Winton in Westmorland. Almond's school, Loretto, had been founded in 1827 by Rev Thomas Langhorne of Crosby Ravensworth, also in Westmorland. His son John was a master at Loretto with Almond, and Charles James Langhorne was a Snell Exhibitioner with Almond in 1850.

[19] For more on this see Chapter 8, and Hutchinson 2008, p555.

[20] Allan, *A Manual of Mineralogy*.

[21] It was our intention to publish these photos here but the reproduction costs demanded by the National Galleries of Scotland were prohibitive.

[22] Two teams representing England and Scotland met at Kennington Oval on 5 March 1870, drawing 1-1. Although the Scots (captained by Kirkpatrick) were all London residents, they did have Scottish birth or ancestry.

[23] Aged 37, Kirkpatrick kept goal for Wanderers against Royal Engineers on 23 March 1878. He broke his arm after 15 minutes, yet carried on and his side won 3-1.

[24] On 27 March 1871, Scotland defeated England by one goal and a try to one try. The match was played at Raeburn Place in Edinburgh, the Academical sports ground which opened in 1854.

[25] *The Scotsman*, 31 March 1892.

[26] *Caledonian Mercury*, 9 May 1836.

Chapter 6

INTERLUDE: WHO WAS MRS GORDON?

THERE IS one mysterious reference to the Foot-Ball Club with connections and confusions enough to put a glint in the eye of any decent conspiracy theorist. It has significance as it is the only known printed mention of the Foot-Ball Club in John Hope's lifetime.

In 1846 the *Metropolitan* magazine published a three-part serial called *The Sortes Scottianae or Two Leap Years* by a Mrs Gordon.[1] The title of the serial is borrowed from the *Sortes Virgilianae*, sortes meaning 'lots' in the sense of 'drawing lots'. It was a method, used since Roman times, to predict the future by opening the works of Virgil at random and seeing which lines appear to the eye first. In this story, the works of Sir Walter Scott, in particular *Rokeby*,[2] were used in place of Virgil.

Mrs Gordon tells a romantic tale of Edinburgh life, its opening scene set on a summer's afternoon in June 1824. The leading male character, Grantley Forbes, meets two older gentlemen on Bruntsfield Links, just as they 'paused to observe a match in process of being played there by the Foot-ball Club'.[3] It is clearly a match between members, rather than with another team or club, and the name is hyphenated, exactly as John Hope would have written it.

Yet anyone hoping for a sporting insight will be disappointed as there is no further mention of the club, and neither football nor Bruntsfield Links appear elsewhere in the story. It is a tantalising glimpse which prompts a number of questions.

Why that location? The club never played on Bruntsfield Links, although Greenhill Park, its home from 1831-36, was just beyond its southern edge. Why football? Golf and cricket were more commonly played there. Why the specific date of 1824, the year that Hope formed his club? Other than needing a leap year for the sake of the title of the story, it could have been any leap year. And most pertinently, why the specific title of the Foot-ball Club?

Looking deeper into the story, there are allusions elsewhere which could link to John Hope and his circle. Grantley Forbes is training to be a

WS, and there are references to the Courts of Justice and the hours at which they sit. He has a brother in the army in Ireland, while the leading lady, Sybil Lindesay, and her father, the Colonel, have connections with India. One of the two gentlemen says he usually walks to Wardie, which was the Hope family's suburban home, and there is mention of a Mrs Hope living in the New Town. The inescapable conclusion is that the author had some inside knowledge.

So, who was the author, named only as Mrs Gordon, and what did she know of football?

Bibliographers over the last century have been unable to untangle the mystery. The wrong author was credited in an obituary, an exchange in *Notes and Queries* in the 1920s failed to come up with an answer, and when we asked the Rare Books Department of the National Library of Scotland, they were not sure.[4] She has remained anonymous, until now.

There are several clues. Mrs Gordon is described on the title page of *The Sortes Scottianae* as 'Authoress of *The Fortunes of the Falconars*', a book which used an unusual spelling of the surname, and which again links to Hope's club as Henry Craigie, a founding member in 1824, married Jessie Pigon Falconar of Falcon Hall in Edinburgh in 1839.

In *The Fortunes of the Falconars*, published in 1844, Mrs Gordon is described as 'of Campbeltown' and also as 'authoress of *Three Nights in a Lifetime*'. That was a novel set in the north of England, published in May 1832 and bound in the same volume as *Inishairlach*, set in the Scottish Highlands after the '45 rebellion. Further investigation reveals Mrs Gordon wrote other works of historical fiction, including *Man and the Animals* (1840), *Helmsley Hall* (1846), *Kingsconnel* (1850), *Musgrave* (1851) and *Sir Gervase Grey* (1854).

Despite this prolific output over two decades and all these cross-references, none of these books reveals her first name. It is a frustrating omission as Mrs Gordon could be one of several people in Edinburgh society, all with interwoven connections. There was also the possibility that the name was invented, in an era where ladies often wrote under pen names.

One writer who appears, at first glance, to be a likely candidate was Mary Wilson Gordon. Born in 1814, she was the daughter of John Wilson, Professor of Moral Philosophy at the University of Edinburgh, a prolific writer under the pen name of Christopher North, notably while writing *Noctes Ambrosianae* (see Chapter 2) and a leading light in the Six-Feet Club (see Chapter 3). He had a summer home at 11 Boswall Road East Cottage, close to the Hope family's Wardie Lodge.

Mary Gordon was highly intelligent and took an active role in her father's academic and literary life. She married the advocate John Thomson Gordon in 1837, and wrote a biography of her father, *Christopher North, a memoir of John Wilson*, published in 1862. She knew men such as James Moncreiff and Sheriff Robert Dundas Cay (both members of the Foot-Ball Club), Sir David Brewster and John Gibson Lockhart. She also knew Maria Edgeworth, the influential Anglo-Irish writer, whose works Hope was known to have read and who, in her novel *Belinda* (1801) had a chapter headed *Sortes Virgilianae*.

It all fits – except for the crucial fact that her own family stated that she never wrote novels. So, it appears she can be discounted.

Another author of that surname was Margaret Maria Brewster Gordon, whose obituaries in 1907 credited her with the novels by Mrs Gordon. Born in 1823, this daughter of the great Scottish scientist Sir David Brewster did write historical fiction, such as the novel *Elinor Mordaunt* in 1860, a biography of her father, *Home Life of Sir David Brewster*, published in 1870, as well as a number of improving and religious works, all of them under her own full name.

Margaret Maria Brewster was an intelligent woman who was her father's companion and helper in Edinburgh's scientific and legal circles. They knew and corresponded with Sir Walter Scott, Thomas Charles Hope (John's uncle) and Henry Witham (father of George, who played with Hope's club). In the early 1830s, John Hope was a member of the British Association for the Advancement of Science, an organisation which the Brewsters strongly supported, and he attended their lectures on botany.[5] Serendipitously, after Margaret and her father attended a British Association meeting in 1847 in Oxford, they met Arthur Kinnaird, father of the first superstar of association football and later President of the FA, Lord Kinnaird.

Yet for all these credentials, the dates are wrong as Margaret Maria Brewster did not give up her maiden name until 1860 when she married John Gordon. Her obituaries were mistaken.

It is clear that neither of these two highly qualified and connected lady authors wrote the reference to a football club playing in Edinburgh in 1824.

A third option was suggested by examining another of Mrs Gordon's published works. In *The Fortunes of the Falconars* she is given the specific name Mrs Gordon of Campbeltown, and the *Metropolitan* magazine also saw the need to clarify her identity when it reviewed this book: 'The name being so extensively used, it may be proper to state that

Mrs Gordon of Campbeltown is the lady to whom we are indebted for this lively work.'[6]

After much searching for Gordons in Kintyre, this turned out to be a red herring as the publisher had made a spelling error. It became apparent that the suffix in fact related to the Gordons of Campbelton, who took their name from the family estate in Kirkcudbrightshire.

In 1811 William Gordon of Campbelton married Charlotte Douglas Dalrymple, born in 1792, third daughter of Colonel George Dalrymple, 19th Regiment of Foot (later known as The Green Howards and the Yorkshire Regiment). Her maiden name suggests a possible football connection as Lieutenant Sir Hew Dalrymple captained a team from the 71st Light Infantry in a 20-a-side match in Edinburgh in 1836, and scored the winning goal.[7]

William Gordon, a sporty type who was a steward of Dumfries Races, died in London in 1823. His widow returned with her eight children to Edinburgh, where she lived initially in Charlotte Square, then moved to the city outskirts at Portobello in the 1830s, remaining there until her death in 1870.

Mrs Gordon of Campbelton was clearly well off, was of the right age, and would have had the means to expend her leisure time writing novels. Yet on other counts, her credentials to be the author do not add up: there is no mention in contemporary media that she is involved in Edinburgh society, and no obvious link between her and the Hopes, or to the other places and people mentioned in the books. Just like the other Mrs Gordons in nineteenth century Edinburgh she cannot be asserted as the mysterious author.

Her true identity appeared to be intractable but just before this book went to press the pieces of a particularly challenging jigsaw fell into place with the realisation that there was a *second* Mrs Gordon of Campbelton living in Edinburgh.

This is because when William Gordon of Campbelton died, the family title passed to his 11-year-old son Alexander. Ten years later in 1833 he married Sarah, daughter of John Lawson of Cairnmuir WS, who therefore also became Mrs Gordon of Campbelton.

This time our investigation into her credentials led in a decisive direction, although it took a wide-reaching examination of her family background to establish concrete links between this Mrs Gordon of Campbelton and the elusive author.

The most pertinent of these was that her younger brother William Lawson was a loyal Foot-Ball Club member from 1831-36, the years when its home was at Greenhill Park, adjacent to Bruntsfield Links. She must, surely, have been aware of his sporting activities and where he played football, hence her specific reference to a match taking place on the city's principal recreational space.

For the legal scenarios necessary for the story, she could draw on her father's experience as a Writer to the Signet, and also on one of her husband's brothers, Thomas, who was at Edinburgh Academy from 1825-31 alongside other future Foot-Ball Club members, before qualifying as a WS in 1840.[8]

The clinching evidence was found in an obscure 1856 travel book, *Castles near Kreuznach*, written by Janet Robertson, who dedicated the work to Mrs Gordon, 'her attached relative'. This vague reference made sense on the discovery that Robertson was the author's maiden aunt, as her sister Isabella had married John Lawson of Cairnmuir in 1808.

The mystery has been solved. Sarah Gordon of Campbelton (1809-1890) was the author of this reference to the Foot-Ball Club in 1846 amidst her range of other historical novels. Her early works, all short stories, were published anonymously (as the Bronte sisters did at almost the same date) and it was only long after she married, from 1844 onwards, that she published under her married name.

She can hardly have realised at the time that her inclusion of the Foot-Ball Club in her serial would resonate almost 200 years later as the only contemporary printed record of its existence. Conversely, it would be the mention of the club that led to this discovery of her identity, which had eluded historians until now.

Mrs Gordon's allusion to football being played in Edinburgh has provided us with a unique glimpse of the Foot-Ball Club in action. And, if nothing else, she has provided evidence that a game of football in a public park was considered a perfectly normal part of the city's close-knit middle-class society.

---

[1] *The Metropolitan Magazine*, London and Edinburgh (March, May, June 1846).
[2] Walter Scott, *Rokeby* (1813).
[3] *Metropolitan*, March 1846, p339
[4] Correspondence with John Hutchinson.
[5] Jamie, p22
[6] *Metropolitan*, March 1844, p89.
[7] *The Scotsman*, 23 April 1836.
[8] There is a further sporting link as Thomas Gordon's grandson, Roland Elphinstone Gordon, was a Scotland rugby internationalist in 1913; he was killed in action in WW1.

Chapter 7

'MR PRINCIPLE': POLITICS, RELIGION AND THE DEMON DRINK

BY THE late 1830s, John Hope was past the first flush of youth. His interest in running the Foot-Ball Club was waning, and subscriptions were becoming harder to find.

His horizons expanded considerably after he qualified as a Writer to the Signet, departing the following month on an extended tour of Europe from December 1829 to November 1830 when he visited France, Italy, Malta, Switzerland, Austria and Germany.

Back in Edinburgh, although of an age to marry and start a family, instead he threw himself into work, as his time and energy were required for his father's thriving law practice, based in the family house at 31 Moray Place. He became interested in new topics and attended improving lectures in the University and elsewhere on politics, philanthropy, social issues and most of all religion.

While Jamie's biography is the primary published source of information about this process, further insight into Hope's daily life comes from an unpublished account by David Campbell, a lawyer who was later apprenticed under him and lived with the other apprentices in the house in Moray Place.[1] Campbell's memorial is highly instructive as, unlike Jamie's broader work, he concentrated more on the man, his way of life and his philosophies.

For example, when Hope's father started to pass on the family properties to him in 1832, when he was just 25, Campbell remarked it was because 'his profession and business habits qualified him for the management of such property'. This acquisition of the lands of St Leonard's was the beginning of a substantial portfolio that would make Hope a very rich man, although it was not such a gift as it sounds. The boom days of New Town expansion had ground to a halt after the banking crisis of 1825/26, which affected many sectors and particularly Edinburgh's publishing industry. House-building in the city only gathered momentum again in the 1850s with the growth in working-men's housing and commercial buildings.[2]

This upheaval was just one sign that the city was changing. The university, for decades the epicentre of the Scottish Enlightenment and still an intellectual powerhouse, had begun to feel competitive pressure after the foundations of the Universities of London in 1826 and Durham in 1832. They took away many of the English non-conformist students who had been barred from Oxford and Cambridge by the Test Act, which was itself was repealed in 1828. Among other notable events in the city, Burke and Hare were tried for murder in 1828 and the National Monument on Calton Hill, intended to commemorate Scotland's dead of the Napoleonic Wars, was abandoned due to lack of funds in 1829.

Conversely, over in the west, Glasgow was expanding rapidly into an industrial giant, reinvesting the wealth it had acquired from tobacco, sugar and slaves into coal, iron, railways, cotton and manufacturing. Over the next sixty years Glasgow saw a massive increase in its power and influence, becoming the 'Second City of the Empire'.

Hope undoubtedly sensed these changes and embarked on municipal politics after it was transformed by the Scottish Reform Act of 1832, which extended the franchise, and the Burgh Reform Act of 1833, which gave greater power to town councils. With the same robustness that he displayed on the football field, he threw himself into the Conservative cause and was appointed as the party's district convenor for the Edinburgh Town Council election of 1834. His devotion to detail, listing and canvassing voters methodically, paid dividends and the candidates he supported were elected convincingly. Bolstered by this success, he busied himself registering Conservative voters but got carried away at the next election in 1836 to the extent that he was outed in *The Scotsman*, which sided with the Liberals, for his 'disgraceful conduct' in persuading voters to vote for his party.

'Intimidation has always been a Tory weapon,' the paper thundered, 'and of the systematic way in which it was employed in the fifth ward at this election we have striking evidence.' And just in case there was any doubt about that 'evidence' or who was behind this behaviour, the paper did not hold back: 'We adverted in our last to the disgraceful conduct of a person at the polling station in the fifth ward, without naming him. The individual was Mr John Hope, W.S., Moray Place. The various letters which we have since received show the great disgust which his conduct has excited. His practice was to lay hold of any voters whom he thought he might use freedom with, at the door, and to coax, or urge, or dictate to them to vote for Messrs Ritchie and Watson. Had the electors been his menial servants, or had they been idiots, incapable of knowing right from wrong, he could not have treated them with greater contempt. So outrageous was his conduct, that he was three or four times seized with the view of being turned out of the room, and he was once floored in the staircase when laying hold of a voter. The persons present were not less astonished at the meekness with which he bore the most offensive epithets, freely applied to him by individuals. The Poll-Sheriff at last called in two policemen to restrain his disorderly conduct, which savoured more of the violence of a drunkard than of the zeal of a rational partisan.'[3]

Jamie, of course, managed to turn the incident to Hope's favour, praising his 'remarkable power of self-control' when criticised and 'his power of self-forgetfulness, his absorption of self, in the cause he had at heart.'[4]

Hope would continue in this bullish fashion for the rest of his life but held back from standing for political office for many years, preferring to take a supporting role until his election to Edinburgh Town Council in 1857. And, although he acted as a Conservative election agent for his kinsman Hon. Charles Hope in the Linlithgowshire elections, he never stood for Parliament.

As he left his youth behind, there was a growing restlessness, an obsessional and socially awkward side to Hope, who had previously enjoyed a relatively carefree life. In 1838 he began to have what Jamie called 'serious religious impressions', and he embarked on a life lived by his own strict principles, adopting a new attitude which induced him to 'do battle for God and the right'.[5] He systematically read *The Bible* and commentaries on it, and his religious devotion extended far beyond Biblical analysis and keeping the Sabbath as he became obsessed with the 'evils' of Popery. He started to approach people in the street to preach to them and, if necessary, to try and change their views.

He was so convinced of his own rectitude that he even referred to himself as 'Mr Principle' in a letter to his sister Julia in 1840.[6] She had been the first to leave the family when she married ten years earlier, and wrote to him to try and understand the changes she had noticed in him.

He replied: 'You ask me to tell you what I am about. Part of my proceedings you will have heard of, for I have not gone to the balls, nor am I feeding at the feeds.' He went on to give her several pages of his ideas on education, religion and alcohol, then described a sermon he had heard against what he calls the 'gif-gaf' dinners: 'I feel always that these dinner-parties produce no friendships, that they are heartless and formal – false smiles and forced conversation – and that large sums of money are spent, which would gladden the firesides of many poor people who have not yet in their lifetime received their good things, upon expensive dishes, because at the dinner season they are rare. All this may be the custom of the world, but it does not follow, on that account, that it is a good custom.'[7]

Others received missives on a similar theme as his letters became more and more strident vehicles for his religious and moral ideas. Typically, he started a letter with a passing reference to affairs of the day, then wrote at great length about the need for prayer and religious study, for a strict daily personal routine, exercise and temperance; it was enough to put off any prospective wives (he never married) and even his own family.

Campbell notes with precision that Hope became a total abstainer on 5 November 1839 to set an example to a trainee lawyer, Alexander Aitken, of whom he was very fond: 'A former apprentice had gone to ruin through drink, and fearing a similar fate for his 'Dear Saundie', unless precautionary measures were taken, he [Hope] induced him to enter into a compact, that neither of them would touch, taste or handle intoxicating drink. The other protégés were also encouraged to become abstainers.'

He also provided Aitken with accommodation, encouraged him to write essays (one of which, dated June 1839, was entitled 'Principle'), and got him to take up cricket. Aitken enjoyed the sport: 'We had half a holiday today, which suited very well – we began about half past 12, & played till 4 o'clock; I have just had dinner, & think I shall again go out at half past 6 o'clock when the club is again to be on the ground.'[8]

From this point on, Hope embarked on lifelong teetotalism. The temperance movement enjoyed widespread support at the time and Hope became so committed to abstention that he never missed an opportunity to spread the word, whether through the British League of Juvenile Abstainers, or by insisting that any employees must also be total abstainers. Even the church did not escape, and he condemned vociferously the use of alcoholic wine at communion, a stance which provoked many an argument with Edinburgh congregations over the years.

He was also encouraged by the progress of temperance in the USA, which was given legislative backing from 1851 with the passing of the 'Maine Law'. Maine was the first state to ban the sale of alcoholic beverages except for 'medicinal, mechanical or manufacturing purposes' and its example was soon followed by several other state legislatures.[9]

Hope not only abstained from alcohol and tobacco, he decided to live a simple, frugal life. He dressed plainly and practically, ate little and took plenty of exercise, while rising and going to bed early. By 1845, he had given up all stimulants, even tea and coffee, and would drink only milk or water, while his preferred food was oranges. In a letter to Rev. James Bell, he noted that his 'tea' consisted of 'tapioca and some boiled milk and some honey comb and half a roll'. He added that he had, by this time, given up drinking tea itself but wrote at length about still calling the meal 'tea'.[10]

Putting his own principles into practice, Hope started to help what he saw as the 'deserving poor' by providing training and accommodation for selected protégés in his home, both as individuals and in groups. However, there was a catch, as first they had to agree (in writing) to conform unequivocally to his abstentionist principles.

A family divided

Meanwhile, just as he embraced religion and total abstention, his domestic life was turned upside down. After his sister Julia left to marry in 1830, eleven members of the family all lived (and worked) together at 31 Moray Place until a rapid series of events left Hope entirely on his own.

The death of his sister Jane in 1839 was closely followed by that of his uncle John (the major) in 1840, his father James in 1842, and uncle Thomas Charles (the professor) in 1844.

The outcome was that Hope became head of the family, inherited the townhouse and took charge of all the family property, making him one of the richest men in Edinburgh, yet he was soon left to his own devices. Three of his sisters married in 1844-45, then his brother James moved out, taking with him the last two unmarried sisters, Charlotte and Fanny.

The reason was that his siblings had found him impossible to live with, according to Campbell's account: 'They considered Mr Hope too strict in his views on how the Sabbath should be kept in the house. The brother and sisters wished more liberty in this and other matters, and they all left Mr Hope and took up their permanent residence at Wardie Lodge.[11] He urged them to stay in Moray Place, promising that he would not be a check on them. He had not charged since his father's death. They might entertain, & do just as they pleased, he would only stipulate for a quiet Sabbath. His pleadings were of no avail. They looked upon him as a recluse, & mad for teetotalism, but he maintained that he was nothing of the kind. He only wished they would examine for themselves the reasons by which he had been convinced.'[12]

Hope had undoubtedly become an eccentric bachelor, but whether he was eccentric because he was a bachelor or the other way around is impossible to say. Certainly his 'holier than thou' attitude to his brother and sisters drove them away.

Over at Wardie Lodge, James was still technically John's business partner, but made it clear he was his own man. He married Gertrude Elphinstone in 1850 and as well as having seven children he provided for his two unmarried sisters and Gertrude's younger sister Anna. The household was supported by no less than 13 servants (nine women and four men).

James preferred the life of a gentleman lawyer and Hope once lamented 'James is a great trial to me'.[13] He did not hold back in accusing his brother of working little, spending too much, getting drunk, taking insufficient exercise and, apparently, not bathing enough. In one bitter response James accused John of sacrificing clients, the business, and everyone to himself, and closed the letter with this sting: 'Drunkenness is a bagatelle compared with selfishness'.

Despite their personal antipathy, the business between the two brothers somehow muddled along. The partnership was finally dissolved in 1864, but for years afterwards James continued to interfere with John's practice and work against him. Hope was remarkably sanguine about this, and in one generally chatty letter about other members of the family he writes over six pages detailing their doings, but of his brother he says only 'My brother James is as usual.'[14]

'That the brothers were living at daggers drawn was notorious in Edinburgh for many years,' noted Campbell, and the bitterness was clearly still there after Hope's death, by which time James was living in some style at Belmont House, a grand villa off Corstorphine Road.

Lifestyles apart, the root of this bickering was that much of the family property had gone to John, not just as the eldest but because it was plain to see that he was the man who would make the most of it. Understandably, the siblings were jealous and the unhappiness within the family sparked a decade of litigation in the 1850s, particularly over legal bills and his sister Charlotte's trust. She was disabled, possibly epileptic, and John maintained that the others were keeping her away from him.[15] It was probably true: Hope became virtually estranged from his family.

It must have been a traumatic time as in a few short years Hope's immediate household was reduced from eleven adults to only himself. However, although it was a large property he made sure he never rattled around on his own and he always had at least a housekeeper, manservant and maid, and in the 1851 census he is listed at 31 Moray Place with William Dunkeld (23, unmarried house servant) and two sisters, Elizabeth Rorison (40, widowed housekeeper) and Margaret (38, unmarried house servant). He also began to fill the house with his deserving boys and apprentices, not to mention legal staff and frequent guests ranging from his own extended family to the young members of the British League of Juvenile Abstainers, who became part of his 'family'.

This leads of course, in our very different world, to all kinds of questions about the propriety of such arrangements, which would not be acceptable today. It may seem odd to today's eyes that any employer or mentor could go to such lengths to encourage a particular form of behaviour in a pupil or trainee, and doubly suspicious when legal apprentices are boarded in the upstairs bedrooms of the boss's house and office. Yet, while Hope was for many decades considered 'difficult' and 'eccentric', never once did his many critics accuse him of impropriety (at least, not in any writing that has survived). Instead, he leaves a clear impression of being a strict but generous employer, who paid the going rate[16] and who would dispense holidays, travel, educational fees, job references and even money in times of dire need.

Hope explained his personal motivation in helping young men: 'I feel a special interest in this apprentice movement. Children are interesting & are comparatively easily managed, but how interesting is the young apprentice, entering on life, entering the workshop to labour at the same bench with the veteran infidel, and how sad to think that the fair blossoms of boyhood are so soon damaged by such associations & how soon they are initiated in vice of all sorts and degrees.'[17]

It would seem that, like so many Victorian men, Hope associated with other men and boys because he felt he understood them and was more comfortable in their company, rather than because of any sexual attraction to them. He was socially gauche and apparently asexual, driven by his work.

The British Empire at the time was full of men like this and Julian Glover, in his recent biography of Thomas Telford, *The Colossus of Roads*, bemoaned a similar problem of trying to understand a work-obsessed bachelor, how difficult it was to get behind the work and achievements to appreciate the feelings of the man himself, given that most of his correspondence was work-oriented and there were few eye witnesses to his personal life.[18]

In fact, Telford (1757-1834) was a close family friend, a contemporary of Hope's father and who built roads with his soldier uncle. Hope corresponded regularly with Telford and considered him an 'uncle', and remarkably they even talked about football. When Hope went on his grand tour of Europe in 1829-30, he stayed with Telford on the way and later wrote to him to say 'Often have I thought with pleasure on those happy weeks. Ever will I remember the 18 Nov in Cardiff, the 22 at Ludlow when football was the subject of conversation.'[19] Telford gave him a specific task while in Italy, which was to report back on the design of the 13th century aqueduct at Spoleto – which he did, despite having to contend with deep snow and glaring sun.

The logical working man

Having joined his father's legal practice in 1826, Hope took it over on his father's death and developed it into a large and successful business through his own hard work and dedication.

Campbell, who came into the practice later (and eventually succeeded to it), was full of admiration for his industry and perseverance: 'He was at work from early morning – often before six o'clock, and he remained working till late at night. He never seemed to tire of the work he was engaged upon; whether framing or revising deeds or other documents or drafting an important letter, or doing other matters professional or non-professional – going over the work again and again, putting it aside and afterwards resuming it until he had made it as complete as he possibly could. His relaxation often seemed to consist not in an entire freedom from active work, but in the changing from one piece of work to another.'[20]

Hope's dedication to work did not diminish until his dying days, and Campbell remarked that he checked and signed off his final set of accounts on 4 May 1893, just six days before the onset of his fatal illness.

He also noted that his boss could be a hard taskmaster: 'Mr Hope was a strict disciplinarian, and would not tolerate slovenliness of work, irregularity, or want of punctuality in his clerks or others. He often remarked when complaining of the carelessness of someone or other employed by him that he knew what he wanted, and had given his instructions distinctly, and he must have them carried out. Still, though thus strict, he in several instances, had compassion on broken-down clerks, giving them employment in the hope of helping them to do better. While he reprimanded severely, it could not be said that he had a bad temper. On the contrary, his temper was very even, and he had a strong control over himself even when much annoyed.'

In the context of the contested will (see Chapter 10), Campbell had a great deal to gain from presenting Hope in a favourable light. Nevertheless, he gave a clear and detailed picture of his personal eccentricities, particularly his determination to be logical and rational in all aspects of his life, irrespective of what others may say.

'Throughout his life Mr Hope was fond of outdoor exercise. He walked because the exercise and fresh air were in themselves a pleasure to him, but he also frequently expatiated upon the good he thus derived to his powers physical and mental. He insisted upon all over whom he had any control taking what he termed 'frequent and systematic exercise in the open air'. His connection with the Volunteers afforded him much walking exercise.

'As a rule, Mr Hope's clothing looked somewhat peculiar, some might say eccentric. He wore a high soft felt hat, conical in shape, of Tyrolese fashion. Till 1875, he wore a tall silk hat, but when abroad that year, he was so much pleased with the lightness and comfortable appearance of the soft felt hat which he saw made in Homburg that he bought one there. He found the wearing of this hat so pleasant that he never afterwards wore any other kind.

'On similar grounds of comfort and also safety, he had the collar of his overcoat made of extra depth, so that on being turned up it covered and completely protected his ears as well as his neck from wind and cold. In dress as in many other matters, Mr Hope looked to comfort more than appearance, and was not concerned whether the articles he wore were, or were not, considered fashionable.'[21]

With a man like this in charge, life at the office in Moray Place was never boring, and was described in detail in a fascinating newspaper profile published in 1855, when Hope was at the height of his powers and a well-known figure in Edinburgh and Scottish society.

The reporter started out with a flattering comparison: 'Mr John Hope, Dr Alison and Dr Guthrie are three Scottish Howards of the day; and of these three Graces, Hope in this instance is the greatest without doubt.'[22] This was quite a comparison, as all were famous men in their fields, and reflected of the esteem in which he was held by some of his contemporaries. Dr Thomas Guthrie (1803-1873) was a Free Church minister and famous philanthropist, temperance reformer and founder of the Ragged Schools; his statue stands in Princes Street Gardens. Dr William Pulteney Alison (1790-1859) was a distinguished doctor, professor in the University of Edinburgh, philanthropist and social reformer, who emphasised the connection between poverty and disease. John Howard (1726-1790) was the great social and penal reformer.

The author takes the reader in whimsical fashion on a visit to Hope, starting in the waiting room (the Dining Room): 'Here the sideboard and tables are loaded with newspapers, pamphlets, periodicals, tracts, treatises, and everything of this sort, with paper, pen, and ink, which may sometimes be needed. A man, it is said, may be known by his library, so here we have an index of Mr Hope's mind. All these various productions point, like so many guns in a battery, against Popery, alcohol, tobacco, and opium.'

There is then a description of the contents of some of these pamphlets and also of some of the wide range of people sitting in the waiting room preparing to plead their cases for help from Hope. After a while: 'At last bang goes the main-door, and we are admitted to Mr Hope's own den, fortunately find him in fine trim, walking up and down the room, whistling like mavis, and tossing his half crowns from his hand into the air, and catching them again, and laughing and talking at the full gallop.

'Hope's workshop is spacious, well-filled, and orderly, and on the table there are a variety of neat bunches of papers, docqueted: Popery, No.291; British League of Juvenile Abstainers, No.324; Teetotallers, No.287. Again there are Agenda – Send an order on the Bank of Scotland for fifty pounds to Dublin; visit my school, No.16 for instructing the working communities in mental, moral, and religious training; buy two thousand new tracts to be given on Thursday to my scholars. N.B. Inquire first if all continue to abstain from intoxicating liquors, tobacco, and opium; see, also if the school fee of sixpence per month for each pupil should not be lowered generally, remitted in any particular instance.'[23]

It is a quirky and not exactly an unbiased portrayal, but most of the elements mentioned in other portrayals of the man are included, and amplified.

100

Philanthropy and fresh air

With his growing wealth and with less inclination to support his siblings, Hope was able to extend his generosity to a wide range of causes encompassing his favourite charities and the deserving poor, with a particular focus on children.

His impact on the youth of Edinburgh was summed up by the admiring journalist in 1855: 'Let the reader stroll down of a summer evening to the large park of playground which Hope has generously provided for the recreation of his juvenile abstainers near Comely Bank below Stockbridge, and he will see it as crowded and busy as a bees' skep – everybody running roaring in grand style; or let the reader see him on his appointed day once in the year in St Andrew's Church. There the galleries are crowded with the parents, and the area filled below with the teachers and scholars, listening now to a lecture and applauding whatever pleases them best – their singing full chorus, 'We'll win the day' or 'We'll no give up our Bible'. Or let the reader attend one of Mr Hope's No-Popery meetings in the Music Hall, he being seated in the chair, surrounded with the elite of Scotch worthies, lay and clerical, and the meeting being addressed first with a Protestant champion from London and Liverpool, and then from Dublin; all speaking to the tune of one hundred pounds apiece, paid frankly out of the private purse of Mr Hope; or let the reader select one of Hope's grand field days which he has at a time, when ten thousand youthful abstainers are convened, in the open air, from every corner of Scotland, to do homage to Mr Hope, as their great patron leader. And now we ask our reader, are we not fully warranted in repeating that Mr John Hope deserves to be designated both a great and a good man?'[24]

That lengthy tribute reflects Hope becoming a vocal advocate of fresh air and healthy exercise for the young, particularly if it involved his beloved football. In 1840 he wrote a long and detailed letter to Rev Henry Grey, who was to lecture at St George's Church, giving advice on the advantages and disadvantages of various 'amusements' and their relative costs. 'Shinty is the cheapest; but there is a danger of hurt from the club. Football is next cheapest; but such questions as the extent to which tripping, shinning or kicking are to be allowed have to be arranged.'[25]

Hope appears to have spent a lot of time looking for suitable fields for football around the city, long after his own Foot-Ball Club no longer needed one. Even when he wrote to the directors of John Watson's School in 1840, principally about a field for the club, he asked them to look at the wider perspective: 'I may mention the regret I have often experienced from the difficulty of finding places near Edinburgh for healthy recreation to which the young men of Edinburgh are exposed. I feel confident that the directors would confer a great benefit upon the young men in their offices if the field in question was devoted to healthy recreation. At a small expense, to be raised by subscription, the field could be levelled sufficiently for all purposes; and it might be put under some management by which the desired object might be secured.'

He did have a narrow target audience at that time: 'The privilege would, of course, be confined to those connected with the law. I am sure it would be for the interests, both of the masters and the young men, that the latter had such a means of recreation, rather than walking about Princes Street idling their time.'[26] However, before long Hope became convinced of the wider benefits of healthy recreation for both rich and poor, and the need for more public playing fields in the city.

In 1847, for example, he wrote one of his long, multi-purpose letters to the Caledonian Railway Company. In asking for a job for one of his total abstainers, he tried to persuade the Company only to employ total abstainers on the grounds that passengers would think it safer and insurance companies would lower their premiums, went on to suggest that they set up special milk trains to Edinburgh and thereby lower the price (which had risen 50% in the previous year), and advised them to provide drinking water for passengers at stations.

Then, he concluded: 'The Company must have constant spare Engines, or rather Engines during intervals unemployed. It would be vastly popular if the Company were to employ these leisure intervals in conveyancing the townspeople on a Saturday afternoon out to play ground or football ground, or cricket ground, in third class carriages, at say, a halfpenny or say a penny the trip. The neighbourhood fields may be got at a moderate rent. This is a subject on which I have long set my heart, and in conjunction with early shop shutting, another subject on which I am strongly impressed, would, I conceive, do much to elevate the working classes.'[27]

His desire to improve the health of the masses was not simply focussed on playing fields. His largesse included paying for holidays for recuperation from illness; overseas travel for those whom he thought would benefit; and year after year he took British League members to Leadhills[28] for holiday, fresh air and hearty activities.

Environmental improver

Hope's mission to make lives healthy went far beyond fresh air and exercise. As ever, he saw the bigger picture and became a keen campaigner on environmental issues, following a practical, holistic approach to improving the living and working conditions of the people he saw around him. He advocated measures which improved not just the physical quality of the workmen's houses in the city, but also the environment around the people who lived in them, ideas which were decades ahead of the government enquiries into the health of the population which were held towards the end of the century.

For example, he was angered by the pollution of the Water of Leith by the Caledonian Distillery and campaigned for years to clean it up. It was not just the effluent running through the city that concerned him, he was perturbed that it derived from the production of alcohol.

As a large property owner, the provision of cheap housing for the working classes was of particular interest. In typical Hope fashion, he put his ideas into effect. In 1858, he made a thorough study of housing in Edinburgh and elsewhere. He wrote letters to *The Scotsman* and Heriot's Hospital, then worked out and put into practice a scheme for building, then leasing houses to workmen, so they could benefit from any price rises, rather than the landlord.[29] The momentum was taken from his plan only by the creation in 1861 of the Edinburgh Co-operative Building Company, which built the Stockbridge Colonies and other mutual housing developments, many of which survive today.

He was a staunch supporter of half days on Saturdays for working men, vocally backing the Half-Holiday Association when it was established in Edinburgh in 1854 (and no doubt encouraged by its close links to the temperance movement, which wanted to ensure the workers did not spend their newly-gained free time in the pub).

He called for free education for all, long before the Education Acts of the 1870s, and had many other ideas for social improvement, advocating bathing pools near workers' houses, proposed government financial aid for Clyde shipbuilders when trade was slack, and encouraged weather reports to be printed in daily newspapers.

John Hope was different from many other Victorian reformers and campaigners, in that he was willing to develop his radical ideas then back them up with his own immense wealth and energy. This made him a formidable force for good in mid-nineteenth century Edinburgh.

---

[1] *Draft Memo of Information respecting the late John Hope Esq WS*, David Campbell WS, hand written, 1894. GD 253/14/5
[2] The half-completed Hopetoun Crescent, which his family tried to develop, is an example of this. For further details see Rodger's *The Transformation of Edinburgh*.
[3] *The Scotsman*, 5 November 1836

[4] Jamie, p29

[5] Jamie, p38

[6] Letter dated 19 December 1840, quoted in Jamie, p36.

[7] Jamie, p31. 'Gif-gaf' appears in the author's glossary of Sir Walter Scott's *Tales of My Landlord* (1831), meaning 'give and take'.

[8] Alexander Aitken letter to Hope, 18 June 1839, GD 253/26/4/9

[9] Maine Road in Manchester, later the home of Manchester City's football ground, was given its name in honour of the Maine temperance movement.

[10] Letter dated 24 February 1845, GD 253/381/4

[11] Wardie Lodge was the Hope family summer residence, built around 1830 on the north side of Edinburgh overlooking the coast at Granton. It has now been incorporated in St Columba's Hospice.

[12] Account by David Campbell GD 253/14/5

[13] Letter dated 1845

[14] Letter to General Sir James A Hope, 25 December 1871; GD 253/7/1

[15] GD 253/15/1

[16] See, for example, the list of wages paid to his clerks in the 1850s. GD 253/15/1

[17] Letter to Rev Dr Muir, 6 September 1847. GD 253/6/1038

[18] Julian Glover, *Man of Iron. Thomas Telford and the Building of Britain* (Bloomsbury, 2016)

[19] Letter from Rome dated 20 February 1830, GD 253/184/3/2. The authors are indebted to Alec Hope for bringing this to our attention.

[20] Campbell memorandum, quoting a letter dated 9 June 1848, timed *Morning ½ p6,* GD253/14/5

[21] Campbell memorandum, GD253/14/5

[22] Published initially in the *Northern Standard*, it was reprinted in the *Fife Herald*, 4 January 1855.

[23] *Fife Herald*, 4 January 1855.

[24] *Fife Herald*, 4 January 1855.

[25] Jamie, p83

[26] Jamie, p99

[27] Letter to JJ Hope Johnstone, 21 June 1847, GD 253/6/963

[28] Leadhills had been owned by the Hopes of Hopetoun for well over two hundred years and the mines were a major source of their wealth.

[29] Jamie, p336

Chapter 8

FOOTBALL'S REVIVAL IN 1850s EDINBURGH

AFTER THE demise of the Foot-Ball Club, there was a hiatus in football activity in Edinburgh and it would be another decade before the game became popular once more among adults in the city.

From the few contemporary references to football in the 1840s, it is clear that scratch matches were occasionally organised among students and adults.[1] Played before the great divide between the two codes, these games were simply referred to as 'football', but the general impression is of a non-handling game, different from the rugby based game which the Edinburgh schools developed later under the influence of masters and boys from the south.[2] Other sports continued to prosper in the city at this time, notably golf and cricket in summer, curling in winter, but the enthusiasm for athletics which had arisen in the 1820s seems, like football, to have abated for a while.

Elsewhere, the first flutterings of organised football were being heard, and basic rules were printed and circulated at Rugby School (1845), Eton College (1847) and Cambridge University (1848). These beginnings have long been considered by football historians as the genesis of the modern game, and it is true that football blossomed in England in the 1850s, embarking on the changes which would result in the association and rugby games we know today.

However, it is important to recognise that Edinburgh also played a significant role in the game's development at this time, with the world's first football trophy, printed rules, organised games for girls and the first inter-school matches.

It would have been understandable if John Hope, having thrown himself into his work and causes, had ceased any involvement in football. However, he found an opportunity to revisit his youthful enthusiasm, by creating opportunities for boys (and then for girls, too) to play the game, working on the principle that sport was an excellent means of recruiting and retaining energetic youthful followers for the fight against drink and the 'evils' of Popery.

105

He therefore combined his interest in fresh air and exercise with his mission to educate children and elevate the working classes, a passion he maintained for the whole of his life. The first step was to create an organisation that would bring all this together.

The British League of Juvenile Abstainers

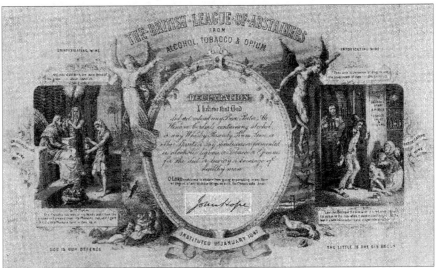

John Hope's signed declaration card for the British League of Abstainers from Alcohol, Tobacco & Opium.

In the autumn of 1846, Hope started to organise and fund meetings for boys that would show them the path to a healthy, respectable and God-fearing adulthood, untainted by the Victorian curse of drunkenness. There was already a well-established Edinburgh Temperance Society, founded in 1833 as part of the nationwide temperance movement, and Hope's plan was to 'catch them young' and provide children with a blueprint for life that would elevate them from poverty and despair.

After a couple of well-attended meetings confirmed the movement would enjoy enthusiastic support from children, Hope formally inaugurated the British League of Juvenile Abstainers on 1 January 1847 and employed two paid officials. They launched a programme of weekly lectures for boys, held in church halls in some of the poorest areas of the city, at venues including Adam Square, Water of Leith, St John's, Davie Street, St Stephen's, Niddry Street, Young Street and West Port. Each member signed a declaration: 'I believe that God did not intend any Beer, Porter, Ale, Wine or Cordials containing alcohol, or any Whisky, Brandy, Rum, Gin or other Spirits or any spirituous or fermented or alcoholic

106

liquors, or Tobacco or Opium, for the diet or luxury or beverage of healthy man.'

The League was not the first juvenile temperance body in Scotland[3] but it became by far the most popular. Talks on temperance were bolstered by the circulation of Hope's own printed lectures on the evils of drink, but what made the gatherings attractive was the use of music. This was an important part of proceedings, and the League developed its own collection of rousing temperance songs, based on popular choral tunes of the day. Some of them were by Dr Joseph Mainzer,[4] but the children adopted EP Hood's hymn *We'll Win the Day*[5] as the British League anthem. This verse gives a flavour of its sentiments:

When drunkards reeling through the street,
In all their sin we sadly meet;
We'll kindly speak, we'll deeply pray,
And shout in their ears, we'll win the day!

By the end of its first year the League had 3,300 members in Edinburgh who attended about 20 regular meeting places. All its activities were free of charge and although Hope at first tried to get subscriptions and donations from prominent citizens, he found the effort was far greater than the reward. He soon resigned himself to subsidising most of the costs himself, which amounted to at least £600 each year (and was estimated to be several thousand pounds in later years).

The most popular of all the League's activities were the mass excursions to the countryside, which became known as 'John Hope's Trip'. These were, for decades, the only chance to see the world beyond the city boundaries for thousands of boys and girls from the Canongate, the Pleasance and other deprived areas of Edinburgh.

The first outing was in April 1847 when Hope arranged for 700 children to visit the Royal Botanic Garden. It was a great success and, in order to encourage other friends and acquaintances to offer the same facilities, Hope asked Professor John Hutton Balfour, the Keeper of the Garden, to write a letter of commendation for his children. Balfour responded: 'I am happy to say that the children who visited the garden on the 23rd instant conducted themselves in a most exemplary manner. No injury whatever was done to anything either in the garden or in the hot-houses. Your arrangements were in every respect admirable, and the excellent training of the children is shown by the fact of the 700 having passed through all the houses without causing the slightest damage.'[6]

Duly encouraged, three months later Hope chartered two trains to take 1,255 boys and girls, supervised by 47 adults, on an outing to Dalkeith Park, just south of Edinburgh. They played football, archery, cricket and other ball games and to Hope's delight 'by the blessing of God there was not a single accident.'[7]

The template having been established, similar trips were organised each summer for many years. It became a major undertaking as each excursion had to be meticulously planned with special trains, arrangements for ticketing, travel to and from the stations, and a lively programme of refreshments and games when they reached their destination.

The *Illustrated London News* published these engravings of the great procession of young abstainers in 1851, parading through the centre of Edinburgh to Holyrood Palace

This was never more evident than in July 1851, when the League hosted a mass gathering for around 20,000 juvenile abstainers who travelled on special trains from around Scotland to the capital, where they were joined by thousands more from Edinburgh itself. In glorious weather, the boys and girls were taken in processions on a programme of visits to the major sights in the city, fed with a vast supply of buns, were universally well-behaved and polite, and loudly cheered John Hope when he spoke. It was such a momentous event that the *Illustrated London News* devoted considerable space to two large engravings of the processions along Princes Street (tailing back up the Mound to the Castle) and the visit to the Palace of Holyroodhouse. In their extensive report they hailed the outstanding success of the gathering and praised Hope for the work that went into it.

To organise large numbers of children on such a scale meant a relentless attention to detail. For every outing, Hope had a leaflet printed giving the children their travel instructions, the pick-up points, programme of activities, what they were going to see and, in particular, laying down a strict code of behaviour. The League superintendents and assistants marshalled the children in St Andrew Square, boys on one day, girls on another, and marched them to Waverley Station with assembly name boards on poles, colour-coded to match their tickets for those who couldn't read. Each year there was a different song, learned by heart, sung by the children as they marched, then added to the League songbook.

A flavour of these trips was captured in 1855: 'To see Mr Hope in full feather we must accompany him and his eighteen hundred scholars, in an excursion train engaged for the purpose to spend a long summer day in country, and to lunch with them on the lawn at Hopetoun House, or somewhere in East Lothian. On these occasions he succeeds in making himself the merriest boy among them, full of fun and frolic, beaming with benevolence, and delighted seeing so many shining faces – clapping one on the back – gripping another kindly by both hands, lifting up a third in his arms, and carrying or kissing all the little urchins, if every one of them were his own and only child.'

The excitement can be gauged by a look at the detailed and varied programmes put together each year. The 1848 *Pleasure Excursion* went on Saturday 5 August to Gosford in East Lothian, the estate of the Earl of Wemyss and March. A special train left the North British Railway Station at 10 am and returned from Longniddry before 7 in the evening. The leaflet described the estate and the lakes, fountains, islands and rustic bowers that the children ('our young friends') would enjoy, as well as 'the field where the various games are to be played'. Unfortunately, there is no description as to what these games were.

In 1850, the League had its outing to Ravelston on Tuesday July 30, and although this time no instruction leaflet survives, there are nine verses (with chorus) extolling the rural delights of Ravelston and Corstorphine Hill. Two of the verses give an idea of the games played:

So lightly skipping o'er the green
With rope and hoop we'll play;
Or eager stand with bat in hand
*   To drive the ball away.*

Thus will the time in harmless games
*   Most sweetly pass away*
Till all retire in fond desire
*   To meet some other day.*

The leaflet for the 1852 trip to Hopetoun House, seat of his kinsman the Earl of Hopetoun, sees the event split into two, Saturday 31 July for Girls and Young Women and Tuesday 3 August for Boys and Young Men. Again, in numbered paragraph by numbered paragraph, meticulous attention is given to the details of the train journey, what the children will see, when they can pick up buns and the availability of drinking water etc. This time, there are specific references to the games to be played.

20   When the refreshment is over, the bugle will sound, and you will all resume your places at the poles, with your Superintendents, who will then proceed with you to the grounds for the Games.

21   The Games for the females will consist of Hoops, Skipping-ropes, Balls, &c, &c; and the Games for the males will consist of Foot-ball, Cricket, Hand-ball, Leap-frog, Cross-tig, Races, Kites, &c., &c. It is also hoped a small Balloon may ascend each day.

22   The Boys are particularly reminded that the space for each game of Foot-ball will be indicated by poles - that each game must endeavour to confine the ball within that space - that the ball must be driven between the poles - that it is 'poor play' to kick the ball out of bounds, but when that occurs, it must be picked up and carried within bounds again.

23   Mr Hope requests that no physical force be employed, but that the law of kindness be used, and none other, in keeping order.[8]

The football he describes here cannot be anything but a primitive form of soccer, harking back to his schooldays, with the ball 'driven between the poles' to score a goal and no reference to carrying or handling, except when the ball was out of bounds. The Hopetoun excursion song has the following final verse:

And when we all come singing back
From Hopetoun's happy halls,
From cricket, and our foot-ball games,
Our hoops,
In hill and dale; and how we sang
The anthem for our Queen.

The whole day sounds great fun, even by modern standards. There is little of the overbearing patronising tones which so often went with this kind of outing in Victorian times and Hope appears genuinely keen to ensure that everyone knew what to do, behaved well, had a really good time, and then, when back to Edinburgh, told their friends about it to encourage more young people to join the League. He was always proud of how well behaved his Juvenile Abstainers were.

Thereafter, the excursions followed annually on a similar basis, visiting Dirleton, Tyninghame, Melrose, Dalmahoy and Gosford again. When an unforeseen peril arose, a stern warning was inserted into the 1855 leaflet: 'As special care will be taken to exclude ginger-bread men, and the sellers of painted trash which creates thirst, and injures the stomach, those who wish bread, in addition to the two buns, may purchase it at the British League cart at cost price.'

There was always great concern about safety, particularly getting on and off trains, as detailed in the instructions for the trip to Peebles in 1862: 'It is the duty of the Railway Company to have all the offside doors of all the carriages locked, both for the going and returning journey, but the League superintendents alone will open the carriages when the train arrives at Peebles.'

Amongst the variety of activities, a key component was football, which took an increasing role in these outings. The instruction leaflet for the 1859 trip to Tyninghame introduced a paragraph headed 'Football Arrangements' which emphasised how important an aspect this had become.

Six Balls. Each Superintendent hour about.
1st, Mr M'Intyre, to exchange with Mr Paton.
1st, Mr Hall, to exchange with Mr Scott.
1st, Mr J. M'Gibbon, to exchange with Mr Macrae.
1st, Mr M'Adam, to exchange with Mr Corbett.
1st, Mr Smith, to exchange with Mr Robertson
1st, Mr J.D. Cox, to exchange with Mr Jamieson.

When 2 o'clock arrives take it each half hour, and see that the last in charge takes the ball to the cart.

Any of the League superintendents are at liberty to give, for a time, their foot-ball in charge of any of the Edinburgh friends, who have gone out to assist us, but only to those who will make a proper use of them; but the League superintendents remain responsible for the balls.

Variations on this complicated arrangement were used in following years.

In 1861, for the first time, football was specifically mentioned for the excursion for girls at Gosford: 'A supply of footballs will be found at the League cart. The Assistants are requested to apply there for the same, and to do what they can to promote the games and the happiness of the children.'[9] This is significant as one of the earliest known references to football being a suitable game for girls.

It was clearly not a one-off as in the 1864 trip to Melrose, in the instructions for both boys and girls, Hope wrote: 'It is expected that each Superintendent and Assistant do all he can to promote the games mentioned in the Programme. The footballs especially require attention; and it is expected that the party having charge of the ball during the last half hour will make a point to see that it is taken to the League cart.'[10]

Given that, by this time, the League had over 2,200 boys and 2,200 girls going on its trips, arranging them was a great achievement in organisational terms. Yet perhaps the most remarkable aspect of these excursions were the highly organised games which included football of the non-handling variety, played to a uniform set of agreed rules. Football in this form was enjoyed by thousands of the very poorest boys and girls of Edinburgh, before the Football Association was founded, and long before the public schoolboys of the south ceased to haggle about the merits of their own particular set of playing rules.

The British League had a much wider remit than these annual gatherings, of course, and its weekly meetings attracted large numbers of young people through the year. This was quantified in 1863 when Hope noted that 451 males and 46 females had enrolled during the first six months of a ten-month session, aged from 12 to 54, although most were between 14 and 24. Other years 1,200 to 1,500 enrolled in different classes, and this continued until 1873 when the function was taken over by the Governors of George Heriot's Hospital.

The movement had enormous benefits for thousands of the most disadvantaged in the city, as the League's education programme developed over the years to include classes for apprentices and evening classes in book-keeping, shorthand, drawing, music, history and sewing. There were debates – mostly, it must be admitted, on anti-Catholic topics – and pupils were encouraged to develop their skills in public speaking, particularly at the annual prize-giving soirees.[11]

Hope was a passionate believer in the power of education for self-improvement, and spent large sums of money on teachers, books, paper, pens and pencils. From 1851 onwards, he paid two music teachers to attend 40 Edinburgh day schools and give lessons in music and singing, to relieve what he believed to be the monotony of school lessons in a five-and-a-half-day school week. These continued until 1881 when the function was taken over by the School Board.

Football in Edinburgh in the 1850s

The revival of football among the wider population of Edinburgh started in 1851 at the university. There was a sudden flurry of reports, published somewhat incongruously in the London-based *Bell's Life* rather than the Scottish newspapers, of football matches played by students. It is impossible to tell whether these reports were a result of more matches being played, or simply an enthusiastic student journalist, but the protagonists appear to have been a mix of English medical students and former pupils of the High School and the Academy. They found worthy opponents in the soldiers garrisoned at Edinburgh Castle.

The first report in *Bell's Life*[12] related to a momentous game which produced the world's first known football medal. It was played on 25 January 1851 in the Queen's Park (next to Holyrood Palace) between the Edinburgh University Foot Ball Club and soldiers of the 93rd Regiment.[13] The reporter gushed: 'The students looked all confidence and appeared active, fine, athletic fellows. The Highlanders, with Lieutenant and Adjutant McDonald[14] as their chief, took their places coolly but with resolute determination, arranging themselves in a manner which displayed excellent training.'[15]

They kicked off at half past two, 20-a-side, for the best of five games (goals), with ends changed each time a goal was scored. Two hours later the soldiers were declared the winners by three games to nil, which reflected the fact that they were no strangers to football, as the previous month they had played a large-sided match amongst themselves at Spark's Cricket Ground.[16]

What makes this contest particularly noteworthy is that the teams had agreed beforehand that the losers would present the winners with a silver medal. This beautiful prize is inscribed with the match details on one side, and engraved on the other with a detailed scene of soldiers challenging for a ball against students in ordinary outdoor clothes. Now on display in the Argyll and Sutherland Highlanders' regimental museum in Stirling Castle, it is recognised as the world's oldest football medal.

The medal was engraved by the silversmith James Mackay, whose son Robert was at the High School with John Hope and had been a member of the Foot-Ball Club from 1824-26; he may have been able to advise his father on the appropriate design.

Silver prize medal presented by the Edinburgh University Foot Ball Club to the victorious soldiers of the 93rd Regiment, who won their challenge match in January 1851. This is now recognised as the world's oldest football medal, and for good measure is the first known picture of men playing football wearing kilts. (The Argyll and Sutherland Highlanders' Museum)

Reverse of the medal presented in 1851 (The Argyll and Sutherland Highlanders' Museum)

The students were not done yet. The following month *Bell's Life*, perhaps via the same correspondent, published a report under the heading 'University of Edinburgh Foot Ball Club', of a 24-a-side match played on 'the Links', not stating whether this was Bruntsfield or Leith. It was staged between 'the Scotch and English members composing this club', and is the first known example of a football match of any kind being played according to nationality.

The game started at two, the teams wearing distinguishing colours 'on the Scotch side by a green badge, and on the English by a red', and it was agreed that they would play for three hours. The Scots scored first with 'a lucky hit', then the English scored twice and were declared winners by the umpires when five o'clock struck. The writer counted 500 spectators, named seven players from each side and the two umpires, and provided one of the most complete football reports of its day.[17]

The final report in *Bell's Life* that spring was of a match played on Leith Links on 21 March 1851 between 'the members of the Edinburgh University club and the gentlemen attending the Veterinary College'. It was won 2-0 by the former after two hours' play and the writer noted that 'the arrangement of the forces from the University was decidedly superior, and throughout their play was of a much higher order. This is mainly attributable to the good practice the side has been in since the commencement of their season.'[18]

Thanks to these anonymous articles, we know that the University Football Club in 1851 was well organised, practised regularly and had a programme of fixtures. There is also a reference to a proposed match between sides from the Universities of Edinburgh and Glasgow, 'the first time the rival clubs have competed together'. Unfortunately, no report of this match has been found, if indeed it took place, and there are no further accounts of students playing football in Scotland until the late 1850s.

Football in the Stockbridge Playground

In 1854, John Hope commissioned the first Scottish printing of rules on how to play football. As part of a philanthropic experiment to bring fresh air, exercise and temperance to the youth of Edinburgh, he took the initiative to lay out a football pitch in a large field which he modestly called a playground. He had taken a lease on ten acres of agricultural grazing land on the north side of the city, off Raeburn Place, which was part of the Rocheid family's Inverleith estate.[19]

His field was known as Inverleith East Haugh and by an extraordinary quirk of history, the adjoining ten acres of Inverleith West Haugh was leased to the Edinburgh Academical Club as a sports ground, and opened three days earlier, thus creating one of the most important sporting clusters in the city.

Hope inaugurated his Public Playground for Stockbridge on Saturday 20 May 1854 – the Queen's birthday – for the members of the British League and their friends. The aim of his project was 'that the young men of the trades might have a place where they should have their games of cricket, football, quoits, and the like, without inordinate expense'.[20] Although Jamie called it 'an experiment', the venture followed well-trodden paths of getting young men and women out of the city centre and into the fresh air at a reasonable cost, providing them with 'innocent and harmless amusement and association, and healthy exercise'. The whole enterprise was under the temperance auspices of the British League.

INAUGURATION

OF

THE PUBLIC PLAY GROUND AT STOCKBRIDGE,

BY THE

MEMBERS OF THE BRITISH LEAGUE AND THEIR
FRIENDS,

(IF THE LORD WILL,)

ON SATURDAY, THE 20TH MAY 1854,

THE QUEEN'S BIRTH-DAY.

A PUBLIC PLAY GROUND having been secured at Raeburn Place, Stockbridge, it is proposed (if the Lord will) to open it publicly on Saturday, 20th May,

THE QUEEN'S BIRTH DAY.

We trust that the Lord Almighty, the Giver of all good, will favour us with suitable weather and kind protection, and that all the members of the British League, with their companions and friends, will meet with us on the occasion, and that the proceedings of the day may conduce to much enjoyment, and the advancement of the British League.

It is also our anxious wish, that those members of the League who are no longer juveniles, and who have, from various causes, been prevented from attending the weekly and other meetings of the League, should accompany us to the Inauguration of our Play Ground, not only to keep up their connexion with the League; and afford us the pleasure of again meeting them, but that they, being now grown up, may take some share in assisting us to carry out the arrangements of the day.

We will also be glad to see with us on that day all Abstainers, and all who take an interest in the welfare of the young, especially the parents and guardians of those connected with the British League. We also invite all our friends, old and young, from the villages in the immediate vicinity of Edinburgh, to share with us our day's enjoyment. But we would remind all visiters, that this is a British League festival, to be conducted on British League principles, and that therefore not only are all alcoholic liquors and tobacco excluded from the play ground, (an invariable rule of the play ground,) but all who join us must abstain from these articles entirely on the present occasion, and if they cannot do this, they are requested not to join us.

We would also recommend that all take a good breakfast

RULES

OF

THE PUBLIC PLAY-GROUND

AT

STOCKBRIDGE.

THE ONLY ENTRANCE IS FROM RAEBURN PLACE.

All Parties, by entering the Play-Ground, agree to conform to the Rules, and subject themselves to the authority of the Park Keeper.

1. HOURS WHEN OPEN.

For Males.—Every Morning from 6 till 9, and on the afternoons of Monday, Wednesday, and Friday, from 4 till dark, and on Saturday from 1 o'clock till dark.

For Females.—On the afternoons of Tuesday and Thursday, from 4 till dark.

Note.—If the females cannot avail of the Play-Ground, more in future than they have done in the past, the afternoons reserved for them, will be given to the males, and the Play-Ground will thus become a Play-Ground for males and children only.

For Children of both Sexes.—At all the above named hours, when the field is not otherwise occupied.

2. WHO ADMISSIBLE.—All persons well behaved and not unsuitable, are admissible without charge on the proper day, but no Alcohol, or Tobacco, or Snuff, or Opium, nor persons under the influence or smell of these articles are admissible; and, if they enter, they are liable to be turned out.

Note.—It is expected that the young men who avail of this Play-ground, though not yet themselves abstainers, will so far conform for the time to the principles of the British League, as not to smoke either in coming to or leaving the Play-ground. The object is to admit all, and not to exclude any

The front page of the inauguration booklet and the set of rules for the Stockbridge
Playground which opened in 1854

On top of the cost of the lease, Hope spent about £100 to fence the area, mark a 60 yard 'racetrack', provide water, erect football goalposts and install a sentry box for a watchman. In his appeal to the Lord Provost and Magistrates to attend the opening, he intimated that the children of the British League would march in procession to the park from their respective meeting-places in the city. As it turned out, neither the Lord Provost nor the Magistrates graced the large public gathering with their presence, but testified their approval by subscribing £10 out of public funds.

The inauguration ceremony was a success: 'There was appropriate speaking; to the Queen a loyal address was voted; and the children sang *We'll Win the Day*. The agents of the League were there to superintend the games; and when the day was over, the talk throughout the town was of John Hope's Park.'[21]

Jamie went on to describe Hope's reaction: 'Not only on the opening day, but on the other days, the agents of the League were present; and Mr Hope himself was often there, as pleased as man could be. One day was set apart to be 'the day of the kites', the great event of that day being the setting off of a gigantic kite, which was named 'The British League'. On another day, as he tells his sister in a letter, he beheld 'a puddick race'

117

(leapfrog), in which twenty-five or thirty boys competed, and by which he was intensely amused. He was also once a delighted spectator of a mimic war. A mound in the field was supposed to be Sebastopol.[22] One party, who were supposed to be British, attacked it with a football; and the Russians upon the mound did their best to drive it back. Or he would watch the cricketers or other players, and as they laughed and shouted in their merriment he experienced the keenest enjoyment.'

The park had a detailed schedule of opening times, and interestingly it made provision for women. Men could use it every morning before work from 6 till 9 and on the afternoons of Monday, Wednesday and Friday from 4 till dark, and on Saturday from 1 till dark. Women were allocated the afternoons of Tuesday and Thursday, from 4 till dark.

Hope went to great lengths to ensure that the users of the park behaved as he would wish them to do and published a booklet, *Rules of the Public Play-Ground at Stockbridge*.[23] In it, he specified: 'no swearing or improper language – no fighting or quarrelling – no betting, or playing for money, or anything whatever – no tripping, no dogs, nor anything to annoy, can be permitted.' He was clearly worried, and rightly so, about maintaining good relations with the landlord and constantly made references to the need for good behaviour lest the lease be revoked. There were dire warnings for any miscreants: 'The most serious offence is climbing on the walls or flakes or trespassing on the avenue to Inverleith House. Any boy crossing the Water of Leith and climbing up the wall and crossing the avenue, and over the flakes into the field, or leaving the field in this way, will be punished with the utmost severity, for that of all others may lead to the loss of the park and thus hundreds of well-disposed parties might be punished for the offence of a few bad boys.'

The was a local peculiarity in *Rule 6, The Sheep &c*, due to it being grazing land: 'The stock must not be chased or disturbed. The object is to get the grass thoroughly ate down in the first instance, after which it will be easily kept down, and short grass will be much more comfortable to play on than long grass. It will also dry much sooner in a wet day.'

Most pertinently, Hope gave instructions to the park users on the type of games they should play, with guidance on how they should organise themselves, as these extracts from the rule book reveal:

Rule 9. THE GAMES — The Games already sanctioned are Foot-Ball, Cricket, Quoits, Foot-Racing, Hand-Ball, Tig, Cross-Tig, and all ordinary Games where no implements are required. Games by which parties may be led to strain or injure themselves from competition in feats of strength, or from bragging each other, such as throwing the stone, or hammer, are not permitted.

118

Of particular interest in the context of football's origins, Rule 9 was supplemented by Hope's detailed description of how he believed football should be played:

9. THE GAMES.—The Games already sanctioned are Foot-Ball, Cricket, Quoits, Foot-Racing, Hand-Ball, Tig, Cross-Tig, and all ordinary Games, where no implements are required. Games by which parties may be led to strain or injure themselves from competition in feats of strength, or from bragging each other, such as throwing the stone, or hammer, are not permitted.

The Game of Foot-Ball is strongly recommended, as giving most exercise and fun in a short time. There must be no kicking of shins, nor tripping—for these are apt to produce quarrels and hurts, and do not form part of the game. The ball is not " hailed," unless it is sent *between* the posts, by one of the side whose duty it is to send it through, and unless it touch the ground. If the ball is sent through by one of the other side, it is not "hailed." The ball should not be kicked out of bounds. When this occurs, it should be lifted up by the hand, and brought within bounds. The party thus lifting it, is entitled to a " free kick," but the ball must not be lifted *by the hand* from the ground at any other time. The British League Cap, to distinguish sides, cost 2d, is recommended. Beware of kicking the ball over the fences. Mr GRAY, saddler, 18, South Hanover Street, can supply round cases of stout grain dressed shoe leather for 3s. 6d. each. They will be found cheapest in the end, and save bladders.

John Hope promoted his code for football of a non-handling, non-hacking kind in the 1854 Rules of the Public Playground at Stockbridge.

Here, in 1854, is an easily understood set of rules which found many echoes when the laws of association football were written in the following decade. It is football of the non-handling, non-hacking kind, with defined playing boundaries, a method of scoring between goalposts, and contested between two teams wearing distinguishing colours.

These rules also provide a tangible link to the Foot-Ball Club's fledgling rules of 1833, and even further back to Hope's football days in the High School Yards.

The remainder of the booklet is of great interest, particularly Rule 11 which looks forward to future developments in the game with the idea that players from workshops, offices and shops should get together to form clubs to play against other teams, to bring in new members and to wear distinguishing clothing.

119

10. IMPLEMENTS OF AMUSEMENT.—All parties must provide their own Implements for sanctioned Games. The Town Council having kindly granted the loan of a Sentry Box for the Park-keeper, parties may deposit their implements in it, *at their own risk*, but the Park-Keeper is not responsible for their safety. All implements so deposited, must be securely tied together and labelled with the name of the depositor. All gratuities to the Park-Keeper are prohibited; his accepting them would cause him to lose his situation.

11. CLUBS.—It is suggested that those in the same Shop or Establishment, or at all events, those in the same occupation, who, by getting free at the same hour, may be able to join in the same Games at the same time, should form themselves into Clubs for Games. The Club can secure a preference to a piece of ground for a sanctioned Game at a specific hour, for two meetings in the week. If the Club meets oftener than twice in the week, it must occupy, on those extra occasions, the ground which, at the time, may happen to be vacant. Persons not in Clubs, on coming to the Park, should not stand merely looking about them, but should introduce themselves to each other, and get up Games among themselves, or ask to be allowed to join others then engaged in Games, if there be room.

Hope's rules for the Stockbridge Playground went beyond advocating good behaviour and how to play, as he foresaw the need for organised events and pitch hire.

To enable clubs and groups to play football, it was possible to hire a pitch, in much the same way that local councils maintain municipal football pitches to this day:

Rule 12. ALLOTMENT OF GROUND — The Ground has been arranged for Foot-ball, Cricket, Quoits, and Foot-Racing. The plan can be seen at the British League Office, 53 Rose Street, and ground secured there between 7 and 8 evening, Saturday excepted. Clubs failing to use their ground for two successive days, forfeit their preference. Parties wishing ground on which to play, but who have not secured ground, may play on any space which may be unsecured and vacant at the time.

The Stockbridge Playground was well used and it all went swimmingly, yet to Hope's intense frustration the landlord refused to renew the lease the following year, and allowed the land to revert to grazing. It is not clear from Hope's papers why he was knocked back by the Rocheid Estate, and although he made pleas to Rocheid's agent, the newspapers and even the Lord Provost, it was to no avail. The complicated legal position of the Rocheid family inheritances, and the owner living in Germany, may have been a factor.[24]

It could be argued that this rejection of Hope's scheme had a profound influence on the future development of football in the city. His preference for a kicking, non-handling form of football never had the chance to take root, while the Edinburgh schools soon came to adopt the handling code we now know as rugby football.

Then and now: Thomas Shepherd's 1829 engraving of Edinburgh New Town from the north west has the open fields of Stockbridge in the foreground and St Stephen's Church prominent on the left. Although his exact perspective is no longer available due to house-building, the view today reveals the same cityscape, while the fields have become Edinburgh Academical Club's Raeburn Place rugby pitch (venue for the first international in 1871) in the foreground, and the Grange Club's cricket field immediately behind.

121

At the same time as the Stockbridge Playground was cut off in its prime, the Edinburgh Academy sports ground next door was taking off. It had opened on 17 May 1854 to great fanfare, hosted cricket that summer, then in the autumn the attention of the boys turned to football. This was the catalyst for a decisive moment in the history of Scottish sport.

Although a form of football had been played for many years by boys at the Academy, as it had in the High School, it was a rough and disorganised playground activity. The creation of a dedicated sports ground with grass pitches prompted a desire for greater organisation, and the solution was provided a newcomer to the school, 16-year-old Francis Crombie.

Although brought up and mainly schooled in Edinburgh, Crombie had spent the previous two years as a boarder at Durham School[25] where Rugby football was played. He was in the enviable position of having a booklet of printed rules of football, together with the knowledge of how they should be applied and from then on, the Academy boys adopted Rugby football as their preferred code.

Their example was followed by the other principal schools in Edinburgh, which by the end of the decade had not only started playing against each other, but had also taken the game into adulthood and to the universities.[26] The earliest recorded representative football match was contested in December 1857 between the Academical Football Club – former pupils of Edinburgh Academy – and students from the University. It was played over four Saturdays before a result was achieved, the Academicals winning in mid-January by three goals, largely due to 'three of four of their number who had learned the drop kick and played the game in England.'[27] The following month saw the first inter-school match, between the Royal High School and Merchiston Castle.

For fully twenty years the Rugby code remained the dominant, almost exclusive, form of football in Edinburgh and the city's first football clubs of the modern era were all based on the principal schools and their old boy networks, all playing to Rugby rules. This advance could not have taken place without support and cooperation from the city's educational leaders, who saw the benefits to schoolboys and to society of what the *Saturday Review* in 1857 first called 'Muscular Christianity'. They encouraged their boys to improve themselves through sporting competition.

It was not until 1873 that association football was first played in Edinburgh. As we shall see in Chapter 9, that belated introduction gave another opportunity for John Hope to promote the kicking, non-handling game he had always preferred.

[1] For example, *Bell's Life*, 11 April 1841, contained a brief announcement that gentlemen's servants in Edinburgh had challenged the city's waiters and the chairmen to 'a game at football for their own sum'. However, there is no corresponding match report in the paper.

[2] Hutchinson (2008), p555. Also, see the print of students playing football in the quadrangle of United College in St Andrews, wearing top hats and gowns in Charles Rogers' *History of St Andrews* (1849), p117

[3] The first juvenile temperance society was formed in Paisley in 1830.

[4] Joseph Mainzer (1801-51) was a German music teacher who wrote music to be sung by massed choirs. He lived in Edinburgh in the 1840s and although he wrote choral music for Church of Scotland Psalms, he was in fact an ordained Catholic priest. It is not known if John Hope was aware of this.

[5] Edwin Paxton Hood (1820-1885) published this song in *The Book of Temperance Melody* (1848).

[6] Letter dated 30 April 1847, quoted by Jamie, p184.

[7] Jamie, p185

[8] GD 253/181/2

[9] *Memorandum for Assistant Superintendents* for the excursion for girls, Saturday 29 June 1861, GD 253/181/2

[10] GD 253/181/1

[11] Public speaking was a valued skill. It was later often said that the trades unions in England were full of Methodists because they had honed their public speaking skills in the annual Anniversary in the chapels.

[12] *Bell's Life*, 2 February 1851

[13] The 93rd was later renamed the Sutherland Highlanders, of 'Thin Red Line' fame at Balaclava in 1855, and then amalgamated with the Argylls in 1881.

[14] This is almost certainly William Donald Macdonald (1827-62), who was appointed Adjutant in January 1851.

[15] *Bell's Life*, 2 February 1851

[16] The *Stirling Observer* of 26 December 1850, quoting the *Witness*, gave a brief report of a match played by men of the 93rd Highlanders, between two sides of 37 against 31.

[17] *Bell's Life*, 9 March 1851

[18] *Bell's Life*, 6 April 1851

[19] Rocheid's Inverleith House is now within the Royal Botanic Gardens. The original avenue to Inverleith House is now Arboretum Avenue, which runs parallel to the Water of Leith, and the original gate-posts are still to be seen beside the south Lodge House.

[20] Jamie, p301-2

[21] Jamie, p302-3

[22] It was one of two mounds in the area both marked as 'ancient bow butts' on Edinburgh maps. This one was flattened by the Grange Cricket Club about 1871 when they moved to Raeburn Place, to create a level playing surface. The other was on the Academy's playing area and survived until 1947 as a popular vantage point for watching rugby matches. Edinburgh Academy continued to call the area the Mound Pitch.

[23] GD253/181/1

[24] After an earlier James Rocheid, proprietor of the Inverleith Estate, died insolvent in 1825 the estate passed through three generations: his son James (a Foot-Ball Club member in 1827/28 and a Royal Archer) died in 1840 in Germany having married a baroness; his son Charles died in 1864 in Germany having also married a baroness. The terms of the will of the first James Rocheid were then contested and it was not until 1869 that his inheritance

123

was resolved. The ownership of 96 acres of prime land in North Edinburgh passed to the next Charles Rocheid, born in 1853, and he began selling off this land in the 1870s almost as soon as he reached his majority.

[25] Francis Crombie was sent to board at Durham in 1852 with his elder brother Alexander when the private school in Edinburgh they were then attending closed suddenly. Both of them had previously attended Merchiston Castle School.

[26] Hutchinson (2008), p554

[27] *Edinburgh Evening Courant*, 19 January 1858

Chapter 9

VETERAN CAMPAIGNER

WHEN JOHN Hope got the bit between his teeth, there was no stopping him. His preferred tactics were to wear people down, to drown them out, and to grind them into submission. Compromise was not in his vocabulary and his strident views were anathema to many.

Yet Hope also built a reputation as a generous philanthropist and committed educationist, contributing freely to numerous charities, exotic and mundane: 'for the education of Hindoos', 'for Jewish females' and for various Irish causes, as well as making smaller donations to hundreds of local widows and others in need, all carefully recorded in his accounts book.

The source of his wealth is worth examining. Despite all his undoubted eccentricities, Hope had a good head for business and his property portfolio extended right across the city to land, shops, houses, gardens, commercial premises and yards around Rankeillor Street, St Leonard's Street, Clerk Street, East London Street, Annandale Street, Hope Crescent, Haddington Place and the Gayfield area including the football pitch known as Gayfield Park, as well as the British League offices in Rose Street.

This is quantified in Rodger's table of land ownership in the city in 1872 which lists him at 15th out of the city's top 20 by acreage (including the railway companies, the Town Council and major charitable trusts). What is more, the high rental that Hope could obtain from his properties made him one of Edinburgh's richest men, as the gross annual value of those acres and the value of the holding per acre placed him sixth and fourth respectively.[1] The total annual rent he received in 1885 was £3,695.[2]

Great wealth cannot, of course, guarantee good health, and while Hope was generally blessed throughout his long life, he kept in close contact with his doctor and became something of a hypochondriac. Campbell described Hope's logical response to medical advice: 'It should be mentioned here that, agreeable to his doctor's wishes, Mr Hope in the later years of his life, kept a record of the nature and frequency of his stools; and in order the more readily to detect the presence of red dust – the forerunner of gravel – urine was kept for some days in the chamber pot for that day, standing in his WC, to admit of the sediment, if any, showing itself. This might by some be considered eccentric procedure, but there was an intelligible reason for it, as to which Mr Hope's doctor can well speak.'[3]

Hope was an eager patient, he noted: 'For some years before his death, Mr Hope, acting on his doctor's instructions, remained indoors during the entire winter months, and the more effectually to carry out these instructions – given to prevent him catching a cold – Mr Hope kept to his bedroom flat, at one end of which was his bedroom, and at the other end his business room. To make up for this enforced confinement, Mr Hope spent about three months holiday during the summer and autumn.'

During those holidays he travelled abroad most years, and was particularly attracted to German health spas, in search of a remedy for his indigestion (probably caused by his diet) and rheumatism. One lasting reminder of this is the portrait he had taken by a photographer in Bad Neuenahr spa in 1865, which he then had printed up as calling cards (see page 5). He must have had hundreds done, as large numbers remain in boxes in the National Records of Scotland.

Rather eccentrically, Hope often took to his bed for an hour or two each afternoon to rest and stretch, yet still kept on working. He had bells within reach to summon his clerks, and received visitors while lying down and in his dressing gown – which could be unnerving for those who were not aware of his habits.

In the Town Council

In November 1857, at the age of 50, Hope was elected unopposed to Edinburgh Town Council for the ward of St George's, which covered the Dalry and Fountainbridge area. One senses that he would have relished an opposing candidate to debate with, as Jamie described how he planned to approach his new responsibilities by drawing up a detailed memorandum of his 'sentiments', in which he declared himself a root-and-branch reformer of abuses. This reads like an election address, but although it was not needed, it was a clear statement of Hope's aims and priorities in life.

Two long-standing campaigns define him: total abstention from alcohol and tobacco, and a virulent anti-Catholicism. By modern standards the latter, in particular, paints him as bigoted and unforgiveable, although in Hope's lifetime he was far from being a lonely voice and his views have to be seen in the context of his times.

Jamie, as a Church of Scotland minister, was understandably sympathetic: 'He was an out-and-out Protestant, educationist, and abstainer. He would abolish patronage, and bring back the people to one church, making the way easy for the dissenting bodies to come back. He was for religious education, and for compulsory education. He would withdraw all Popish endowments, and have the nation, by missionaries, and by royal preachers, set itself to convert to Christ the Roman Catholics and the heathens at home and abroad. He declared himself ready for any extension of the Protestant franchise; but he would refuse it to Papists, on the ground that they were not qualified to rule, not being civilly or religiously free, but in subjugation to priests, bishops, and Pope.'[4]

Hope's new-found position and influence as a councillor gave him greater opportunities to pursue some familiar themes. The fleeting success of the Stockbridge Playground spurred him on to his next venture in the promotion of open spaces for working men, women and children. He liked instant action, and was prepared to use his considerable wealth to move things along a little quicker than some committee-led projects naturally moved.

This was abundantly clear after members of the Half-Holiday Association approached him about the opening of East Princes Street Gardens for recreation. Instead, he suggested they try to resurrect the idea of the park in Stockbridge in which he had invested so much time and money. Although an approach was rejected by the Rocheid Estate, the negotiations put Hope into contact with Charles Macpherson, the council's Superintendent of Streets and Buildings, which set up one of the comic double acts of this story.

Macpherson clearly had his own working ways and pace (or lack of). Jamie, not a man for outlandish humour, saw the funny side when Macpherson was instructed to examine the ground at Stockbridge. 'To assist him in his report, Mr Hope, to whom the whole subject was very familiar, wrote suggesting many details as to water supply, drainage, football posts, blue clay for quoits, etc.' This affronted Macpherson's dignity and he retorted 'Are you a sub-committee?' Hope, not known for his sensitivities, noted ruefully, 'I may be going too fast'.

Yet although a return to Stockbridge Park did not materialise, amazingly the Town Council did open a new 8-acre public park in 1859 on the other (south) side of Raeburn Place, subsequently extended in 1864 to 15 acres. Hope found an unlikely ally in a political opposite, Councillor James Crighton, a Liberal and anti-temperance man, who called for the park to be extended further, and in 1869 Hope was delighted to be asked by Crighton in a meeting of electors, 'Will Mr Hope support a public park for Stockbridge?' To loud laughter, he responded 'Do you suppose Mr Hope will turn back on what he has already said? Don't you know that the park which is there is called Hope Park? Don't you know that, sir? Have you forgot that I had the first park – that I had a park at Stockbridge before you ever thought of parks? You are but a humble follower of me.' For dramatic effect, the newspaper report added 'Renewed laughter and uproar, which continued for some time.'[5]

This open space became known as John Hope's Park and in the following two decades served as a pitch for the emerging Stockbridge football teams, not to mention cricket and shinty. However, after the council's lease expired in 1891 the park was built over to create housing where Dean Park Street, Comely Bank Avenue, Comely Bank Road and Dean Park Crescent stand today.[6]

Meanwhile, the original Playground at Stockbridge did have a sporting future, as the Rocheid family leased the land in 1871 to the Grange Cricket Club, who in turn bought it outright in the 1890s. It is still their home today.

Hope was also influential, through the Council, in creating a public park in the Meadows which was, indirectly, relevant to the development of football in the city. The east end of the Meadows, also known as Hope Park after one of his ancestors, was where Hearts, Hibs and some of the earliest clubs in the city played their first games in the mid-1870s.

Again, the establishment of this park involved the hapless Macpherson, who had hired contractors to lay out the ground without taking into account Hope's attention to detail and his obsession with getting things done rationally and logically. The contract specified that the main road through the Meadows should be laid with 'metal' (small stones) capable of passing through a two-inch ring, and that the whole of the ground should be levelled. When Hope walked by to inspect the work in progress, it seemed to his eye that the metal was too big, but the workmen assured him it was fine. Determined to prove his point, he commissioned a blacksmith to make an iron ring of exactly two inches diameter, went back to the Meadows and found that many of the pieces of stone would not pass through. He promptly summoned Macpherson and insisted the contractor abide by the terms of his agreement.

Similarly, he was not impressed by the contractor's efforts to level the ground and wrote to Macpherson: 'I was at the Meadows, west end, today, and observed some covering up of turf which had been cut in the space between the old walk and the belt of trees. The man said the cut turf was broken and would not lift. This was not correct, for I made him lift it, and it did lift. There was also a considerable covering up of turf uncut. The man said it was on stony ground and would not lift. I made him try, and told him if he couldn't cut it I would myself; and sure enough he cut the turf, and it was quite suitable for lifting. In consequence of what I have seen I have no confidence in these men, or in their no-turf stories.'

Acknowledging that lifting turf on a hot day is hard work, he advised Macpherson to employ more workers to get the work done properly and added, to ensure he could not wriggle out of his responsibilities: 'Will you please bring this letter to the next committee meeting, and remind me to speak of it?'[7]

This whole episode, trivial though it may seem, reflects Hope's determination never to take 'no' for an answer, while at the same time caring for the well-being of the individual. He would immerse himself in the details of a project, but could also see the bigger picture which was, in this case, that public parks were needed in Edinburgh and, in no small measure through his constant prodding and badgering, were duly created.

He was, in some respects, a true radical, with no time for cant or privilege. In particular, he was opposed to his fellow councillors granting themselves perks at the expense of their electorate. For example, he organised Peoples' Demonstrations for ordinary working families to celebrate the marriages in 1858 of the Princess Royal and 1863 of the Prince of Wales, when the Town Council had only proposed an elegant dinner for themselves. As he said: 'The working classes have, I hope, loyal feelings, and those feelings ought to be encouraged; but if no provision be made for the working classes manifesting those feelings – if they be treated as not having any sympathy with the sovereign, or any loyalty – then seditious and republican sentiments are begotten.'[8]

Football for the Volunteers

At dawn on the first day of July 1916, Colonel George McCrae led his men of the 16th Royal Scots over the top on the first day of the Battle of the Somme, the bloodiest day in the history of the British Army. McCrae's battalion was made up of footballers from Hearts, Hibs, Falkirk, Raith Rovers and other clubs from the east of Scotland, together with a wide range of supporters and volunteers, and from that day on it became part of the history and folklore of the city.

Four decades earlier, in 1872, the same George McCrae was aged 11, a poor orphan. Desperate to join John Hope's cadets, he was rejected because he was too small. He persevered, and six years later he was accepted. It transformed his life and he went on to be a highly successful Volunteer, businessman and city councillor. As City Treasurer he restored the city's finances after a century of neglect, as a trusted government official and MP he was knighted for services to his country. And finally, he was Colonel of his own regiment.

McCrae's progress was exactly what Hope would have wished for the hundreds of waifs and strays and deserving poor of Edinburgh who wanted to better themselves. Had he witnessed McCrae's success, Hope would have been very proud.

Hope himself became involved in the Volunteer movement in 1860 as a Captain of the Edinburgh Rifle Volunteers (ERV), in the wave of enthusiasm for volunteering following the Crimean War and the deterioration of diplomatic relations with France. The threat of invasion, real or perceived, coupled with a bellicose view of Britain's increasingly imperial role worldwide, started a trend which continued beyond the end of the century and indulged the Victorian love of pomp and circumstance, military bands and uniforms.

Hope saw an opportunity to set up a company within the ERV, Protestant and teetotal, to expand and develop the already successful work of the British League. As Jamie noted, 'He deemed it worthy of espousal for many reasons. He was a sturdy patriot; he was fond of military display; he saw that the drill would afford exercise and healthy recreation for office-lads and working men; and he believed that there would be many social benefits through the bringing together, for a common purpose, of various classes of men.'[9]

British League cadets in the 1860s

No.16 (Abstainers) Company was run on strict temperance principles, hence their nickname 'The Water Rats', and took its place at the Great Review of Scottish Volunteers on 7 August 1860 with three officers, including Hope as Captain, 47 non-commissioned officers and privates, and one bugler. Hope, as always, wanted the best for his boys and was willing to pay for it, so to ensure that 'The Water Rats' company was open to all boys with the necessary talents, rich or poor, he insisted that there be no entrance fee or charges for the uniform. His uniforms had to be the best (with their badges of a lion's head spouting water), their drill had to be the best (and they were regularly commended for it at official inspections), and their Captain the best (although Hope did not have a naturally commanding voice, he worked hard to improve his ability to command his men). He demanded the highest standards in attendance, efficiency and shooting, and made sure that the local newspapers knew about the company and printed reports of their abilities.

Having set up the senior company, Hope turned his attention to creating a cadet branch, feeding off his British League boys. They too began drilling in the Corn Exchange and Hope arranged for them to have carbines and dressed them in a red Garibaldi shirt, blue knickerbocker trousers and strong sailcloth leggings, dyed brown, all designed by the artist Joseph Noel Paton. The success of the enterprise is reflected in the 120 cadets who paraded in Hope's old High School Yards on 5 July 1862, with an accompanying drum and flute band.

One of the prizes awarded to cadets for efficiency was a good stout pair of boots, and so popular was this incentive that in a period of 22 years, 2,064 pairs were distributed, all paid for by Hope at a cost of well over £1,000.

Soon, the roll of No.16 Company was at its maximum and Hope was passing potential recruits to other companies, so he approached the Lord Provost for permission to form a Third Corps. When this was approved in 1867, Hope resigned his Captaincy of No.16 Company and was gazetted Captain of the new Third ERV Corps, which took its place among the Edinburgh volunteers, resplendent in scarlet and blue uniforms.

1867 was also the year that Queen's Park, Scotland's oldest existing association football club, was founded, the first challenger to the established order of clubs and schools playing football to Rugby rules. The new code took several years to spread to the east but when it did, men from the Third ERV were quick on the uptake. They attended an exhibition football match played on 27 December 1873 at Raimes Park, the Royal High School FP's ground at Bonnington Toll, between two select teams of Glasgow players. The game was, apparently, of poor quality but the men, and particularly Sergeant Alex Lamont, were so fired up with enthusiasm that they set up their own team, with the direct encouragement of Hope. The founding meeting of the Third ERV, one of the first association football clubs to be formed in the city, was on 24 February 1874 in the British League office in Rose Street, and it was sanctioned by the regiment on condition that the football did not interfere with drill. Blue and white was chosen as the colour of the jersey.

John Hope kicked off their first match on the Meadows.

Third ERV football team in 1875

Third ERV became a founding member of the Edinburgh Football Association in 1875, alongside Heart of Midlothian, Hanover and Thistle (who had been playing a mixture of football and handball). Alex Lamont the captain was dubbed 'The Father of Edinburgh Football' and when he emigrated to Australia in 1884 'to better himself', Hope wrote a glowing reference to a relative in Australia. Lamont's medals are now on display in Edinburgh Castle along with other memorabilia of 'The Water Rats'.

Queen's Park stoked the fire by travelling over again to play a representative Edinburgh side, and association football – by then the handling and non-handling games were being differentiated – took off in Edinburgh.[10] Other new teams soon followed such as White Star, St Andrew, Brunswick, Swifts and Hibernian, and membership of the Edinburgh FA rose rapidly from four clubs in 1875 to 12 in 1878 and 28 in 1880.

Third ERV won the first Edinburgh Cup, beating Thistle 6-0 in 1876. The trophy, later the East of Scotland Shield, was presented to John Hope by the team captain 'amid loud applause' at the Corps' annual soiree at the Freemasons' Hall. At the same meeting, Major Hope himself awarded prizes to his cadets for shooting, attendance and proficiency at drill.[11]

Third ERV was the first team in Edinburgh to abandon the old 'short dribble and backing up' style of play, and to develop the more effective passing game, which they learned from matches, and defeats, in Glasgow. They were also the first Edinburgh club to have their own ground, at Powburn (in the Mayfield area), and a 'stripping box' (changing hut). Their ground was also used for Edinburgh FA matches.

With their background as abstainers, the club encouraged the Edinburgh FA to hold its meetings in temperance hotels, and, less laudably, were known for being overtly Protestant. However, it did not follow that they were anti-Catholic. Frank Watt, a player and then secretary of Third ERV, was the first secretary and prime mover of the Edinburgh FA, and sympathetic to the admission of (Irish Catholic) Hibernian because he could see the crowd-pulling potential of local derbies.[12]

One historian of the period, writing in a paper on bigotry against Catholics in football,[13] has quoted the story of the game between Third ERV and Hibernian on 19 October 1878 in the second round of the Scottish Cup, where Third ERV, losing 3-0 after half an hour, had two men injured and conceded the game, which was then continued as a 'mixed friendly'. What he failed to mention is that both teams then repaired to the Young Men's Catholic Association in St Mary's Street Halls for tea, divided perhaps by their religion, but united in their firm belief in teetotalism.[14]

The football club continued until 1879, when some of the Volunteers, feeling that football was interfering with drill, closed the club down. That was the catalyst for some of the players to choose football over volunteering and move on. Frank Watt joined Swifts then moved to St Bernard's, a rising club which had played on the Meadows, Powburn and John Hope's Park in Stockbridge, before settling at Logie Green. The team's greatest moment came when it won the Scottish Cup in 1895, and it played in the Scottish League with diminishing success before being dissolved in 1943.

Given Hope's keen active encouragement of the Third ERV football team in the 1870s, the question arises why he had not taken steps in the previous decade to set up football team for the Abstainers Company or the British League. He had decades of playing football behind him, and had been so enthusiastic about artisan teams playing each other at his Playground in 1854 and on the new playing areas created in Edinburgh thereafter. Had he taken this step in the 1860s, the development of what was to become the association game in Scotland would have moved much faster in the east. It is particularly surprising given that the Glasgow equivalent of the Third ERV was Third Lanarkshire Rifle Volunteers, who founded their football team in 1872 and played as Third Lanark in the Scottish League until 1967.

There was already contact between the two volunteer companies at a military and also at a shooting level: following the formation of the City of Edinburgh and Mid-Lothian Rifle Association in 1861, regular shooting matches took place between Edinburgh and Glasgow teams. In 1863, Edinburgh beat Glasgow 379 to 337, and in 1864 a match took place in Stirling between Third Lanark RV and First Edinburgh RV, repeated in 1865.[15] But why was this healthy competitive spirit not also manifest at football? That is perhaps a secret waiting to be discovered in Hope's voluminous correspondence.

Hope finally retired from his command as a Lieutenant Colonel in 1883, and five years later, as part of a raft of army reforms, all the volunteer corps were assimilated into the territorial regiments of the line. When Third ERV became the Fourth Volunteer Battalion The Royal Scots (Lothian Regiment), Colonel William Martin, a British League boy who rose through the ranks to take over command from Hope, his mentor, wrote to his men: 'Both in name and uniform we shall therefore in future be connected with, and a part of, the oldest regiment in the service'.[16]

As well as Colonel Martin and Major George McCrae, another who went on to great things from the Third ERV was Joseph McNaughton, who began as a cadet in No.16 Company in 1863 and rose to become a Captain. 'In the career of each of these three officers,' said Jamie, 'Mr Hope took a warm and personal interest'.[17] They exemplified the spirit of rising from lowly beginnings to greatness, through help and hard work, which appealed so much to him.

Extreme Protestantism

It is difficult, in our politically-correct, anti-sectarian world, to understand the depth of anti-Catholic feeling in Britain in the nineteenth century. By our standards, John Hope was a bigot and a Protestant extremist of the worst kind because of his fierce condemnation of what he saw as the evils of Popery. Yet it has to be acknowledged that at the time his views were shared by millions of otherwise sane and compassionate people in all parts of Britain.

The tension between Roman Catholic and Protestant in Edinburgh goes back to the days of Mary, Queen of Scots and John Knox in the 16th century, and flared up with the occupation of the city by the Jacobite army in 1745. Bonnie Prince Charlie's brother, Henry Benedict, the last of the generally recognised Stuarts, died near Rome in 1807, the year that John Hope was born. In the Victorian era, the sight of a Catholic Stuart marching through the city at the head of a predominantly Catholic army was only just out of living memory.

On a British level, the 'Irish Question' and Catholic emancipation had been vexing Westminster politicians most keenly since the Napoleonic Wars, when Ireland was seen as Britain's Achilles Heel in the fight against the French, as Irish nationalists saw an opportunity to redress hundreds of years of oppression. In the 1820s, George IV (like his father) feared that Catholic emancipation would threaten his coronation vows to uphold the Protestant Church, and there was a widespread belief in the country that Catholic allegiance to Papal Jurisdiction, rather than the king and parliament, was tantamount to treason.

As the flagging Irish economy forced mass emigration, into Scotland came thousands upon thousands of Roman Catholic migrants, hungry, poor, ill-educated and very much under the influence of their priests. They poured into the slum districts of Edinburgh's Old Town, notably the east end of the Cowgate and the Canongate, to feed the labour demands of the ever-growing industries. They were met with hostility and social exclusion, some of it bolstered by the force of the law.

However, there were also voices of moderation and Prime Ministers from Pitt to Peel appreciated that reform in Britain was part of the solution for Ireland, as well as the correction of an ancient wrong. Anticipating a more stable and more tolerant society, they proposed measures which would relieve Scottish and English Catholics, as well as Irish ones and non-Conformists, of the burdens of exclusion from public office and the universities, and from controls on property ownership. The process of emancipation culminated in the passing of the Sacramental Test Act in 1828 and the Roman Catholic Relief Act in 1829, but anti-Catholic fervour remained so strong that Sir Robert Peel lost his parliamentary seat, and the Duke of Wellington fought a duel with the Earl of Winchelsea, who had accused him of 'insidious infringement of our liberties'.

The tensions simmered over in 1845, when the question of a Westminster government grant to a Roman Catholic seminary at Maynooth in Ireland provoked a huge furore, particularly in Scotland. There was an Anti-Maynooth Conference where Rev John Cummings of the Church of Scotland contrasted what he called Protestant virtue and Catholic vice as

135

'liberty and slavery, truth and a lie, love and bloodshed, light and dark, heaven and hell'. This was strong stuff, prompting Queen Victoria herself to step in: 'The bigotry, the wicked and blind passions it brings forth is quite dreadful, and I blush for Protestantism!'[18]

Hope had no such qualms and wrote voluminous letters to all and sundry to persuade them of the evils of supporting a Catholic college. One of these to a fellow lawyer ended 'It strikes me ... that alliances with Rome, in any degree, are like the alliances that Israel and Judah formed with Egypt, ending in the captivity as their punishment for not trusting in God.'[19]

The government stood firm and Maynooth College received its grant, yet Hope continued to protest, suggesting as late as 1858 that there was a causal relationship between the Maynooth grant and the Irish Famine which followed, through God's displeasure.[20] He had actually visited the college while on holiday in Ireland in 1851 and noted that the new building was still 'unoccupied, unfinished, and unfurnished'. He cynically suggested that British government grants were being misused and that there would undoubtedly be requests for more.[21] Many agreed with him.

This was not a time for the religiously faint-hearted. And to further complicate the situation, in 1843 the Church of Scotland had turned itself inside out with the Disruption, whereby over 400 of its ministers (nearly half) voted with their feet and their consciences, left their churches, manses and incomes to set up the Free Church of Scotland. Fortunately for them they were followed by large numbers of their congregations, who set about creating an entirely separate church structure with its own buildings, manses and incomes to pay for it all. The dividing issue was the question of patronage and the right of congregations to choose their own minister, free from the influence of local landlords or the state. The result has been a fiercely independent Church of Scotland, which guards still the right of congregations to choose their ministers, but which has twice as many buildings around the country as it needs.

Hope was curiously calm about this momentous event and remained faithful to the moderate conservative element of the established Church of Scotland, but still managed to count a number of the breakaway evangelicals in the Free Church as his friends and acquaintances, as they agreed with him on the other issues of the day which agitated him so much. Indeed, in his memorandum upon entering the Edinburgh Town Council in 1857, he said that he was in favour of abolishing patronage and the recreation of one church in Scotland, inclusive of all dissenting bodies.[22]

His fervent anti-Catholicism never left him, backed by his belief in the power of education to achieve his aims. His reasoning was, as always: 'Allegiance rendered by Papists to the Sovereign [is] subordinate to the allegiance they render to the Pope.' He summarised this in 1854 when he chaired a No Popery meeting in the Music Room in Edinburgh's George Street with the two-fold aim: 'That our duty to God, and the preservation of our own civil and religious liberties, requires the immediate exclusion of Papists from Parliament, and from all power, place, and pay at home and abroad. That it is the duty of our nation to see that every subject of the British Crown be forthwith possessed of and taught to read and understand the Bible in his own native language.'

Given the tenor of some of his public speeches, he made a not entirely believable assertion that he felt 'Love for the Papists personally, and prayer for their conversion, a duty, while we oppose the Romish system'.[23] And went on: 'I am for gentleness and kindness, in order to win the Roman Catholics'.[24]

Paradoxically, while Hope could speak with entrenched bigotry on the subject in general, he would happily donate a great deal of money to organisations as varied as the Hibernian Female Schools Society, a society for the Education of the Sons of the Irish Clergy and one for the training of Connemara weavers. He saw education as the way to solve what he saw as the problem: 'teach the masses', 'educate the people'; in other words, alert them to the evils of Popery, and they will understand. It is worth remembering that he also played football in his youth with George Witham, a known Roman Catholic from a Jesuit school.

In 1851, the General Assembly of the Church of Scotland set up a committee on Popery, which, to Hope's frustration, did very little. By 1857, after a great deal of ineffectual clerical huffing and puffing, Hope was appointed secretary of a Special Mission, partially to harness his energies but primarily, one suspects, to utilise his financial clout. The aim of the Mission was to bring light through preaching, publishing and education 'to the most ignorant and bigoted Romanists in our country', and to counter what they saw as the rising power and influence of the Roman Catholic Church.[25] Not surprisingly, the pace quickened with Hope's input, but not to everyone's satisfaction and in 1859, the original committee came to an end. The Church paused to consider its operations and how far they might be conducted 'in a less objectionable form', as Jamie delicately put it.[26] When all the accounts were rendered, the committee spent £5,234, of which the committee was responsible for £1,267 while Hope himself had contributed £3,967.[27]

Perhaps the clearest statement of Hope's philosophy is to be found in a little leaflet he published for session 1856-7, entitled *To The Young Men of Edinburgh*. It encouraged boys to attend free classes in The Young Men's Saturday Evening Popery Class for Mutual Improvement, held at the British League Office, 53 Rose Street, at 7 o'clock.

The objects which the class has in view are simply these:

1   The improvement of young men in the art of speaking, the acquirement of knowledge, and the fluent, natural, and intelligent communication of that knowledge to others, conjoined with kindly criticisms upon the productions, and endeavours to correct and amend the defects in style and manner of its various members.

2   To give its members a thorough practical knowledge of Popery in all its aspects, whether social, civil, or religious, and cultivate the mind by subjects of paramount interest and importance, embracing by no means a limited or uninteresting field of literature.

Hope gushed: 'As we live in eventful times, when every system is being cast into the crucible of searching investigation, it is not only a privilege, but a duty incumbent upon all, to avail themselves of every means put within their reach for the purpose of being kept upon a level with the time.' He outlined what his classes would achieve: 'It is sincerely hoped that all young men, into whose hands this may fall, will be induced to join us and share our advantages. The old adage still holds good, that 'as iron sharpens iron, so the mind the mind'; and what more pleasant, what more interesting, what more conducive to the development of the intellectual faculties, than a Mutual Improvement Class, the members of which meet together, feeling the inspiring bonds of a brotherhood in pursuit of knowledge, each one anxious to impart what he knows to others, eager to pick up and treasure in the storehouse of memory that knowledge which may be possessed by his neighbours, and ever willing to help forward and nourish the intellectual and spiritual wellbeing of all? Come, then, with us, and help onward our mutual good.'[28]

The classes were theoretically open to everyone, but although there was no mention in the Constitution of members having to be Protestant, there was a catch: children joined in groups at local Church of Scotland and Free Church halls, so there was clearly a selection process.

In this and so many causes, Hope would use his considerable personal energy and financial resources to make things happen yet, in doing so, he alienated his fellow travellers who did not share his commitment and whom he believed were moving too slowly. This was a pattern of intolerance which was repeated throughout his life.

138

[1] Rodger, p117

[2] GD 253/16/3

[3] Campbell memorandum, GD 253/14/5

[4] Jamie, p332-3

[5] *Edinburgh Evening Courant*, 27 October 1869

[6] For more details see Rodger, *The Transformation of Edinburgh: Land, Property and Trust in the Nineteenth Century* (2001).

[7] Jamie, p335-6

[8] Jamie, p412

[9] Jamie, p385

[10] Details, often contradictory, on early football in Edinburgh come from a variety of sources including the *Edinburgh Athletic Times,* 23 September 1895, p3; *Scottish Athletic Journal,* 22 December 1882, p10; *Scottish Sport,* 24 January 1890, p9; et al.

[11] *Edinburgh Evening News*, 3 April 1876

[12] Frank Watt was one of the first men to make a career out of football, going on to Dundee and, in 1895, to Newcastle United where he and his son, also Frank, inspired a fine set of league and cup winning sides either side of WW1.

[13] GPT Finn, *Faith hope and bigotry, case studies of anti-Catholic prejudice in Scottish soccer and society*; in Jarvie and Walker, *Scottish Sport in the Making of the Nation* (1994).

[14] Quoted in Alan Lugton, *The Making of Hibernian* (1995), p37.

[15] William Stephen, *History of the Queen's City of Edinburgh Rifle Volunteer Brigade, Edinburgh* (1881), p142

[16] Quoted in Jamie, p540

[17] Jamie, p541

[18] Queen Victoria, letter to (her uncle) King Leopold of Belgium, dated 15 April 1845.

[19] Letter dated 17 April 1845, quoted in Jamie, p128

[20] Jamie, p383

[21] Jamie, p265 and 282

[22] Jamie, p332

[23] Quoted in Jamie, p280

[24] Quoted in Jamie, p312

[25] GD 253/18/8

[26] Jamie, p316

[27] Jamie, p317

[28] GD 253/181/2

Chapter 10

FINAL YEARS AND LEGACY

WHEN JOHN Hope resigned his commission from the Third Edinburgh Rifle Volunteers at the age of 76, he was slowing down a little but was determined to remain on the Town Council and stood for election one last time.

He had a proud record as a councillor and in 1884 he looked back on his achievements in his final Address to the Electors of St George's Ward: 'I entered the Town Council in 1857 as a root & branch social and sanitary reformer.'[1] He reminded them how he had worked hard for Saturday half-holidays for all workers and earlier closing for some trades, particularly grocers and bakers; for better housing and greater washing facilities for working families. To the surprise of few, he retained his seat.

140

Many of his great causes had indeed made progress or had been resolved. The need to elevate poor children from the slums was still there, but the Education Act of 1872 had greatly improved the situation. Workers' housing was still bad, but municipal reforms in Edinburgh such as the 1867 City Improvement Act had led to slum clearance programmes which were making inroads into a century or more of neglect. The Saturday half-holiday had been won for most workers. The Boys' Brigade,[2] founded in 1883, to some extent took over where Hope's cadets had been, while the Volunteer regiments were absorbed into the territorial army in 1888. And although the No-Popery movement was still active, it was relatively subdued after the passionate peak of the 1840s and 50s, and it would be a long time until sectarian strife erupted in west central Scotland, during and after the First World War.

Most of all, he was proud of his campaigning to provide parks and recreation areas for working families. There were now playing fields all over the country, free of charge, which allowed football teams to proliferate in a way that Hope could not have imagined (though he would have been horrified by the march of professionalism). In that same Address to Electors he says: 'I am out and out in favour of public parks. About 1854 I started the Stockbridge Park, and carried it on till the landlord took it from me. So much was I in favour of Parks that in 1874 I requested a young man in the law on whom I had a claim for such assistance to prepare the draft of a Bill to be submitted to Parliament enacting that every village in the country should have a playground, under proper regulations, at all events every village which was big enough to have a licensed public house.'[3]

He had expanded on his ideas in a letter to Lord Cranbrook, a cabinet minister, in 1879: 'I take the liberty to suggest another idea, which, I believe, would be highly popular in the Lowlands and in the cultivated and enclosed portions of the Highlands of Scotland. It is that an Act of Parliament be passed, requiring the heritors or ratepayers of each parish in Scotland to provide for each village in their respective parishes, where such does not exist, a level-drained public playground and relaxation ground, of extent in proportion to the size of the village, and sufficient for football, cricket, quoits, croquet and athletic exercises, and having a smooth, dry footpath all around its external limits, with some benches for the use of the elder inhabitants, who might not join in the games, but whose presence might be for good.' With his customary attention to detail, Hope went on to advocate specific nights for football and cricket, that sheep should keep the grass short, and naturally that no alcohol be consumed near these playgrounds.[4] He concluded: 'Some towns, such as

141

Edinburgh, are already well provided, but there is a great want in rural villages, and such a provision would be a great boon to the working classes, and show to the people of Scotland how desirous their real friends are for their welfare.'

His lifelong campaigning against alcohol was successful, to a point, and in 1881 over three thousand abstainers from Edinburgh, Leith and the surrounding area signed an address of appreciation to him. It read: 'Your great educational enterprise on behalf of young men and young women has not only been warmly appreciated by us as abstainers, but in this we believe you have earned the gratitude of every right-minded citizen. From 1851 till the passing of the Education Act now in force, a period of more than twenty years, your evening schools placed within the reach of apprentices the blessings of a free and comprehensive secular education, combined with the advantages of religious and temperance instruction; while your special classes for the acquirement of particular branches of knowledge, which you still carry on, have enabled many of the sons of working men to attain to positions of public trust and usefulness.'[5]

It amounted to a remarkable accolade, but there remained one aspect of temperance which Hope continued to be exercised about, and which he was determined to tackle in these last years: the use of wine at communion. Few people today could be animated by the question of whether churches offered fermented (alcoholic) or un-fermented (non-alcoholic) wine to their congregations, but in the 1870s and 1880s it was hugely divisive. Church elders resigned or left, congregations were in uproar and meetings were held to debate whether 'the fruit of the vine' as described in *The Bible* was alcoholic or not.

Hope's unwavering stance over the use of unfermented wine at communion was laughed at and frequently misunderstood by both Church of Scotland members and outsiders. It caused him to sever his connections with St Andrew's Church, and although he then became a member of the Kirk Session at St Luke's Church in Young Street, in time his name was again removed from the roll of communicants.

There was no official reason given, other than the stipulation under Church Law in Scotland that this was to be the consequence of failing to attend Session meetings and communion for three consecutive years. In fact, Hope had tried unsuccessfully to persuade the congregation to give up fermented wine at communion.[6] With his usual care, he kept all the postcards advising him of the meetings of the Kirk Session, and the many letters which the Minister, Rev Ranald Macpherson, had sent to him, attempting to arrange meetings to discuss the matter. Clearly, Macpherson did not want to lose so influential and wealthy a member of his congregation, and it appears that several other elders were 'at one' with Hope, who opposed what he considered 'Mr Macpherson's high-handed conduct'.[7]

When Hope stepped down from the Town Council in 1889 he was clearly past his prime, physically and mentally, although the Lord Provost Sir John Boyd wrote to ask him to reconsider: 'I do not know of anything which I should more deeply regret than your leaving it. In our times there are few who are wholly unselfish in their public service; and you have shown an example which must have had its influence, and which, no doubt, will be acknowledged by-and-by. I do not think that any one has done as much for Edinburgh as you have, working quietly and unobtrusively, but steadily and earnestly, at great cost of time, thought and money, for the best interests of the working class.'[8]

The Lord Provost's words reflected the official city reaction to Hope's work in Edinburgh, and the thousands of men, women, boys, girls and charities he had helped added their own voices. Others were, of course, delighted to see the back of him.

Last will and testament: The Hope Trust

Hope may have been pleased with the plaudits, but he was also faced with the challenge of how to create a meaningful legacy that would last long beyond his allotted span. In his old age, he turned his attention to a matter much closer to hand, and in doing so, he was stirring up trouble for the future.

He was a very rich man, one of the richest in Edinburgh, having amassed an extensive portfolio of property in the city from his father, uncles and other family members, to which he had added while drawing a substantial income as a lawyer. Although he had spent large sums on his philanthropic interests, he had no wife or children to look after and his personal life had been frugal.

He wanted to ensure that, after his death, his money would continue to support the causes he had espoused, directed by people he knew he could trust, and began drawing up the legal documents to establish the Hope Trust.

There is little doubt that Hope himself would wish to be remembered for setting up a trust to promote temperance and the Protestant Church, but it is this area of Hope's life and legacy which still causes controversy in a world concerned with the negative impact of sectarianism in football.

By the end of his life, the church was deeply riven by schism and divisions incomprehensible to worshippers today: Auld Lichters stood

143

against New Lichters; Burghers against Anti-Burghers; the Free Church against the Established Church; the United Secession Church, the United Presbyterian Church, the Relief Church; to say nothing of the Episcopalians, Methodists, Primitive and Wesleyan, Congregationalists and Baptists.

Through it all, Hope firmly believed in the superiority of the Presbyterian version of the Christian faith, as had, in the 1850s, more than half of the rest of Scotland. In that respect, Hope was no different from hundreds of thousands of douce, law-abiding and very respectable fellow Scots. Protestant Scotland saw itself as the embodiment of the Reformation, the country's defence against Roman Catholicism and the overarching authority of the Pope in Rome. The ignorance, illiteracy, poverty and overcrowding of the Irish immigrants coming into Scotland after the Famine reinforced the prejudice.

He planned the Trust in relentlessly logical fashion, as ever, and formulated his legacy with great care over many years: the first Trust-Deed was drawn up in 1862, followed by a Trust-Disposition and Settlement in 1879, then it was all crystallised in 1890 with a Trust-Conveyance of 22 April and a Trust-Disposition and Settlement of 26 July; the dates are important in the light of subsequent events.

The Hope Trust was formally established in 1890 and this was reflected almost immediately with the announcement that 'the classes and meetings hitherto conducted under the title of the British League of Juvenile Abstainers, and sustained by John Hope, will in future be known as the Hope Trust Classes.'[9] A newspaper report estimated that Hope had spent up to £3,000 a year since 1847 to promote education and temperance, so it was a timely reinvention of the British League after 43 years. His legacy would ensure this work would develop under the control of the trustees, although 'the old lines will be followed meantime' with children's abstinence meetings on four nights a week.

It was a fine piece of foresight as three years after the Trust was set up, Hope breathed his last. In May 1893 he caught a chill and took to his bed. After a brief rally, his health continued to decline and he died on 25 June, calmly and in his own home, at the ripe old age of 86. He was buried four days later in the family vault at Greyfriars Kirkyard.

In accordance with his wishes, the funeral was not a lavish affair: there were no flowers or wreaths, the coffin was of strong common wood covered by plain black cloth, and the followers had to walk behind the hearse from Moray Place to the churchyard. Finally, he specified: 'There will be no prayer nor religious ceremony of any kind at the grave.'

144

THE
BURYING GROUND
of
JAMES HOPE, Esq.R

SACRED TO THE MEMORY OF
JANE WALKER
WIFE OF THE ABOVE JAMES HOPE
DIED 6TH APRIL 1822 AGED 36 YEARS

THE ABOVE
JAMES HOPE
WRITER TO THE SIGNET
DIED 14TH NOVEMBER 1842 AGED 73 YEARS

ALSO
THEIR ELDER SON
JOHN HOPE W.S.
THE EDINBURGH PHILANTHROPIST
AND
FOUNDER OF THE HOPE TRUST
DIED 25TH JUNE 1893 AGED 86 YEARS

John Hope's family grave in Greyfriars Kirkyard

145

There were fulsome obituaries in the daily papers, acknowledging his philanthropic work. The *Evening News* summarised him as a 'champion in the causes of the education of the poor, temperance and the anti-Popery crusade.' The *Aberdeen Journal* commented: 'The deep interest he took in education and the welfare of the poorer classes of Edinburgh, and his crusade against intemperance and Popery, made him a prominent figure'. *The Scotsman* published a lengthy account of his life, judging that 'Mr Hope in many ways was undoubtedly a striking personality, of strong imperious will, narrow and restricted in his vision in religious and political matters, but a hearty advocate of social reforms for the improvement of the people.'[10] None of the obituaries mentioned football.

That 'strong imperious' nature did not take long to resurface and the first public note of controversy came when his will was published just a week after his death: 'Mr Hope revokes a settlement and all codicils with two exceptions, and in addition there are six subsequent codicils.' It was evident that he had changed his mind several times about who should benefit and by how much. In the end, apart from some small individual legacies, it was revealed that 'his whole means and estate', worth an estimated £400,000 (the equivalent of at least £50 million today), would be devoted to the support of total abstinence, promoting the use of unfermented wine at the Lord's Supper, and to leading anti-Popery campaigns.

To the horror of his surviving family – his brother James, sister Margaret and several nieces and nephews – they were totally excluded from any bequests. Hope reasoned that they deserved nothing from him as they had not supported his philanthropic work, they had their own income, and they had chosen to live in society, and therefore more expensively.

On the other hand, it was the green light for the Hope Trust to embark on its mission. Based in 31 Moray Place, the house where Hope himself had lived and worked for over sixty years, the four men he appointed as his trustees were all dedicated followers, former British League boys who had risen from poor beginnings and greatly prospered through hard work: David Campbell, an Edinburgh solicitor; William Martin, headmaster at Dalry Public School and who had taken over command of the Third ERV from Hope; and two ministers, Rev David Jamie of Ballingry, who later wrote his biography, and Rev Jacob Primmer of Townhill, a fanatical anti-Popery campaigner.

However, the trustees had a fight on their hands as the following year his brother James launched a legal action to contest the will, on behalf of the wider family. With the Lord Advocate as their QC, they alleged that when Hope drew up the trust deeds in 1890 he was not of 'sound disposing

146

mind', subject to hallucinations and delusions. If so, he had died intestate and they were therefore entitled to a substantial share of his very large estate. The Hope Trustees, on the other hand, saw the whole future of the Trust's work and their own personal positions in jeopardy, and knew they had to ensure that Hope was adjudged to be of sound mind when he had made the various wills and codicils.

The family's first attempt was rejected in June 1895 by Lord Kincairney, who ruled that the claim was 'so defective in specification and definiteness as to be irrelevant'. The following year they presented it again more forcefully to the Court of Session, this time prefixing delusions with the word 'insane'. This was their argument: 'He believed that he had a special and imperative duty to further the cause of total abstinence and to oppose the Church of Rome by devoting his pecuniary resources to these objects, in consequence of commands which he conceived he had received from the Deity by direct communication upon various occasions. These insane delusions dominated his mind and overmastered his judgement'.[11] Again, their motion was rejected by a panel of judges in February 1896, with Lord McLaren pointing out that plenty of sane people believed God had spoken to them.

The family had one last throw of the dice and appealed to the House of Lords, where three judges postulated there was potentially some merit in their appeal, and in July 1898 sent the case back to Edinburgh. This was the signal for a final showdown, a trial by jury at the Court of Session, in which there was a great deal at stake for both parties.

No-one could deny that Hope had been eccentric – all of Edinburgh knew that. Even Campbell admitted that Hope had been difficult, having had to deal with him in business for decades. He accepted that his mentor spoke his mind without hesitation, and made a lot of enemies, but there was no legal bar to being unpopular, and a significant difference between being eccentric and insane.

Both sides were not short of raw material as they lined up over 200 witnesses and ploughed through the enormous volume of Hope's papers, frantically searching for evidence to bolster their cases. The Trustees held the archive, so they had an opportunity to pull out any incriminating or ambiguous letters or documents, but must have been nervous at missing something. They made a pretty good job of it, although in papering over whatever cracks they may have found, they disturbed and reorganised the archive, making it far more difficult for subsequent generations of researchers to make sense of what they found.

Only once is there a suspicion that all was not quite as smooth as it might be. In the section of Campbell's biography of Hope which discussed his household and servants, he refers to James Stenhouse, who was a particularly favoured servant for nearly 21 years, and to whom Hope left a legacy of £500 and his clothes. There is a paragraph added to the description of Stenhouse, in pencil and in a different hand: 'It has been said by Andrew Salmond that if James Stenhouse cared, he could in the witness box prove in five minutes that Mr Hope was mad. This is a vile calumny but it may as well be kept in mind.'[12] Clearly, someone was worried.

This appears to hark back to a mighty argument in the Moray Place office in 1891. Salmond had been close to Hope for many years, both as his building agent and involved in his charity work with the British League, travelling all over Scotland. Hope had paid for him to go on holiday regularly, for which Salmond had written long and profusely grateful letters. Then, out of the blue, he was summarily dismissed by Hope, it was said for being a U.P. (United Presbyterian) and a Liberal. It seems scarcely credible that Hope did not know before then of Salmond's religious and political allegiances, and perhaps this was proof of the old man behaving irrationally. But Stenhouse and Salmond kept quiet.

The trial also dug up negative comments, such as one damning Memorandum, dated about 1896, from Bailie Thomas Sloan of Edinburgh, a man who had crossed swords with Hope over building works in the 1860s when he complained that he often went to sleep during council meetings: 'Mr Hope took very little interest in Town Council business except in so far as it affected his own rights. I do not consider he was a public-spirited man at all. In the Council he was looked upon as a bore. I do not believe he would have been tolerated as he was but for his social standing & the belief that he expended large sums on promoting the volunteer movement temperance etc. He showed great selfishness in using his position as a Councillor & Governor of Heriot's Trust to promote his own interests. He was very suspicious and grasping in all business transactions.'[13]

The trial was originally set for 5 June 1899, then postponed, but over the summer counsel for the family made overtures for settlement, having 'excerpted' (copied) 7,000 pages without finding the golden nugget that would prove their case. The Trustees agreed to pay £15,000 (worth at least £2 million today) to the family in return for a complete withdrawal of the suggestion of insanity, and to prevent over sixty years of dirty laundry being made public. Each side agreed to pay their own costs, and in the family's case they can have had little left over from a lengthy legal battle and a split between several siblings and their descendants.

148

The Hope Trust thought a settlement of less than five per cent of the estate's value was worth paying, to avoid a hugely expensive trial and the risk of defeat, however remote that risk might be. It was clearly confident of success as it had already embarked on its work, delivering lectures and literature on abstinence and religion all over Scotland.

It continued on this path for many years and its mission goes on, although the Trust's remit has been modernised over the years. It still promotes temperance and religious education, just as the British League did in 1847, but now largely through the funding of academic research and by supporting drug and alcohol addiction charities. It remained in 31 Moray Place until quite recently, in 2015, when it moved to an office in Glenorchy House in Union Street in Edinburgh, and now comes under the umbrella of the solicitors Drummond Miller LLP. They are direct successors to David Campbell, who took over Hope's practice as D and JH Campbell, so there is still a clear link to its founder.

With the threat of a court case over, the door was also open for Jamie to publish his copious biography. *John Hope, Philanthropist and Reformer* came out in 1900 and ran to 576 pages, reappearing a few years later in an abridged version which was widely and freely distributed. Campbell's handwritten memoir, however, was tucked away quietly in the archive. All the protagonists would be long dead before anyone looked at it again.

Another trustee, William Martin, commissioned an oil portrait of Hope in 1905, which he presented to the Edinburgh Total Abstinence Society. It is now held by the University of Edinburgh's School of Divinity and is reproduced on the back cover.

John Hope, the man

To those who subscribed to his views and who benefitted from his generosity, Hope was a figure who inspired respect and gratitude. This is at odds with the many negative depictions of his character, and exemplifies how there was no middle ground in liking or disliking Hope.

He was undoubtedly stern and difficult, yet he could be a generous man who was willing to put deserving boys with the right credentials and attitude through school, paying their fees at night classes and helping them through university or apprenticeships.

One was George Wilson, who started studying at Hope's Sabbath class in 1859 and showed promise as a public speaker. Hope saw his potential, sent him to the south of France when his health failed, then on to university to study divinity ten years later. As he ultimately took up his appointment as a minister in Edinburgh, Wilson wrote to Hope: 'I came

149

into the League a poor boy, and I am going out with a noble profession, and all the difference has been owing to your kindness.'[14] He remained a loyal follower to the end and conducted Hope's funeral service in 1893.

For people like Wilson, and perhaps there were thousands like him, Hope could do no wrong. As late as 1942, an old 'Water Rat' reminisced: 'John Hope was considered somewhat eccentric, but many still alive can testify to his kindness of heart shown in his help to boys of humble parentage.'[15]

Jamie, in his preface, highlights the same characteristic of kindness, writing that his book is a memorial of 'a good, kind man'.

Hope undoubtedly saw himself as an agent for social change, both for the individuals involved and for the society in which they lived. He believed passionately in education, free where possible, for all, girls and boys. He believed in the value of music and physical exercise for the development of the whole person, and for a little bit of fun to mitigate the harshness of life which poverty brought. He believed that those who grasped the opportunities he offered could 'improve themselves' and 'get on in life'. Thousands did.

There is no debate about the extraordinary range of his educational activities and the number of young people who benefitted from them, particularly those who came from the poverty of some of the worst areas of Edinburgh. Lawyers, ministers, teachers, soldiers and politicians united to praise his achievements and the thousands of pounds of his own money that he spent on philanthropy and education. That so few girls went on to benefit from the more advanced stages of his education programme and then to go on to the professions is more a reflection of the society in which Hope lived than the wishes of the man himself.

However, his philosophy was also achieved as an agent for social control: he wanted his employees, his League members, his Volunteers and even his footballers to toe the line – his line. He was careful to select good Protestants and encouraged them accordingly towards temperance, to follow his own path.

It also has to be recognised that his implementation of this philosophy was done without some of the more open attempts demonstrated by other philanthropists to buy political favours or votes, to attract potential customers or to cow a potentially disruptive workforce. In his middle years, when he was highly successful and secure socially and financially, Hope had no need to buy favour. Certainly, he wished to influence and change things, but he had all he needed, which gave him the rare privilege of being able to say what he wanted, to anyone.[16]

150

To dig into Hope's personality, however, is a challenge. By drawing together the flimsy strands from letters, behaviour and comments we can only paint an inadequate picture for modern audiences concerned with how Victorians like Hope really felt.

We know relatively little about Hope the social man, for example. He certainly enjoyed the musical side of his British League meetings and Volunteer gatherings, and commissioned music from local composers for them, but the vast bulk of his correspondence is concerned with his business life mixed with church, temperance, education and philanthropy.

As Campbell said, he took relaxation from one kind of work by doing another, while the ever-faithful Jamie noted: 'It would be his remarkable power of self-control, or, rather, his power of self-forgetfulness, his absorption of self, in the cause he had at heart. We shall see him afterwards voluntarily and expressly sacrificing himself for the sake of the cause with which he is identified, while showing at the same time that the combative spirit is strong within him. No man knew better how to 'bottle up' his feelings, as he himself expressed it.'[17]

Many of his idiosyncratic ways seem curiously modern. Hope did not believe himself to be a particularly fluent public speaker and preferred to communicate by the written word, inundating friends, colleagues and those he wished to influence with reams and reams of paper. He would have loved electronic mail.

He was a great believer in the power of the press, and in addition to his hundreds of letters to newspapers, made sure that if any of his organisations had a good story to tell, about his 'Water Rats' for example, then the newspapers knew about it. And, if he had told them about his views on some issue which were then not reported, then he repeated the message incessantly until they took note. Equally, he was acutely aware that some of his young people could not afford to buy newspapers, so was a strong advocate for street posters, bills as he called them, without which he said he could not carry out his operation.[18] It was an early kind of social media.

For a man with such entrenched views, Hope was remarkably well travelled and enjoyed regular trips around Scotland and the UK. For many years he visited Continental Europe and Germany was probably his favourite, thanks to German music and philosophy.[19]

Hope rarely admitted to being happy with anything, but that is not to say he lived a life without joy. He was probably at his most content surrounded by hundreds of laughing children from Edinburgh's slums, running around in the open air and singing their hearts out on one of his excursions to the stately home of one of his aristocratic acquaintances.

Football legacies

There was not a decade in his lifetime in which Hope did not leave his mark on football.

In the 1810s, he learned football at the High School; in the 1820s and 1830s, he was playing with his Foot-Ball Club; from the 1840s through to the 1860s, football was played at his British League outings; in the 1850s, football formed a major element of his Stockbridge Playground and in his work to provide playing fields; in the 1870s his Third ERV helped found the Edinburgh Football Association, playing association football rules; in the 1880s St Bernard's emerged from the Third ERV and went on in the 1890s to win the Scottish Cup, the highest honour in Scottish football.

Hope was born in 1807, the same year as William Webb Ellis, and his football club blazed a trail in Scotland just a year after Ellis's apocryphal pick-up in 1823. His embryonic set of rules for football in 1833 marked a tangible step from the customs and practices of the schoolboy game at the High School to the written laws which codified the structure of football in the 1850s and 1860s. His 1854 Rules were contemporary with the Cambridge Rules, were published several years before the Sheffield Rules, and a decade before the momentous events which included the creation of the Football Association (1863), the founding of Queen's Park (1867) and the publication of Scottish rugby's 'Green Book' (1868).

Clear lines of influence can be drawn throughout the century from Hope's original Foot-Ball Club, through his own social and philanthropic work and also through the activities of those who were influenced by him, his ideas and his associates. The players in his club, as they matured and developed their careers, subsequently had considerable influence – as he did – in every walk of life in Edinburgh and beyond: in the law, medicine, commerce, the armed forces and overseas in the colonies.

Others in the city, such as the Snell Exhibitioners, added their own influences from Oxford and elsewhere, moving through the schools which encouraged sport and led to the flourishing of rugby football in Edinburgh in mid-century. That, in turn, ushered in the growth of the game in Scotland and gave rise to some of the first great names of Scottish rugby, men such as Asher, Maclagan, Morrison and the Don Wauchope brothers. Harry Stevenson, the dashing Academicals and Scotland captain, who played with some of these giants in the 1890s and who developed the concept of the attacking full-back, brought Hope's story to a neat conclusion by marrying Mary, the youngest daughter of William Scott Kerr who had played with Hope in his Foot-Ball Club in the 1820s.

152

This link to rugby football was just one legacy of the Foot-Ball Club. Hope's encouragement of British League girls to play football, in open view of others, was a hundred years ahead of the attitude of many of the sport's leading lights.

His greatest achievement, however, was to incorporate something of the rough tough traditional game of football, and make it acceptable for a rational, civilised world. His club and his rules effectively provided a launchpad for football to flourish, in a format which those new to the game could readily understand, and which allowed those who had enjoyed it at school to continue playing into adulthood.

The study of the development of Hope's Foot-Ball Club goes some way to answering the eternal questions, so beloved of football historians, as to how the modern game of football originated and why football, once established, did not spread faster and to wider socio-economic groupings than it did.

The answer to those questions is perhaps that, what we believed to be the answer many years ago, is still much of the answer today. We can do no more than quote John Hutchinson's own words in the introduction to *The Football Industry*, published in 1982. Under the heading 'A Patchwork of Growth' he listed the prerequisites for the growth of the game: 'the tradition of local amateur football, the extra leisure time and spending money of a growing number of people, particularly in the cities, and the expansion of the transport network'.[20] To that can now be added 'a strong individual or group of individuals to drive the club forward, a pool of like-minded self-motivated players to make extra- or intra-club games possible, and a suitable pitch to play on'.

Hope's club fits this pattern perfectly. He and his fellow members had a tradition of local amateur football from their days at the High School, the Academy and elsewhere; they were young, relatively well-off and professional, so had time, energy and resources to play; they all lived in the city centre so transport was not a problem; the club had the driving force of Hope with the support of his friends and contemporaries; and it found pitches to play on. The club flourished for several years but when one of these crucial elements was removed – when John Hope became less active – the club foundered.

John Hope's club is a very early indication of the criteria needed for the establishment and development of a football club, which became more obviously manifest from the 1860s onwards as the game grew. Specific local factors meant that his club came and went, with no other immediately to fill the void, but this study has demonstrated that the members retained their enthusiasm for the game and passed on that enthusiasm to the next generation. This is exactly why the development of football was 'a patchwork of growth' and why some areas of Britain were slow to develop a tradition of football, some developed a local amateur tradition, and some went on to foster the full, professional, commercial game.

Mens sana in corpora sano

There is one theme which has been flowing gently through this narrative, the concept of the ideal whole person: *mens sana in corpore sano*, a healthy mind in a healthy body, the balance in an individual between sensitivity and intelligence, and strength and vigour, the inner and the outer person.

Later categorised as Muscular Christianity, the origins of this balance go back to Roman times.[21] It found a resonance in the age of chivalry, where Christian knights were strong, honourable and charitable, skilled in martial arts, self-control, courtly ways and poetry. It developed with the ideal of Renaissance Man which came to symbolise that fine synthesis between learning, the arts and manly and combative characteristics. It was seen in the medieval courts of France and Italy and closer to home in the court of James IV, then of James VI, and, in particular of his elder son, Prince Henry.[22]

In the Enlightenment in Scotland, it encapsulated a marriage in fields of learning between the theoretical and the practical: the learned man of science trading ideas with the practical man of experiment. It linked the laboratory-based botanist with the outside gardener, the physicist and chemist with the engineer, the geologist, the surveyor and the boiler-maker. All over the country, it became acceptable for academics to be seen to be getting their hands dirty, mixing mental exercise with physical endeavour.

Therefore a young man of letters, medicine or the law thought it perfectly reasonable to exercise body as well as mind. This was particularly true in a close community such as Edinburgh, where lawyers, doctors, ministers, soldiers and professors were surrounded by like-minded friends, many of whom had shared the same school and university. They joined together to play golf, to curl, to shoot arrows and eventually to play football under a code of agreed rules.

This was rational recreation in an urban environment, a reflection of the earlier concept of self-discipline which characterised the idea of the gentleman, and a firm counterblast to the boorish and uncontrolled traditions of more rural recreational pursuits of their country cousins. It was an expression of masculinity suitable for well-off, civilised, educated, sentient, Scottish city gentlemen, who played out their manly aggressions in a robust but controlled and, to them, socially acceptable manner. That it happened in Scotland before similar ideals took shape in England was helped undoubtedly by the smallness of the country, the poorer more egalitarian society, the less hierarchical nature of its predominant religion, and the opportunities for a 'lad o' pairts' to shine through. This all tended towards a society which, while still stratified, was freer than its southern neighbour from what John Hope regularly called *humbug*.

They wanted their recreation to be a modified, modern kind, in the city's confined spaces which demanded strict rules, hence Edinburgh's place in sporting history as the home of the earliest rules of golf, bowls and archery. This desire for regulated recreation was the message of the Gymnastic Club, the Six Feet High Club and the St Ronan's Border Games and it became the message of the Foot-Ball Club. The members saw sport as an opportunity to be tough and courageous, but also exclusive and elitist where a man could enjoy the comradeship of like-minded fellows.

Hope's formation of a football club in 1824 needs to be seen in its time and social context. He was connected through his family and personal interests with virtually every aspect of life in the city: national politics (as political agent for Charles Hope MP); local politics (as a Town Councillor); the law (he, his father and brother were all Writers to the Signet); the church (he was a church elder and Secretary of the General Assembly of the Church of Scotland Committee on Popery); the military (his father had been a Colonel in the Royal Edinburgh Volunteers and he himself founded, financed and was Colonel of his own Volunteer Battalion); the university (he attended it and his uncle was a professor there); and commerce (as a substantial property owner). He knew and corresponded with most of the important lawyers and ministers in the city at the time of the latter part of the Enlightenment. His father had been a classmate of Sir Walter Scott, his grandfather had been Regius Keeper of the Botanic Gardens. It is hard to imagine anything of consequence happening in the city without one or other member of Hope's family knowing about it.

His Foot-Ball Club created a body of 300 men of the great and good of Edinburgh society who played football and enjoyed it, passing to their sons not only their love of the sport but the idea that this was what gentlemen of their social standing could do in their spare time. This next generation in turn influenced other boys, and Edinburgh school life in the 1850s and 1860s changed the face of football throughout Britain.[23] Football in Scotland developed independently from that played by the languid English gentlemen so often associated with its codification and growth in the latter half of the century.

Hope behaved like a gentleman on the football field, but he was very much a Scottish gentleman. His Christianity was genuine and it was also Muscular and Presbyterian. These two strands, the universality of the concept of rational exercise and the uniquely Scottish no-nonsense approach to sport, come neatly together in the life of John Hope.

[1] Address dated 9 October 1884, GD 253/7/3

[2] The Boys' Brigade, founded by William Smith in Glasgow in 1883, claims to be 'the first voluntary uniformed youth movement in the world'. This is disingenuous when you look at the numbers in the voluntary and uniformed British League cadets twenty or thirty years earlier.

[3] GD 253/7/3

[4] Letter to Lord Cranbrook dated 3 July 1879. GD 253/14 un-numbered bundle

[5] The total number of signatures was 3,163. Quoted in Jamie, p520

[6] GD 253/16/8

[7] GD 253/17/7

[8] Quoted in Jamie, p348

[9] *Edinburgh Evening News*, 3 September 1890

[10] *The Scotsman*, 26 June 1893

[11] Quoted in Jamie, p572

[12] GD 253/14/5

[13] GD 253/15/4

[14] Quoted in Jamie, p472. Wilson's story is told in depth p468-474.

[15] *Edinburgh Evening News*, 25 April 1942

[16] Hope was not the only philanthropist to donate large sums of money to the cause of Protestantism. See for example McDowall, *Sport in History* vol 32 no1, Sept 2012, p405, for the mixed motivation of the Baird family, coal and iron masters in west central Scotland.

[17] Jamie, p29

[18] Jamie, p344

[19] He was not alone in this, and many of the educational reforms in Scotland mid-century were influenced by German thinking. His *alma mater*, the Royal High School, appointed a German Rector, Dr Leonhard Schmidt, in 1845 and began to teach German.

[20] Hutchinson, *The Football Industry*, p18.

[21] The phrase was first used by the Roman poet Juvenal in his *Satires*.

[22] Henry was an archetypal Renaissance Prince in whom learning and arms, the cerebral and the physical were harmoniously combined. *For armes and arts sustaine each others right,* was a line from *Prince Henry's Barriers* (1610), a masque written by Ben Johnson with collaboration by Inigo Jones, quoted in G Parry, *The Golden Age Restor'd, The Culture of the Stuart Court 1603-42*. Manchester University Press, 1981 p71. For more details on the court see CEL Hutchinson, *Prince Henry Frederick; The Ideal Prince?* Unpublished thesis, Department of History, University of Glasgow (2004).

[23] Their influence was far-reaching, to the extent that two Edinburgh Academicals, WH Gordon and WJ Mackintosh, were at the founding meeting of the Football Association in 1863.

Chapter 11

A DIRECTORY OF FOOT-BALL CLUB MEMBERS

Almost three hundred names appear in the membership lists which were compiled by John Hope in nine of the club's seasons (covering 1824-28, 1831-34 and 1836).

This directory list all the members, with a brief biography of those who have been identified with a reasonable degree of certainty. It is followed by a short index of others who worked with and for the club. In some cases the information is sketchy, in others there is too much to include here.

Hope was not always careful in recording his members' names, and would write them down phonetically. The spellings given here are the corrected versions, rather than those which are in the original records. We are acutely aware that identification can be an imprecise science, and although we have taken considerable care to ascertain the facts, we would welcome any comments or corrections.

George Hewitt Ainslie 1827-33
Born 10 November 1809 in Calcutta; died 6 February 1850 at Peelrig, Berwickshire. Lived at 23 Melville Street. Went to Canada in 1830s for a few years.

John Alison 1831-32
Born 8 December 1805 in Dundee; died 19 February 1850 at Brompton, Middlesex. Lived at 8 Forres Street & 35 Moray Place. Lawyer, qualified WS in 1829.

Robert Allan 1824-31
Born 12 November 1806 in Edinburgh to Thomas Allan; died 6 June 1863 in Edinburgh. Stockbroker, also an accomplished mineralogist who travelled widely to collect samples and wrote a Manual of Mineralogy in 1834. Fellow of the Royal Society of Edinburgh. Lived at Windsor Street, York Place & Hillside Crescent.

William Patrick Allardice 1831/32
Born 8 November 1807 in Brechin; died 12 August 1876 in St Andrews. Address given as 25 St Andrew Square (office of Dundas and Wilson). Lawyer,

qualified WS in 1836, later practised in Glasgow. His son Hugh (1857-82) was in the Fettes rugby team 1870-72.

James Anderson 1831
Possibly b1816, son of Adam Anderson. Edinburgh Academy 1829-31.

William Robert Baillie 1831-36
Born 30 November 1812 in Edinburgh to William Baillie; died 9 August 1858 in Edinburgh. Edinburgh Academy 1827-28. Lawyer, qualified WS in 1836.

Frank Baird 1827/28
Possibly Francis Buchan Baird born 25 May 1804 in Edinburgh to Thomas Baird; died 1836.

Thomas Baird 1825-28
Possibly Thomas Baird born 12 December 1802 in Leith, brother of above, medical student at Edinburgh University 1825 & 1826 (did not graduate).

Peter Bairnsfather 1826/27
Born 27 May 1809 in Edinburgh to Hugh Bairnsfather; died 31 May 1890 in St Andrews. Lawyer, qualified WS in 1832. His son Peter Robert Bairnsfather (1850-1919) played rugby for St Andrews University in the 1860s.

Thomas Balfour 1824/25
Born 2 April 1810 at Shapinsay, Orkney to William Balfour; died

30 March 1838 in Edinburgh. Everton School (Liverpool) then Edinburgh University in 1824 (good conduct prize, first class) and Cambridge University in 1826 (did not graduate). Returned to Edinburgh around 1830, became advocate 1831. MP for Orkney and Shetland 1835-37. A biographical booklet was published in 1978 by Kirkwall Grammar School.

William Barker 1831/32
Address given as 25 Dublin Street, which was the home of the surgeon William Brown from 1825-1833, hence Barker was probably a medical student.

Robert Bell 1834, 1836
Born 2 March 1815 in Edinburgh to Joseph Bell; died 9 September 1887 in Falkirk. Edinburgh Academy 1824-30, Edinburgh University. Lived at 29 St Andrew Square. Lawyer, qualified as advocate 1836. Sheriff Substitute of Shetland and Falkirk.

James Beveridge 1827/28, 1831
Born 29 May 1800 in Edinburgh to William Beveridge; died 16 August 1869 in London after cutting his own throat. Lived at 12 Dublin Street. Lawyer, qualified WS in 1826.

John Frederic Bigge 1831
Born 12 July 1814 to Charles Bigge, High Sheriff of

Northumberland; died 28 February 1885 in Newcastle. Edinburgh Academy 1829-30 then studied in Edinburgh, and on to Durham University (BA 1840). Vicar of Stamfordham, Northumberland.

James Blackwood 1832/33
Born 6 July 1814 in Edinburgh to William Blackwood, publisher; died 17 October 1871 in Edinburgh. High School. Lived at 3 Ainslie Place. Lawyer, qualified WS in 1837.

John Blair 1834, 1836
Address given as 4 Randolph Crescent (home of William Scott of Craigmuie). Possibly John Blair (1815-1865) son of Major Patrick Blair, Madras Artillery, who lived at Lynedoch Place; Edinburgh Academy 1824-30, Durham University, ordained 1838.

Adam Bogue 1827/28 Not known.

John Bonar 1831-32
Address given as 33 Melville Street. Probably John William Bonar, born 15 May 1812, son of William Bonar of Craigleith, merchant; died 10 January 1879. Edinburgh Academy 1824-27, later Australia and New Zealand.

Boswell 1824/25 Not known

William Mitchell Boyd 1825-28
Born 29 August 1804 to John Boyd of Broadmeadows,

Selkirkshire; died 9 April 1894 in Madeira. Lawyer, qualified WS in 1828. Lived in Berkshire and London.

William Bruce 1824-31
Born 24 March 1806 to Alexander Bruce of Kennet, by Alloa; died 27 May 1858 in Edinburgh. Lived at 39 Moray Place. Wine merchant, and a Tory activist.

Charles Snodgrass Buchanan 1831-32
Born 4 April 1813 to David Snodgrass Buchanan of Cunninghamhead; died 22 September 1849 near Carlisle. Edinburgh Academy 1826-29. Lived at 8 Ainslie Place. Lawyer, qualified WS in 1838.

S Buchanan 1831
Possibly [Neil] Snodgrass Buchanan, brother of above. Born 29 January 1814; died 21 July 1863 in St Helier, Jersey. Edinburgh Academy 1826-29, then army career as Captain in 93rd Highlanders 1835-1851.

William Cadell 1827/28, 1834, 1836
Born 8 October 1810 to James John Cadell MD of Grange, Linlithgow; died 4 May 1862 at Carronpark, near Falkirk. Lived at 127 Princes Street & 55 Melville Street. Lawyer, qualified WS in 1833. Director of Cramond Iron Works.

Evan Philip Cameron 1824-26
Born 27 June 1810 in Jersey; died December 1862 in Berbice, British Guiana. Edinburgh University, graduated in medicine 1833. Doctor in British Guiana.

Archibald Campbell 1827/28
Probably a cousin of John Archibald Campbell, Clerk to the Signet, who lived at 2 Albyn Place, his address in the register.

Archibald Hamilton Campbell 1831-33
Born 12 August 1819 in Carbrook, Stirlingshire to John Campbell WS of Annfield; died 13 June 1909 in Toronto. Edinburgh Academy 1828-34 and Edinburgh University. Banker, lived at 29 Heriot Row. Went to Canada 1845 for copper mining, then Montreal in 1851 as a bank manager, then went into timber and lumbering.

Brother of:
John George Campbell 1831-34
Born 12 December 1808 in Dunipace, Stirlingshire to John Campbell WS of Annfield; died 1890 in Toronto. Educated privately. Bengal Artillery 1825-28, 2nd Lieutenant, then cashiered for drunkenness. Returned to Edinburgh to work for his father as a clerk. Lived at 29 Heriot Row, later went to Canada. Wrote the last letter to Foot-Ball Club in 1841 from his insurance office at 7 Great King Street.

John Campbell 1825/26 & 27/28
Not known. Address given as McKenzie WS, Charlotte Square

Campbell 1825/26 Not known.

Campbell 1825/26 Not known.

George James Carnegie 1826-28
Born 13 May 1806 in Abercorn, West Lothian to Lieut-Col George Carnegie; grandson of Earl of Northesk; died 20 Dec 1837 in Brussels of typhus. Edinburgh University, studied Rhetoric alongside John Hope, won 1824 prize for merit.

Robert Dundas Cay 1824-27

(National Library of Scotland)

Born 20 August 1807 in Edinburgh to Robert Hodshon Cay, Judge; died 19 March 1888 in Edinburgh. Lawyer, qualified WS in 1833. Member of Royal Company of Archers, won silver arrow in 1831. Photographed by

160

Hill and Adamson in 1843, and by the Edinburgh Calotype Club (above). Registrar of the Supreme Court, Hong Kong, 1844-53.

Henry Robert Chaplin 1825-27
Born 1805 in Lavenham, Suffolk; died 1875 in Great Bentley, Essex. Mr Espinasse's School, Edinburgh in 1823 then Edinburgh University, graduated in medicine 1831. Surgeon. President of Hunterian Medical Society 1832.

Henry Cheyne 1827/28
Born 24 August 1804 to John Cheyne of Tangwick, Shetland; died 27 February 1868 in Edinburgh. Lived at 6 Royal Terrace. Lawyer, qualified WS in 1829.

George Todd Chiene 1826/27
Born 21 August 1809 in Crail, Fife to Captain John Chiene; died 17 June 1882 at Burntisland, Fife. Educated in Crail and at Edinburgh High School. Accountant, trained with Messrs Paul & Mackersy then set up his own practice in Edinburgh and had insurance and investment company connections. Later lived in Fife and was captain of Lundin Links Golf Club. Among family sporting connections, his brother Professor John Chiene was the first President of the Scottish Rugby Union, while his son George was captain of Edinburgh Academical rugby club.

Robert Christie 1831/32
Born 24 July 1818 in Scoonie, Fife, to Charles Maitland Christie; died 29 August 1896 in Durie, Fife. Edinburgh Academy 1828-32. Lived at 8 Heriot Row. Captain, 5th Bengal Cavalry, served in Afghan War, retired injured 1851. Landowner, JP, DL in Fife. Married four times.

Clark 1827/28 Not known.

Clark 1831 Not known.

Clark 1831 Not known.

Alexander Cockburn 1824-27
Born 4 March 1809 in Edinburgh to Robert Cockburn, founder of Cockburn's Port; died 12 December 1888 in Edinburgh. Wine merchant in Edinburgh and London. Lived at 3 Belford Park.

Brother of:
Archibald Cockburn 1824-26
Born 23 April 1807 in Edinburgh to Robert Cockburn; died 22 June 1891 in Chelsea leaving £105,000. Edinburgh University 1823. Wine merchant in Edinburgh and London.

William Colquhoun 1825/26
Possibly William Laurence Colquhoun of Clathick (1809-1861) who was a Royal Archer in 1832 and lived at 15 Charlotte Square; possibly William Hanson Colquhoun (1807-1883), an

161

Advocate in 1829, later Sheriff Substitute in Dunblane and Inverness.

James Connell 1827/28
Born 31 August 1812 in Edinburgh to Sir John Connell, Advocate; died 4 March 1879 in Monks Eleigh, Suffolk. Lived at 34 Cumberland Street. Edinburgh Academy 1824-27. Edinburgh University 1827-31, Glasgow University 1831-32 where he won a Snell Exhibition to Balliol College, Oxford (BA 1836). Ordained 1836, minister of several parishes including Hammersmith 1860-71 and Monks Eleigh 1871-79. Author of many religious tracts and sermons directed against Popery.

Twin brother of
John McNeil Connell 1827-33
Born 31 August 1812 in Edinburgh to Sir John Connell; died 1861 in Canada. Edinburgh Academy 1824-27. Lived at 34 Cumberland Street.

Henry David Cook 1831/32
Born 19 May 1814 in Laurencekirk to Dr George Cook of St Andrews; died 16 June 1882 in Strathpeffer. Lived at 47 Castle Street. Indian Civil Service (HEICS) from 1834, became magistrate and judge. Member of Royal and Ancient Golf Club 1835. Latterly lived in Portobello.

Cousin of:
John Cook 1831-36
Born 21 May 1813 in Edinburgh to Walter Cook WS; died 4 December 1891 in Edinburgh. Lived at 25 Drummond Place. Lawyer, qualified WS in 1836. Member of Royal and Ancient Golf Club 1836. Treasurer to Donaldson's Hospital, chairman of SPCK.

William Cooper 1831
Born 28 March 1808 to Samuel Cooper of Failford; died 31 December 1880 in Edinburgh. Lawyer, qualified WS in 1832.

Copeland 1826/27 Not known.

John Moore Craig 1827-1831
Born 11 October 1809 in Glasgow to John Craig, merchant of Prestonholm and Leith; died 10 February 1845 at Cape of Good Hope. Lawyer, qualified WS in 1834. Bankrupt in 1840 and went to South Africa.

Brother of:
Robert Mark Craig 1826-28
Born 10 May 1808 in Glasgow to John Craig, merchant of Prestonholm and Leith; died 1881 in Tipperary. Member of Speculative Society 1827-30. Manufacturer, Prestonholm Spinning Mill, Lasswade until 1853 when he sold up and went to Ireland.

Henry Craigie 1824-28
Born 24 January 1807 in Quebec to Hon John Craigie, Commissary and Storekeeper General for Lower Canada; died 19 April 1867 in Edinburgh. Came to Edinburgh after death of father in 1813. Lawyer, qualified WS in 1829 but gave up professional work to become a Christian philanthropist. Lived after marriage to Jessie Pigon Falconar at Falcon Hall, Morningside. His biography 'Christian Stewardship' (1871) has no mention of school or sport.

Brother of:
Laurence Craigie 1824/25
Born 13 February 1808 in Quebec to Hon John Craigie; died July 1869 at Peel, Isle of Man. Came to Edinburgh in 1813. Advocate, member of the Manx Bar. Declared bankrupt and in 1851 was in debtor's prison.

James Crawford 1825/26
Born 17 December 1808 to Alexander Crawford of North Berwick; died 17 November 1863 in Edinburgh. Edinburgh University. Lawyer, qualified WS in 1833. Legal Agent for the Free Church of Scotland.

John Crawford 1826/27
Not known.

Robert Crawford 1825/26
Not known.

Crichton 1827/28 Not known.

John Cumming 1826/27 and 1831
Born 1812 to William Cumming of Riga, shipping agent. Edinburgh Academy 1824-25, Edinburgh University.

Archibald Cunningham 1831
Born 13 September 1811 to Colonel Cunninghame of Thorntoun; died 23 October 1856 in Edinburgh. Edinburgh Academy 1826-27. Advocate, called to the Scottish Bar 1834.

Cunningham 1824/25
Not known.

Thomas Davie 1824/25
Not known.

Robert Dennistoun 1824-26
Born 28 March 1807 in Glasgow to Robert Dennistoun; died 4 February 1880 at St Helier, Jersey. Lived at 14 Royal Circus. Went to Demerara and Trinidad where he inherited estates from his father. Latterly lived in Torquay then Jersey.

Brother of
Richard Dennistoun 1824-26
Born 8 May 1806 in Glasgow to Robert Dennistoun; died 20 March 1848 in Glasgow. High School. Lived at 18 Atholl Crescent. Lawyer, qualified WS in 1829.

J Dickson 1826-28 Not known.

John Dickson 1834 & 1836
Born 30 October 1817 in
Edinburgh to Walter Dickson WS;
died 6 December 1909 in Perth.
Edinburgh Academy 1825-32.
Lived 3 Royal Circus. Lawyer,
qualified WS in 1843, practised in
Perth from 1848.

Brother of:
Thomas Goldie Dickson 1836
Born 7 August 1819 in Edinburgh
to Walter Dickson WS; died 28
July 1905 at Castle Douglas.
Edinburgh Academy 1828-35.
Edinburgh University. Lived at 3
Royal Circus. Chartered
Accountant. Lieutenant, City of
Edinburgh Rifle Volunteer Corps
on its foundation in 1859.

William Dickson 1825/26
Born 1810 in Edinburgh to James
Dickson; died 31 May 1881 in
Edinburgh. Accountant and
Actuary. Succeeded his father as
Secretary of Edinburgh Life
Assurance Company 1834-67.
Lived Brandon Street, then 10
Royal Circus. Member of Royal
Archers 1833.

Christopher Douglas 1831/32
Born 13 February 1811 in
Edinburgh to Alexander Douglas
WS; died 11 November 1894 in
Edinburgh. Lived 17 Drummond
Place and 13 Atholl Crescent.
Lawyer, qualified WS in 1834.

Andrew Dudgeon 1824-28
Born 28 February 1805 to John
Dudgeon of Craig Lodge,
Haddington.

Brother of:
Robert Dudgeon 1831
Born 17 March 1813 to John
Dudgeon of Craig Lodge,
Haddington. Unmarried and at
Craig Lodge in 1851.

A Duncan 1824/25 Not known.

John Duncan 1824/25
Born 23 November 1806 to John
Duncan; died 21 June 1900 in
Edinburgh. Lived in Princes
Street, Dundas Street and Grange
Road. Qualified WS in 1833.

Duncan 1826/27
Not known (possibly same as one
of the above)

James Dunsmure 1831/32
Born 23 April 1814 in Edinburgh
to James Dunsmuire MD; died 16
October 1886 in Edinburgh. High
School. Edinburgh University,
graduated in Medicine 1835.
Lived at 26 Castle Street. Surgeon,
Fellow of the Royal College of
Surgeons (President 1866-67).
Member of Royal Archers, won
Musselburgh Silver Arrow 1866.

Samuel Dyer 1831
Born 13 July 1817 in Reading,
Berkshire, to Rev John Dyer,
Baptist minister; died 1 August

164

1843 in Macao. Edinburgh Academy 1826-32. Lived at Raeburn Place. Went to Hong Kong to set up a shipping business but died within a month of arrival.

James Ritchie Dymock 1824/25
Born 29 September 1807 in Edinburgh to William Dymock WS; died 6 February 1883 in Edinburgh. Tea and wine merchant. Town councillor, JP, manager of Royal Infirmary, Blind Asylum and treasurer of Magdalene Asylum.

John Elliot 1824-27 Not known.

John Elphinstone Elliot 1826/27
Born 27 May 1810 in Southdean, Jedburgh, to James Elliot of Wolflee WS; died 1 January 1890 at Ponteland, Northumberland. Lawyer, qualified WS in 1833. St Catharine's College, Cambridge (BA in Divinity 1841). Minister of Whalton, Northumberland 1843-80. Changed surname to Elliot-Bates on marriage in 1843.

George Esplin 1830s
Born c1813, died February 1848 in Glasgow. Accountant.

Alexander Ewing 1831-33
Not known.

Samuel Robert Fergusson 1831
Born 29 May 1812 in Pitlochry to James Fergusson; died 26 September 1890 at Strathtay,

Perthshire. Lawyer (apprentice to James Hope), qualified WS in 1835. Managed the Colonial Bank in London.

William Foulis 1831/32
Not known.

Edward George 1832/33
Born 26 January 1812 in Ramsgate to Robert George; died 1 October 1868 at Surbiton. Edinburgh University (graduated in Medicine 1835). Lived at 5 South College Street. Doctor, practised in Sandgate, Kent.

Dugald Gilchrist 1831
Born 13 February 1804 in Dornoch to Dugald Gilchrist of Ospisdale, Sutherland; died 1 December 1834 in Edinburgh. Lived at 21 Broughton Street. Lawyer, qualified WS in 1829.

Gilmour 1825/26 Not known.

Gordon 1825/26 Not known.

Gordon 1825/26 Not known.

James Graham 1827/28
Not known. Address given as 30 Great King Street.

Colquhoun Grant 1826/27
Not known.

Patrick Grant 1825/26
Born 2 June 1804 in Edinburgh to James Grant WS; died 18 April

1870 in London. Lawyer, qualified WS in 1825. Sheriff Clerk of Inverness-shire 1835-70, amateur historian of the Highlands.

Grant 1827/28 Not known. Possibly same as above.

Gregory 1825/26 Not known.

Robert Hamilton 1824-36
Born 23 January 1807 to John Hamilton, Receiver General of Customs; died 21 June 1872 in Edinburgh. Lawyer, qualified WS in 1830.

Robert Cray Hamilton 1824/25 Not known.

Hamilton 1831 Not known.

Robert Allan Harden 1826/27
Born 28 November 1803 in Edinburgh to John Harden; died 9 January 1875 in Edinburgh. Lived at Doune Terrace. Indian Civil Service (HEICS).

James Heron 1831-36
Born 2 March 1811 in Ayr to James Heron, merchant; died 23 November 1849 in Glasgow. Lived at 47 North Northumberland Place and 8 Hope Street. Lawyer, qualified WS in 1835.

Joshua Middleton Hewitson 1825-28
Born 26 December 1806 in Newcastle-upon-Tyne; died 20

March 1831 at Naples, Italy. Quaker.

Hodson 1825/26 Not known.

Andrew Hogarth 1824-31
Born 25 February 1806 in Coldstream to David Hogarth; died 22 March 1884 at Worthing, Sussex. Lawyer, qualified WS in 1829.

Brother of:
George Hogarth 1824-28 and 1832-33
Born 6 March 1810 in Coldstream to David Hogarth; died 30 November 1890 in Cupar. Banker. Town councillor and Provost of Cupar. Captain in Fifeshire Volunteers.

James Hope 1831-32
Born 1 July 1818 in Edinburgh to James Hope WS; died 10 July 1903 in Edinburgh. Edinburgh Academy 1826-33. Lived at 31 Moray Place, later Wardie Lodge. Lawyer, qualified WS in 1840. Director of Bank of Scotland and Standard Life Assurance Company.

Brother of:
John Hope 1824-36
Born 12 May 1807 at Dalry House, Edinburgh, to James Hope WS and Jane Walker of Dalry; died 25 June 1893 in Edinburgh. High School, Edinburgh University 1824-26 (did not

graduate). Lawyer, qualified WS in 1828. Lived at 31 Moray Place. Philanthropist, town councillor. Founder of the Foot-Ball Club and of the Hope Trust.

James Alexander Hunt 1831-36
Born 10 October 1817 in Edinburgh to James Hunt; died 10 October 1890 in Dunfermline. Edinburgh Academy 1828-31. Lived at 13 Moray Place and at Pittencrieff, Dunfermline. JP in Fife.

Brother of:
John Hunt 1831-32
Born 13 February 1816 in Edinburgh to James Hunt; died 10 June 1841 in Dunfermline. Edinburgh Academy 1828-30. Lived at 13 Moray Place. Advocate.

Brother of:
William Hunt 1831-36
Born 19 August 1814 in Edinburgh to James Hunt; died 6 September 1860 in Dunfermline. Lived at 13 Moray Place and at Pittencrieff.

Alexander Hunter 1831-32
Born 19 May 1816 in India to Richard Hunter, Bengal Civil Service; died 7 January 1890 in Edinburgh. Edinburgh Academy 1824-31. Edinburgh University, graduated in medicine. Lived at 21 Queen Street and 18 Belgrave Crescent. Surgeon Major, Madras.

Brother of:
Richard Hunter 1831/32
Born 20 June 1817 in India to Richard Hunter; died 29 June 1844 in Calcutta. Edinburgh Academy 1825-29. Lived at 21 Queen Street. Lawyer, qualified WS in 1838.

Jacob Dickson Hunter 1831
Born 10 September 1809 in Calcutta to Oswald Hunter, surgeon; died 31 January 1889 in Portobello. Edinburgh University 1824-1831, graduated in medicine. Surgeon, RCSE, FRCPE.

J P Hunter Laurie 1826/27
Not known.

Archibald Inglis 1824/25 and 1827/28
Born 1 December 1801 in Edinburgh to Dr Andrew Inglis; died 3 January 1889 in Edinburgh. Edinburgh University 1818-24, graduated in medicine. Surgeon. President of the Royal College of Surgeons 1853-55. Professor of Midwifery, University of Aberdeen. Medical Registrar for Scotland.

Brother of:
John Inglis 1824-26
Born 13 August 1805 in Edinburgh to Dr Andrew Inglis.

James Irvine 1824/25
Born 13 April 1809 in Lerwick, Shetland, to Alexander Irvine;

died 8 May 1877 in Edinburgh. Lived in Cumberland St and Pitt Street. Lawyer in Edinburgh.

J Irvine 1826/27 Not known Possibly same as above.

George Vere Irving 1833-36
Born 9 October 1816 in Edinburgh to Alexander Irving (Lord Newton); died 29 October 1869 in London. Edinburgh Academy 1824-31. Lived at 27 Heriot Row and at Elvanfoot, Lanarkshire. Lawyer, called to the Scottish Bar as Advocate in 1837. Noted antiquary, president of the British Archaeological Association. Captain in Lanarkshire Volunteers.

J Irving 1825-27 Not known

James Jardine 1825-31
Born 7 October 1810 in Edinburgh to Sir Henry Jardine WS; died 15 November 1839 in Edinburgh. Lawyer, qualified WS in 1834.

Robert Wellwood Johnston 1831-36
Born 12 September 1814 in Tulliallan to Lawrence Johnston of Sands; died 4 October 1893 at Cleish House, Kinross. Lived at 9 Walker Street. Became a farmer on the family estate at Sands, Tulliallan and in 1893 was described as the 'veteran sportsman, the Horatio Ross of the Ochils' when he shot 30 brace of grouse on his moors.

Thomas Johnstone 1831-36
Born 29 November 1812 in Edinburgh to Thomas Johnstone, solicitor. Edinburgh Academy 1824-28 and Mr Espinasse's School 1828-29. Lived at 37 Albany Street.

Brother of:
William Johnstone 1832-36
Born 21 September 1814 in Edinburgh to Thomas Johnstone, solicitor; died 10 May 1848 at Douglas, Isle of Man. Edinburgh Academy 1824-28 and Mr Espinasse's School 1828-29. Lived at 37 Albany Street. Lawyer, qualified as Advocate 1836.

Patrick Small Keir 1824-28

Born 9 May 1810 in Edinburgh to Patrick Keir (or Kier) of Kinmonth; died 29 November

1889 at Kindrogan, Perthshire. Edinburgh University, studied Law and became Advocate but never practised. Lived at 32 Charlotte Square, Edinburgh and Kindrogan House, Perthshire. Member of Royal and Ancient Golf Club 1831. Member of Highland and Agricultural Society for over 50 years.

James Ker 1831
Born 2 June 1817 in Edinburgh to James Ker of Blackshiels; died 7 November 1854 in Sebastopol. Edinburgh Academy 1825-31, school in England 1831-34, Military Academy (Edinburgh) 1834-36. Lived at 24 Royal Circus. Military career with 19th Regiment of Foot from 1838, rising to Captain in 1846. Died of wounds received in the Battle of Inkerman during Crimean War.

Brother of:
John Archibald Ker 1831
Born 19 September 1818 in Edinburgh to James Ker of Blackshiels; died 21 June 1915 in Edinburgh. Lived at 24 Royal Circus, later 10 Great King Street. Edinburgh Academy 1826-31; Loretto 1831-33. Civil Engineer, for 12 years in Public Works Dept, Ceylon.

William Scott Kerr 1824/25
Born 3 October 1807 in Edinburgh to Robert Kerr of Sunlaws; died 25 April 1890 in Edinburgh. High School. Trinity College, Cambridge (matric 1825, BA 1829). Landed proprietor, Sunlaws House, Roxburgh; Chatto, Roxburgh; and Drummond Place, Edinburgh. JP.

Kinloch 1824/25
Possibly Samuel Kinloch, born 17 November 1805 in Edinburgh to Henry Kinloch; died 1874 in Edinburgh. Jeweller and gold chaser.

David Kinnear 1826-28
Born 17 March 1807 in Edinburgh to George Kinnear, banker; died 20 November 1862 in Montreal, of dysentery. Edinburgh University (graduated in Law), called to the Scottish Bar 1829. Went to London, then emigrated to Montreal in 1835 where he was Justice of the Peace and Stipendiary Magistrate, also partner and chief proprietor of the Montreal Herald.

Brother of:
James Kinnear 1827/28
Born 2 December 1810 in Edinburgh to George Kinnear, banker; died 21 July 1849 in Cadiz, Spain. Lawyer, qualified as WS 1832. Lived at 21 Coates Crescent.

Charles Sharpe Kirkpatrick 1832/33
Born May 1813 to Sir Thomas Kirkpatrick; died 9 October 1867

in Libertad, El Salvador.
Edinburgh University 1829-32,
Cambridge University 1833,
emigrated to Canada 1834,
returned 1844 when he became 6th
Baronet of Closeburn,
Dumfriesshire. His son James
Kirkpatrick (1841-99) was captain
of the Scotland association
football team in 1870 and an FA
Cup winner in 1878.

George Fulton Knight 1824-28
Born 8 June 1808 in Edinburgh to
George Knight, English teacher at
the High School; died 13 February
1891 in Manchester. High School
and Edinburgh University. Free
Church Minister, East Wemyss.

Lamont 1825-28 Not known.

W Landreth 1826-28 Not known

William Lawson 1831-36
Born 9 February 1812 in
Edinburgh to John Lawson of
Cairnmuir WS; died 11 June 1847
in Ontario, Canada. Edinburgh
Academy 1826-28. Lived at 4
Royal Terrace and 9 Howard
Place. Brother of Mrs Gordon the
author (see chapter 6).

**Robert William Learmount
1826/27** Not known.

**George Gordon Browne Leith
1831/32**
Born 26 January 1812 in Armagh
to Sir George Leith; died 1887 in

Hamilton, Ontario. Edinburgh
Academy 1825-27. Lived at 41
Melville Street. Went to Canada.

Robert Lockhart 1824-26
Not known.

Edmond Logan 1824-28
Born January 1804 in Montreal,
Canada to William Logan, baker;
died 24 January 1865 in
Edinburgh. Royal High School
(Dux 1819). Lawyer (apprenticed
to James Hope), qualified WS in
1830. Lived Princes Street and at
Clarkstone, by Polmont.

Brother of:
Henry Logan 1824/25
Born 10 February 1807 in
Montreal; died 21 April 1838 in
London. Royal High School
(writing medal 1819). Went to
London in 1825 to work for his
brother William (later Sir William
Logan, father of Canadian
geology).

Logie 1831 Not known. Address
given as 7 North St David Street.

Hugh Lyon 1831/32
Born 30 March 1812 in Edinburgh
to George Lyon WS; died 8 July
1891 in Edinburgh. High School,
Edinburgh Academy 1824-27.
Glasgow University, Edinburgh
University. Solicitor in Supreme
Court. Lived at 26 Royal Crescent
and at Glenogil, Forfarshire.

Brother of:

Thomas Lyon 1831/32
Born 4 February 1814 in
Edinburgh to George Lyon WS;
died 21 December 1870 in India.
Edinburgh Academy 1826-28.
Lived at 26 Royal Crescent, later
an indigo planter in India.

Justin MacCartie 1831/32
Born 1815 to Justin MacCartie of
Carrignavar, Co Cork; died 20
February 1900 at Carrignavar.
Edinburgh Academy 1827-30.
Lived at Inverleith Row. Lawyer
in Ireland, Barrister in Dublin.
Brother of:

Robert MacCartie 1831
Born 1810 to Justin MacCartie of
Carrignavar, Co Cork; died 31
August 1867 in Plymouth, Devon.
Edinburgh Academy 1825-28.
Lived at Inverleith Row. Landed
proprietor, Brussels and Plymouth.

David McCulloch 1824/25
Born 1806 at Anwoth,
Kirkcudbrightshire to James
Murray McCulloch; died 12
September 1858 in Bombay.
Merchant in India.

Brother of:

Walter McCulloch 1824-36
Born 21 November 1807 at
Anwoth, Kirkcudbrightshire to
James Murray McCulloch; died 25
March 1892 at Ardwall. High
School, Edinburgh University.
Lawyer, qualified WS in 1830.

Noted athlete and boxer. Lived at
10 Forres Street, 139 George
Street, then Dumfries. Lord
Steward of Kirkcudbrightshire.

McDonald 1824-27 Not known.

Robert Macgregor 1831
Not known. Address given as 4
Royal Terrace.

Ewan MacIntosh 1825/26
Not known.

E Mackay 1825/26 Not known.

Robert Mackay 1824/25
Born 6 March 1807 to James
Mackay, jeweller and silversmith;
died 11 May 1872 in Edinburgh.
Lived at 10 Shandwick Place.
Lawyer, qualified WS in 1831.

Mackenzie 1826/27 Not known.

James Hay Mackenzie 1831-36
Born 30 September 1809 in
Edinburgh to Colin Mackenzie
WS; died 16 February 1865 in
Edinburgh. Lived at 29 Charlotte
Square and 10 St Andrew Square.
Lawyer, qualified WS in 1831.
Deputy Keeper of the Great Seal.

John Ord Mackenzie 1826-28
Born 18 March 1811 in Edinburgh
to Richard Mackenzie WS; died
14 March 1902 at Dolphinton,
Peeblesshire. Lawyer, qualified
WS in 1832. 'Father of the Writers
to the Signet' in later years.

Brother of:

Kenneth Mackenzie 1831/32
Born 17 July 1812 in Edinburgh to
Richard Mackenzie WS; died 16
September 1880 in Edinburgh.
Edinburgh Academy 1824-28,
Edinburgh University 1828-31
(did not graduate). Lived at 31
Abercromby Place and
Northumberland Street. Chartered
Accountant, formed Mackenzie
and Spens with William Spens
(below). Royal Company of
Archers 1835. President and of
Edinburgh Academical Club and
Academical Cricket Club in 1854,
helped to establish Raeburn Place
cricket and football ground.

**John Maclean Mackenzie-
Grieve 1826/27**

Born 29 March 1810 in Edinburgh
to Dr Andrew Mackenzie Grieve;
died 5 January 1891 in Paris.
Lived in Queen Street and Hutton
Hall, Berwickshire. Captain in the
Life Guards. Moved to Paris
where he was a founding member
of the French Jockey Club,
caricatured in *Vanity Fair's* 'Men
of the Day' in 1877.

James MacKnight 1834-36
Born 23 September 1810 in Ratho
to Rev Thomas MacKnight; died 6
November 1878 in Edinburgh.
High School. Lived at 12 London
Street. Lawyer, qualified WS in
1833. Commissioner of Police
1840-56, town councillor 1856-78.

George Maclachlan 1827/28
Born 25 June 1803 to Donald
Maclachlan; died 7 August 1877 at
Castle Lachlan, Argyllshire.
Lawyer, qualified WS in 1826,
partner in Maclachlan and Roger.
21st Chief of Maclachlan.

McLachlan 1824/25 Not known.
Possibly same as above.

A D McLean 1826/27
Not known.

Steuart Macnaghten 1831
Born 20 June 1815 in Madras to
Sir Francis Macnaghten; died 28
June 1895 in Southampton.
Edinburgh Academy 1826-31
(Dux 1831). Dublin University
(MA). Barrister in Middle Temple.

Knighted 1890. JP and DL for Hampshire.

Hector Archibald Macneil 1825-32

Born c1807 to Captain Archibald Macneil of 75th Regiment; died 11 April 1875 in Edinburgh. Lived at 6 Wharton Place and 8 Maitland Street. Lawyer, qualified WS in 1830. Captain in Edinburgh Light Infantry Militia.

Ewen Cameron Macneill 1825-27

Born 1805 to Roderick Macneill of Barra; died 1847 in Trinidad. In January 1828, won the foot race at the Highland Club meeting in Bruntsfield. Lawyer, qualified WS in 1828.

McNicol 1826/27 Not known.

Allan Alexander Maconochie 1824/25

Born 10 February 1806 at Kirknewton, West Lothian to Lord Meadowbank; died 29 May 1885 at Kirknewton. Lived at 13 Royal Circus and Meadowbank House, Kirknewton. Lawyer, called to the Scottish Bar 1829, practised as Advocate until appointment as Professor of Law at Glasgow University 1842-55. Judge at Court of Session. Pioneer photographer. Surname adapted to Maconochie-Welwood in 1854. Became Lord Meadowbank in 1862.

Brother of:

Robert Blair Maconochie 1831

Born 21 May 1814 at Kirknewton, West Lothian to Lord Meadowbank; died 4 October 1883 at Gattonside, by Melrose. Edinburgh Academy 1824-28. Lived at 13 Royal Circus. Lawyer, qualified WS in 1837. JP for Roxburghshire and Edinburgh.

I McPherson 1826-28
Not known.

McPherson 1825-27 Not known.

John Anthony Macrae 1831

Born 1 February 1812 to Colin Macrae of Inverinate, Ross-shire; died 23 May 1868 in Edinburgh. Lived at 14 Gloucester Place. University of Leyden (LLD). Lawyer, qualified WS in 1835. Major in Queen's Edinburgh Rifle Volunteers. Chief of Clan Macrae.

Scipio Alexander Mactaggart 1831-36

Born 15 March 1812 in Campbeltown to Daniel Mactaggart; died 25 June 1886 in Inveraray. Lived at 3 Royal Circus. Lawyer, qualified WS in 1835. Practised in Inveraray, Sheriff Clerk of Argyll and Provost. Pioneer photographer.

George McWake 1831
Not known.

Edward Francis Maitland 1824-26
Born 16 April 1808 in Edinburgh to Adam Maitland of Dundrennan; died 23 February 1870 in Edinburgh. High School, Edinburgh University (gold medal for moral philosophy 1829). Lived at Ainslie Place. Lawyer, qualified WS in 1831. Solicitor General for Scotland 1855-62. Appointed a judge in 1862 as Lord Barcaple. Edinburgh Academy director 1853-58.

F Maitland 1826/27
Possibly Frederick Charles Maitland, born 7 April 1812 in Kirkliston to Alexander Charles Gibson Maitland; died 31 August 1890 in East Grinstead. Edinburgh Academy 1825-27, Mr Espinasse's School 1828. Lived in London.

O Maitland 1825/26 Not known.

Maitland Gibson 1826-28
Not known.

Maitland Makgill 1827/28
First name not given, probably one of the five sons of Capt Frederick Maitland Makgill: David (b1801), James (b1806), Charles (b1808), Lewis (b1809), Henry (b1813).

Lieut Joseph Maitland RN 1826/27 Not known.

Erskine Marjoribanks 1831/32
Born 29 January 1812 in Bathgate to Alexander Marjoribanks; died 13 March 1871 in Bathgate. Lived at 4 Carlton Street.

Brother of:
George Marjoribanks 1824-28
Born 2 February 1806 in Bathgate to Alexander Marjoribanks; died 15 June 1828 in Bathgate. Studied medicine, licentiate of Royal College of Surgeons at his death.

Brother of:
Thomas Marjoribanks 1825-33
Born 16 December 1809 in Bathgate to Alexander Marjoribanks; died 6 January 1868 at Stenton, East Lothian. Minister at Lochmaben until 1849, then Stenton.

George Maxwell 1824-27
Not known.

Melville 1824/25 Not known.

E Milne 1826/27 Not known.

George Thomson Mitchell 1831/32

Born 4 September 1812 in Airth to Robert Mitchell; died 19 July 1894 in Blairadam, Kinross. Edinburgh University (MD 1835). Doctor. Lived at 41 Melville Street.

James Moncreiff 1832/33

Born 29 November 1811 in Edinburgh to James Wellwood Moncreiff, Advocate; died 27 April 1895. High School, Edinburgh University. Lived at 47 Moray Place, St Andrew Square then 15 Great Stuart Street. Advocate, called to the Bar 1833. MP for Leith and Edinburgh. Lord Advocate, 11th Baronet, 1st Baron Moncrieff. Founder, with others, of Grange Cricket Club. His son Francis captained Scotland's first rugby team in 1871.

William Monro 1831/32

Born 1815 in Edinburgh to Dr Alexander Monro, Professor of Anatomy and Surgery; died 2 March 1881 at Parkstone, Dorset. Edinburgh Academy 1825-29. Lived at 121 George Street, later in Kirkcudbrightshire. Soldier with 79th Highlanders: Ensign 1834, Captain 1842, retired as Major in 1854. Adjutant of the Galloway Rifle Volunteers.

Alexander Binning Monro 1824-26

Born 22 May 1805 in Doune to David Monro Binning of Softlaw;

died 12 December 1891 in Oxford. Lawyer, qualified WS in 1829. Lived at 43 Moray Place, later at Auchenbowie, Stirlingshire.

Morrison 1826/27 Not known.

Munro 1826/27 Not known.

Andrew Murray 1831-32

Born 19 August 1813 in Edinburgh to Andrew Murray, Sheriff of Aberdeen; died 13 October 1872 at Richmond, Surrey. Edinburgh Academy 1826-29. Lived at 34 Heriot Row, and in Richmond. Chartered Engineer. Chief Engineer of Portsmouth Dockyard, Surveyor of Factories at the Admiralty.

Brother of:
John Murray 1825-27

Born 15 October 1809 in Edinburgh to Andrew Murray; died 17 January 1881 at Murrayshall, Perthshire. High School (gold medal for Greek 1823). Edinburgh University (MA), University of Gottingen. Lived at 126 George Street and at Murrayshall. Lawyer, called to Scottish Bar 1831, practised as Advocate until 1847. Changed surname to Murray Graham in 1859 following an inheritance.

Andrew Dickson Murray 1831/32

Born 19 February 1812 in Edinburgh to William Murray of

Conland WS; died 10 January 1878 in London. Edinburgh Academy 1824-27. Lived at 17 Forth Street, later in Kensington. Lawyer, qualified WS in 1837. President of the Royal Physical Society, President of the Royal Botanical Society of Edinburgh.

Charles Murray 1827/28
Not known (address given as St Bernard's Church).

James Murray 1827/28
Not known (address given as St Bernard's Church).

James Mylne 1824-28
Born 25 March 1807 to George Mylne, manager of Edinburgh Life Assurance Co; died 3 December 1879 in Edinburgh. High School (gold medal for Greek 1821). Lived at 35 Charlotte Square. Lawyer, qualified WS in 1834. Director of Edinburgh Academy 1854-64. Director of the National Bank of Scotland.

Charles Nash 1827/28
Not known. President of Brunswick Cricket Club in 1832.

Andrew Nelson 1831/32
Not known. Address given as 33 Melville Street.

Robert Nelson 1831/32
Not known. Address given as 33 Melville Street, probably brother of above.

George Stewart Newbigging 1825-27
Born 20 October 1810 in Edinburgh to Sir William Newbigging, President of the Royal College of Surgeons; died 25 November 1840 in Paris. Edinburgh University (MA 1831, MD 1837). Surgeon, Fellow of Royal College of Surgeons of Edinburgh.

Brother of:
John Stewart Newbigging 1824-28
Born 20 January 1809 in Edinburgh to Sir William Newbigging; died 25 October 1849 in Jedburgh. Edinburgh University. Lawyer, qualified WS in 1832. Sheriff Clerk of Roxburghshire from 1841.

Brother of:
Robert Newbigging 1824-28
Born 4 March 1807 in Edinburgh to Sir William Newbigging; died 5 January 1833 in Edinburgh. Edinburgh University (1824 logic class, with John Hope). Lived in St Andrew Square. Advocate.

Brother of:
William Newbigging 1824-28
Born 25 July 1805 in Edinburgh to Sir William Newbigging; died 18 November 1829 in Edinburgh. Studied medicine at Edinburgh University 1823-27 but did not graduate.

Nicholson 1824/25
Not known.

Sir John Ogilvy 1827/28
Born 17 March 1803 in Edinburgh
to Rear Admiral Sir William
Ogilvy; died 29 March 1890 at
Archerfield, East Lothian. Harrow
School 1817-21; Christ Church,
Oxford. Succeeded father in 1823
as Chief of the Clan Ogilvy.
Lieutenant in Life Guards 1826-
31. Major-General, Royal
Company of Archers. Liberal MP
for Dundee 1857-74.

Peter Wedderburn Ogilvy 1836
Born 15 November 1815 at
Ruthven, Perthshire, to Peter W
Ogilvy; died 7 September 1847 in
Madras. Lived at 8 Forres Street.
Soldier with 35th Madras Native
Infantry, rising to Captain.

Robert Oliphant 1825-28
Born 23 February 1810 in
Forgandenny to Lt-Colonel James
Oliphant of Rossie; died 14
November 1872 in Chester. Lived
72 Northumberland Street.
Lawyer, qualified WS in 1833.
Member of Six Feet High Club
(golf medal 1828 & 1831); Royal
and Ancient Golf Club (gold
medal 1834 & 1835); Perthshire
Golfing Soc. (gold medal 1834).

John Ormond 1836
Address given as 4 Forres Street,
home of Dr Robert Omond. This is
possibly his brother, Rev John

Reid Omond b 2 August 1804 in
Orkney; died 4 April 1892 in
Monzie, Perthshire. Edinburgh
University (Hebrew class prize
1832). Ordained minister of
Monzie in 1836; photographed by
Hill and Adamson in Edinburgh
after the Disruption of 1843.

Adam Paterson 1831-32
Born 9 November 1814 in
Glasgow to Andrew Paterson,
solicitor; died 21 March 1841 in
Paris, Upper Canada. Edinburgh
Academy 1824-27. Lived at 47
Albany Street. Went to Ontario in
1830s.

John Paton 1825/26 Not known.

Robert Paton 1827/28 Not
known. Possibly brother of above.

Robert Prescott 1831
Born 3 December 1813 in Ireland
to Lt Col Serjeantson Prescott,
Dragoon Guards (killed by a
cricket ball in 1816); died 21
January 1886 at Prestonpans.
Edinburgh Academy 1825-31.
Trinity College, Cambridge (MA).
Lived at Floors Castle, cousin of
Duke of Roxburgh.

John Pryce 1836
Not known. Address given as 13
Howard Place.

George Ramsay 1825/26
Born 3 July 1809 in Edinburgh to
Thomas Ramsay; died 11

September 1887 at North Berwick.
Chartered Accountant, manager of
Scottish Union Insurance. Lived at
5 Charlotte Square.

**Charles Greenshields Reid
1831/32**
Born 13 October 1814 in Portsea,
Hampshire to Captain Charles
Hope Reid, RN; died 12 February
1897 in America. Lived at 9 Saxe
Coburg Place and 2 St Colme
Street. President of Speculative
Society 1839-42. Lawyer,
qualified WS in 1840. Royal
Archers, won the Kilwinnning
Papingo in 1844. Secretary of
Trinity College, Glenalmond
1845-54. Bankrupt 1857, went to
London, then America.

J Rennie 1826/27
Not known.

Frederick Rensworth 1825/26
Not known.

**Donald Robertson 1826/27 and
1831** Not known.
Address given as 108 George
Street (Hogarth's Lodgings).

James Rocheid 1827/28
Born 17 May 1809 in Edinburgh
to James Rocheid of Inverleith;
died 3 March 1840 at Mannheim,
Germany. Lived at 15 Inverleith
Place. He inherited a third of the
Inverleith estate on the death of his
father in 1824. His son Charles, by
his first wife, Baroness Marianne

Danckelmann, was involved with
Hope in the lease of Stockbridge
playing field in 1854. A legal case
about ownership of the estate ran
from 1860-69, after which the
ground in Stockbridge was leased
(and later sold) to Grange Cricket
Club.

James Rolland 1826-28
Born 24 November 1802 in
Edinburgh to Adam Rolland of
Gask; died 20 November 1889 in
Edinburgh. Lived at 29 Melville
Street. Lawyer, qualified WS in
1829.

Brother of:
John Rolland 1826-31
Born 1 December 1814 to Adam
Rolland of Gask; died 26 June
1849 in Edinburgh. Edinburgh
Academy 1826-28. Lived at 14
Shandwick Place. Surgeon.

William Ross 1832-36
Probably William Ross of
Kirkcudbright, who entered
Edinburgh University in 1831.
Lived at 8 Windmill Street, likely
to be student lodgings.

Henry Roy 1831-33
Born 25 April 1813 at Nenthorn,
Berwickshire to William Roy; died
1893 in Edinburgh. Edinburgh
Academy 1824-27. Edinburgh
University (graduated in Medicine
1838). Lived at 22 Drummond
Place, then London, before
returning to Edinburgh.

178

Roy 1825/26 Not known. Possibly the same as the above.

William Russell 1831 Not known.

Sandilands 1824-28 Not known.

George Scott 1825-27
Born 12 June 1804 in Leith to William Scott, brewer; died 12 May 1833 in Leith. Lawyer, qualified WS in 1827. Lived at 2 James' Place, Leith.

George Robertson Scott 1826/27
Born c1809 to George Robertson Scott of Benholm, Kincardine. Lived at 22 Great King Street (home of his cousin William Robertson WS); later known as Captain GR Scott.

John Scott 1831
Born 2 October 1809 to William Scott WS of Teviotbank; died 16 July 1867 at Marienbad, Bohemia. Lawyer, qualified WS in 1832. Lived in Edinburgh and Rodono, Selkirkshire. Acquired Barony of Rodono in 1860.

George Semple 1834-36
Not known. Address given as 8 Forres Street, home of John William Semple, advocate.

Sill 1825-27 Not known.

James Sinclair 1824/25
Possibly born October 1802 to James Sinclair; died 1 March 1876

in Thurso. Advocate, called to Scottish Bar 1827 but did not practise. Magistrate in Forss, Caithness, and Deputy Lieutenant.

W Sinclair 1826/27
Possibly William Sinclair, George Heriot's Hospital; Edinburgh University Latin prize 1831.

Samuel Henderson Somerville 1831/32
Born 1814 to William Somerville of Fingask; died 25 July 1875 in Ragatz, Switzerland. Edinburgh Academy 1827-28. Lived at 13 Nelson Street, later in London, Germany and Italy. Changed surname to May Somerville after marriage. JP and Deputy Lieutenant in Dumfriesshire.

James Souter 1826/27
Born 20 April 1806 in Banff to Stewart Souter; died 18 July 1858 at West Calder. Lawyer, qualified WS in 1830.

Spalding 1825/26 Not known.

John Speid 1831-36
Born 26 June 1814 to Robert Speid of Forfarshire; died 16 May 1861 at Ardovie, Forfarshire. Lived at 2 Comely Green. Lawyer, qualified WS in 1841. Member of Forfarshire Rifle Volunteers.

Archibald Spens 1825-27
Born c1809 to Colonel Archibald Spens, Inveresk; died 24

November 1869 at Portobello, Midlothian. Edinburgh Academy 1824-25. Royal Company of Archers 1827. Honorable East India Company Service, Bombay Civil Service.

William Spens 1824-31
Born 6 September 1807 in Edinburgh to Dr Thomas Spens, President of the Royal College of Physicians; died 22 August 1868 in Partick. High School, Edinburgh University. Lived at 14 Drummond Place. Accountant, founded Mackenzie and Spens with Kenneth Mackenzie (above). Moved to Glasgow in 1839 when appointed Manager of Scottish Amicable Life Assurance.

Brother of
Thomas Spens 1824/25
Born 12 August 1803 in Edinburgh to Dr Thomas Spens; died 4 January 1836 in Calcutta. Edinburgh University 1818-24. Surgeon, Indian Medical Service. His son Thomas Hope Spens (1836-57) was killed in the Indian Mutiny.

Brother of
James Spens 1826-28
Born 28 November 1811 in Edinburgh to Dr Thomas Spens; died 21 November 1856 at Ambala, India. Edinburgh Academy 1824-26, Addiscombe 1827. Joined Royal Engineers (Bengal) in 1828, rose to Captain.

Brother of
John Spens 1831-34
Born 21 January 1816 in Edinburgh to Dr Thomas Spens; died 7 February 1836 in Edinburgh. Edinburgh Academy 1824-1831. Edinburgh University, studied Medicine (gold medal in Natural Philosophy 1835).

Nathanael Spens 1824-27
Born 18 February 1805 in Leuchars, Fife, to Lt-Colonel James Spens of Craigsanquhar; died 22 November 1869 in Portobello, Midlothian. Cousin of the above. Lawyer (apprentice to James Hope), qualified WS in 1830. Royal Company of Archers (joined on same day as John Hope), won silver arrow 1830 and 1834.

Charles William Dunbar Staveley 1834
Born 18 December 1817 in Boulogne to Lt-General William Staveley; died 23 November 1896 in Dublin. Scottish Naval and Military Academy, Edinburgh 1833-34 (prizes for landscape drawing, sketching, etc). 62 Northumberland St. Long military career in many countries, commissioned 1835 and rose to become General Sir Charles Staveley.

Patrick Steuart 1831
Born 1 October 1817 to Charles Steuart WS; died 8 April 1905 at

Moffat. Edinburgh Academy 1827-28. Lived at 3 Albyn Place. Farmer at Middlegill, by Moffat. A noted sheep breeder.

George Stewart 1831/32
Born 12 September 1814 in Stranraer to Lieut Leveson Douglas Stewart RN; died 13 January 1893. Edinburgh Academy 1824-30, Edinburgh University. Lived at 5 Walker Street.

Brother of:
James Stewart 1831/32
Born 2 October 1816 to Lieut Leveson Douglas Stewart RN; died 19 December 1895 in Edinburgh. Edinburgh Academy 1825-31, Edinburgh University. Lived at 5 Walker Street.

James Stewart 1826-28
Details not known. Edinburgh Academy 1824-26. Lived at 109 George Street.

P Stewart 1826/27
Not known.

William Stewart 1834-36
Not known. Lived at 11 Howe Street.

John Frederick Stoddart 1824-26
Born 1805, son of Sir John Stoddart, chief justice and judge in Malta; died 29 August 1839 at Colombo. High School, Edinburgh

University. President of the Speculative Society 1825-27. Advocate, called to Scottish Bar 1827. Judge of the Supreme Court, Ceylon in 1836.

Archibald Campbell Swinton 1827/28
Born 15 July 1812 at Broadmeadows, Berwickshire, to John Campbell Swinton; died 27 November 1890 at Kimmerghame, Berwickshire. Edinburgh Academy 1826-27. Edinburgh University (MA; gold medal for Moral Philosophy 1831). Glasgow University (LLB). Advocate, called to Scottish Bar 1833. Lived at Inverleith Place and Marcliffe Road. Royal Archers 1833 (Brigadier General 1864). Professor of Civil Law at Edinburgh University. Director of Edinburgh Academy 1842-90.

Brother of
James Rannie Swinton 1831
Born 11 April 1816 near Duns to John Campbell Swinton; died 18 December 1888 in London. Edinburgh Academy 1826-31. Edinburgh University. Portrait painter, went to London 1839, studied at Royal Academy. Photographed in Edinburgh by Hill and Adamson, 1843.

Craufurd Tait 1824/25
Born 9 February 1807 in Edinburgh to Craufurd Tait WS of Harviestoun; died 6 April 1828

returning from Bengal. Edinburgh University 1824 (studied rhetoric, did not graduate). Ensign with 28th Bengal Native Infantry but fell ill and died on ship returning home. Elder brother of Archibald Campbell Tait (1811-1882) who was at the High School, later Archbishop of Canterbury and headmaster of Rugby.

George Thomson 1831
Not known.

J A Thomson 1826/27
Not known.

William Thomson 1831/32
Born 1813 to John Thomson, cashier of Royal Bank; died 9 March 1879 at Balgowan, Perthshire. Went to China, bought estate of Balgowan on return. Keen botanical collector.

David James Staig Thorburn 1827/28
Born 31 December 1806 in Lochmaben to Rev William Thorburn; died 19 May 1882 in Gloucester. Edinburgh University (graduated in Medicine, 1827). Doctor, Indian Civil Service (HEICS). Later lived in Cheltenham.

Walter Thorburn 1824-28
Born 30 October 1807 in Edinburgh to Walter Thorburn, cabinet-maker; died 1873 in London. Solicitor at 2 South

Bridge, Edinburgh; later practised in London.

Thomas Tod 1825-28
Born 26 January 1810 in Melrose to Thomas Tod of Drygrange, Roxburghshire; died 8 February 1867 in Edinburgh. Edinburgh University. Magistrate, JP and Deputy Lieutenant in Roxburgh. President of local cricket club.

Thomas Jameson Torrie 1827/28
Born 14 December 1808 in Edinburgh to Patrick Jameson Torrie of Prince of Wales Island; died 7 August 1858 at Roslin. Edinburgh University. Advocate, called to Scottish Bar 1830. Lived at 21 Royal Circus. President of Plinian Society. Fellow of the Royal Society of Edinburgh. His son of same name (1857-1913) played rugby for Scotland v England in 1877.

Trench 1826/27
Not known. Possibly James Trench (1808-54), Edinburgh University; Master Builder and Superintendent of the Edinburgh City Mission; or William Stewart Trench, Edinburgh University (graduated in Medicine 1831); West Indies.

Turnbull 1826/27 Not known.

Charles Underwood 1825/26
Born 1807 in Ross, Herefordshire; died 1 July 1852 in Valletta,

Malta. Edinburgh University (graduated in Medicine in 1830). Ran the Ross Dispensary, then went to Malta in 1846 for his health.

Underwood 1831 Not known. Possibly same as above.

James Wallace 1826/27 and 1831 Born 1 April 1813 in Dirleton to Alexander Wallace of Auchinvole, Kilsyth; died 23 March 1881. Lived at 14 Manor Place. Lawyer, qualified WS in 1838.

Brother of:
William Wallace 1831-32 Born 4 September 1810 to Alexander Wallace of Auchinvole. Lived at 14 Manor Place.

Gerard Wardlaw 1831/32 Born 31 December 1817 in Edinburgh to Lt-Gen John Wardlaw; died 17 February 1869 in Leamington Spa. Edinburgh Academy 1828-31. Lived at 9 Albyn Place. Joined 72nd Highlanders as Ensign in 1834, retired as Captain in 1848.

Brother of:
James Wardlaw 1831/32 Born 11 November 1818 in Edinburgh to Lt-Gen John Wardlaw; died 3 October 1867 at Belmaduthy House, Ross-shire. Edinburgh Academy 1828-32. Lived at 9 Albyn Place. Joined 24th Bengal Native Infantry as

Ensign in 1837, retired to reserve in 1849 as Major. Farmed in the Black Isle.

Brother of:
Robert Wardlaw 1831/32 Born 1816 to Lt-Gen John Wardlaw; died 1 December 1885 in Hastings. Edinburgh Academy 1828-32. Lived at 9 Albyn Place. Joined Dragoon Guards as Cornet 1835, retired as General in 1884. Fought in Crimea, much decorated.

Andrew Watson 1831/32 Born 26 July 1817 in Edinburgh to Andrew Watson WS. Lived at 19 Melville Street.

Brother of:
David Watson 1831/32 Born 10 November 1815 in Edinburgh to Andrew Watson WS. Lived at 19 Melville Street.

Thomas Wylie Webster 1824-27 Born 4 July 1807 to Rev John Webster, Forfarshire; died 29 March 1877 at Bridge of Allan. High School, Edinburgh University. President of Speculative Society 1828-30. Advocate, called to Scottish Bar 1829. Scottish Parliamentary Solicitor, London. Changed surname to Riddell-Webster

George Wedderburn 1834-36 Born 25 March 1817 in Edinburgh to James Wedderburn, Solicitor

General; died 1 May 1865 in Edinburgh. Edinburgh Academy 1825-31. 31 Heriot Row. Lawyer, qualified WS in 1840. Factor to Ogilvy of Ruthven (above).

Brother of:
James Wedderburn 1836
Born 23 September 1814 in Edinburgh to James Wedderburn; died 17 July 1863 in London. Edinburgh Academy 1824-30. Lived at 31 Heriot Row. Assistant Surgeon, Coldstream Guards from 1836, later with Scots Greys.

Weir (friend) 1831
Not known.

William James Welsh 1832/33
Born 1814 to Major General James Welsh, Madras Presidency; died 12 September 1846 in St Louis, Missouri. Lived at Northumberland Street. Died in a fall from his horse.

David Williamson 1824-26
Born 17 November 1803 in Dumfries to Thomas Williamson WS; died 21 July 1843 in Edinburgh. Lived 20 Stafford Street. Lawyer, qualified WS in 1828.

Robert Williamson 1827/28
Not known.

George Witham 1824-26
Born 9 October 1805 in Yorkshire to Henry Witham (formerly Silvertop), botanist; died 8 September 1847 at Lartington Hall, Yorkshire (now Co Durham). Edinburgh University medical student 1823-25 (did not graduate). Lived at Great King Street. Joined 68th Regiment of Foot 1827 as Ensign, rose to Captain by purchase. Succeeded to family estate. Magistrate and Deputy Lieutenant in North Yorkshire and County Durham.

Alexander Wood 1832-36
Born 10 December 1817 in Cupar to Dr James Wood; died 26 February 1884 in Edinburgh. Edinburgh Academy 1825-32. Lived at 19 Royal Circus and Canaan Park, Morningside (home of his cousin John Stewart Wood). Edinburgh University (graduated in Medicine in 1839). Doctor, Fellow of the Royal College of Physicians of Edinburgh (President 1858). Inventor of hypodermic syringe in 1853. See *Alexander Wood MD, FRCPE. A Sketch of his life and work* by Rev Thomas Brown FRSE (1886).

Alexander Wood 1825/26
Born 1 May 1810 to Henry Bennet Wood; died 29 October 1861 in Duns. Classical Academy, Edinburgh 1822-24; Edinburgh Academy 1824-25 (first Dux of the school). Lived at 23 Great King Street. Advocate, called to the Scottish Bar 1834. Sheriff Substitute of Berwickshire.

Brother of:
Anthony Wood 1831-32
Son of Henry Bennet Wood. Lived at 23 Great King Street.

Brother of:
William Wood 1831
Born 1817 in Dalkeith to Henry Bennet Wood; died 10 December 1852 in Musselburgh. Lived at 23 Great King Street.

Andrew Wood 1825-28
Born 1 September 1810 in Edinburgh to Dr William Wood, surgeon; died 25 January 1881 in Edinburgh. Edinburgh University (graduated in Medicine 1831); Cambridge University (LLD 1880). Lived at 9 Darnaway Street. Surgeon, Fellow of the Royal College of Surgeons (President 1855-57).

Brother of:
Thomas Wood 1831
Born 26 July 1812 in Edinburgh to Dr William Wood, surgeon; died 9 September 1879. Edinburgh Academy 1824-28. Lived at 87 George Street. Coffee planter in Ceylon.

Brother of:
William Wood 1831
Born 21 April 1814 in Edinburgh to Dr William Wood, surgeon; died 20 February 1889 in Aberdeen. Edinburgh Academy 1824-29. Lived at 87 George Street. Accountant.

John Wood 1824-28
Possibly John George Wood, born 5 April 1804 in Edinburgh to John Philp Wood, Auditor of Excise; died 14 September 1865 in Edinburgh. Lived at 8 South Charlotte St. Lawyer, qualified WS in 1829.

W Wood 1831
Possibly Walter Wood, son of Dr James Wood. Born 31 October 1812 in Dundee; died 6 March 1882 in Elie. Edinburgh Academy 1825-28. Edinburgh University (MA 1832). Lived at 19 Royal Circus. Ordained 1836, Free Church Minister of Elie from 1845. Possibly William Wood, son of John Philp Wood. Born 21 March 1812 in Edinburgh; died 15 December 1892 in Edinburgh. Lived in Oxford Terrace. Chartered Accountant. Elder in Free Church of Scotland.

James Charles Wyld 1831
Born 11 July 1813 in Leith to James Wyld of Gilston, merchant; died 11 July 1892 in Tecumseth, Ontario. Edinburgh Academy 1824-26, Edinburgh University and Military Academy. Lived at 11 Royal Terrace. Went to Canada in 1834 to farm.

Brother of:
Robert Stodart Wyld 1831
Born 16 April 1808 to James Wyld of Gilston; died 29 October 1893 in Edinburgh. Lived at 11 Royal

185

Terrace. Lawyer, qualified WS in 1833 but did not practise for long. Provost of Queensferry. Edinburgh University (Honorary LLD 1874). Author of philosophical works and *The Memoir of James Wyld of Gilston and his family* (1889).

'Forgot name' 1827/28
Someone who paid their subscription but clearly did not stay with the club for long.

Foot-Ball Club servants and suppliers

James Stewart

Receipt from James Stewart in 1832 for payment of
24 shillings to blow up footballs

Stewart was a retainer of the club from 1827-35, paid one shilling per week with an occasional bonus, to keep the club supplied with balls and manage the stock of equipment. He lived at 2 Howe Street, moved in 1835 to Hay's Court at the head of West Port, then appears to have gone to Helensburgh. He was clearly a favourite of John Hope, who listed some old clothes (1 blue shirt, 1 torn woollen jacket, 1 vest plaid with jersey) and 'told Jane Stewart that her father should have them'.

James Gow

Gow appears to have taken over from Stewart, initially for blowing up balls and supplying bladders, and later with club administration. He is first mentioned in May 1834: 'The subscription for the summer season will be five shillings and it will be collected by James Gow.' In 1839 he was still closely involved: 'James Gow, chairman, 10 Forres Street, will call upon the Old Members of the Foot Ball Club to receive their subscription for the present season.' Gow (1806-1868) was not chairman of the club in a committee sense, the term meant he ran a sedan chair and delivery service. He appears to have fallen on hard times as later he worked as a railway porter.

Stewart and Gow were not always available, and some other helpers are named in the accounts: Gourlay, paid one shilling a week in 1831 for attendance; Hugh Templeton, paid a shilling 'for teaching Gourlay to blow the balls'; James Thomson, a 'Lad to blow up the balls' in 1832; and Muirhead, paid 1s 6d per day for 16 days in 1834.

187

George and Janet Spence
Rented Dalry Park to John Hope from 1824-31. George Spence (1791-1827) had married Janet Smith (1792-1878) in 1811 and together they ran a cow-feeding business from their home in Thornybauk, letting out grass pasture. The agreement appears to have ended after the park was damaged, although the complaint was signed by a George McGill. There is a Spence family memorial in St Cuthbert's Churchyard.

John Girdwood
Rented Greenhill Park to John Hope from 1831-36. John Girdwood was also a cow-feeder living in Thornybauk, where he ran a dairy. He was clearly well educated and literate, writing to Hope in 1834: 'Sir, I have been much disappointed at your calling so much and never had the pleasure of seeing you. I see by your note that you are complaining of the grass rent is too high. I was fully of the mind of giving it at your own rent the first time I heard of your complaint, and I am of the same still. I hope you will go and prosper in your game.'

Duncan Stevenson & Co
Printer to the University, who printed early club memoranda until the company was sequestered in 1829, following the financial crash.

J&C Muirhead
Proprietors of the Edinburgh Advertiser, who printed club memoranda in the 1830s. The company was owned by Claud Muirhead, of Heriot Row.

Sir William Forbes of Pitsligo
Banker to the Foot-Ball Club, through his private bank which eventually became part of the Union Bank of Scotland, and owner of the lands of Greenhill, just south of Bruntsfield Links. His son John, who inherited Greenhill in 1828, was elected a Fellow of the Royal Society of Edinburgh in 1833, having been proposed by John Hope's uncle, Thomas Charles.

John Christie & Son
Breeches-maker and glover, who also supplied the leather cases for footballs. In 1827 he established his shop at 16 George Street, opposite St Andrew's Church.

John Hope's family

On his paternal side:
His grandfather Dr John Hope (1725-1786) married in 1760 Juliet Stevenson (c1735-1802). Five children:
> Robert Hope (1761-c1789) 'bred to the bar but died early in life', unmarried.
> Marion Anne Hope (1763-1837) m. 1797 James Walker of Dalry (1743-1817).
> Major John Hope (1765-1840), unmarried.
> Professor Thomas Charles Hope (1766-1844), unmarried.
> **James Hope WS** (1769-1842), his father – see below.

On his maternal side:
James Walker of Dalry (1743-1817) married first in 1780 Jean Hay-Newton (1759-1792). Three children:
> Francis Walker (1781-1844), known from 1829 as Sir Francis Walker-Drummond, Bart, of Hawthornden; m. 1810 Margaret Anne Drummond (1791-1876).
> **Jane Walker** (1786-1822), his mother – see below.
> James John Walker of Dalry (1790-1856) m. (1) 1825 Lillias Mackenzie (1796-1833); m. (2) 1848 Ellen Dykes (1809-1869).

James Walker married second in 1797 Marion Ann Hope (1763-1837). One daughter: Julia Walker (1798-1874) m. 1823 Sir John Hall, Bart, of Dunglass (1787-1860).

John Hope's parents, James Hope WS and Jane Walker, married in 1805 and had nine children:

John Hope WS (1807-1893), unmarried.

Jane Anne Hope (1808-1839), unmarried.

Juliana 'Julia' Hope (1810-1888) m. 1830 John Watson Barton (1798-1840). Seven children:
> Mary Jane Barton (1831-1908), unmarried.
> Julia Sophia Barton (1832-1903) m. 1854 Rev Charles Augustus Hope (1827-1898).

John Hope Barton (1833-1876) m. 1872 Florence Mary Annabella
Ramsden (1842-1924).
Margaret Barton (1835-1870) m. 1859 Rev Charles Warren Markham
(1835-1896).
Louisa Barton (1836-1926), unmarried.
Caroline Barton (1838-1916) m. 1867 William Clayton Browne
(1835-1907).
Frances Barton (1840-1917), unmarried.

Helen Hope (1813-1887) m. 1845 Rev John Sandilands (1813-1865).
James Walter Sandilands, 12th Lord Torphichen (1846-1915) m. 1881
Frances Ellen Gordon (1852-1943); divorced 1890.

Jamima Hope (1814-1877) m. 1844 Rev Henry Blisset (1808-1893).
John Freeman Blisset (1845-1880), unmarried.
Margaret Jane Blisset (1846-1901) m. 1886 Thomas Millett Dew
(1859-1931).

Margaret 'Maga' Hope (1816-1896) m. 1844 James Alexander Duncan
Fergusson (1812-1864).
Alice Jane Fergusson (1845-1928) m. 1872 Andrew Smythe
Montague Browne (1836-1916).

James Hope WS of Belmont (1818-1903) m. 1850 Gertrude Buller-
Fullerton-Elphinstone (1826-1894). Seven children:
Anna Gertrude Hope (1851-1895) m. 1878 Francis Bertram
Dalrymple (1850-1932).
James Edward Hope (1852-1917) m. 1880 Sophia Edmonstone
(1853-1924).
Clementina Jane Hope (1854-1860) died young.
Mary Constance Hope (1857-1942) m. 1889 Otho Glynn Bolitho
(1844-1911).
Edith Geraldine Hope (1859-1904), unmarried.
John Reginald Hope (1862-1870) died young.
Cecil Arthur Hope (Major) (1865-1934) m. 1889 Eleanor Grove
(1864-1960).

Charlotte 'Cota' Hope (1820-1887), unmarried.

Frances Jane 'Fanny' Hope (1822-1880), unmarried.

Timeline

1807   John Hope born at Dalry House, 12 May
1808   Hope family living at 65 Queen Street
1815   Carterhaugh Ba' Game
1818   Birth of brother James
1822   Death of mother in childbirth
1824   John Hope enrols at Edinburgh University
1824   Foot-Ball Club founded at Dalry Park
1824   Hope family moves to 31 Moray Place
1826   John Hope leaves Edinburgh University
1826   John Hope travels to England and abroad
1827   John Hope becomes a Royal Archer
1829   John Hope becomes a Writer to the Signet
1829   John Hope travels around Europe for a year
1831   Foot-Ball Club moves to Greenhill Park
1832   John Hope begins to acquire property in Edinburgh
1833   Football Rules written down
1836   Last membership records of Foot-Ball Club
1836   Foot-Ball Club moves to Grove Park
1839   John Hope becomes an abstainer
1839   Death of sister Jane
1840   Death of uncle John
1841   Last written evidence of Foot-Ball Club
1842   Death of father James
1842   John Hope enters legal partnership with brother James
1844   Death of uncle Thomas Charles
1844   John Hope becomes head of family
1844-45 Marriage of three sisters
1847   British League of Juvenile Abstainers founded
1848   First country excursion of British League
1850   Marriage of brother James
1854   Hope's playground opens in Stockbridge
1854   Edinburgh Academy opens sports ground in Raeburn Place
1857   Edinburgh Academical Football Club founded
1858   John Hope elected Edinburgh Town Councillor
1860   Third Edinburgh Rifle Volunteers established
1863   Football Association founded in London
1864   Legal partnership with brother James dissolved
1867   Queen's Park FC founded in Glasgow, adopt Association rules
1870   First (unofficial) association football international

1871	First rugby football international, played in Edinburgh
1872	First official association football international
1873	Scottish Football Association founded
1874	Third ERV football team founded
1876	Third ERV founder members of Edinburgh FA
1889	John Hope steps down from Edinburgh Town Council
1890	John Hope establishes the Hope Trust
1893	John Hope dies at 31 Moray Place, 25 June
1899	Legal dispute over John Hope's will is resolved
1900	Rev Jamie's biography of John Hope published

Bibliography

1.   Primary Sources

The primary source for any research into The Foot-Ball Club is the Hope Papers, held by the National Records of Scotland. The overall reference for the archive is GD253, which extends to a vast number of files and in particular his correspondence. Much of this relates to wider business and family matters, and although it contains the odd gem it does not have particular relevance to John Hope's football activity.

The section numbered GD253/183 contains the Foot-Ball Club records which have been digitised and can be consulted as 'Virtual Volumes' on the computer terminals at New Register House in Edinburgh. Below is a summary of the papers which relate specifically to the Club.

GD253/183/1: Foot Ball Book
A handwritten lined notebook in pink marbled cover, 54 pages, containing (in order):
1825/26 membership list
1826/27 membership list
1827/28 membership list
1831 (summer) membership list
1831 expenses
1827/28 expenses
1826/27 expenses
1825/26 expenses
1824/25 membership list
1824/25 expenses

GD253/183/2: A list of the Football Club, April 15th 1831
This appears to be a duplicate of the 1831 membership list, but from April 15 with 39 members. Some spellings are different.

GD253/183/3: Pass Book, Mr John Hope, Football Club
1832/33 season accounts
1834 accounts

GD253/183/4: Foot Ball Book, John Hope
1831/32 accounts
1832/33 accounts

193

1833/34 accounts
Memo of agreement with John Girdwood, 5 Dec 1831, for use of Greenhill Park.

GD253/183/5
Miscellaneous club papers and receipts, 1825-1831

GD253/183/6
Miscellaneous club papers and receipts, 1832-1841
1836 membership list

GD253/183/7
Miscellaneous club papers, notably:
Set of six rules of football
Football memoranda with costs of playing the game
Undated membership lists

2.   Select bibliography of published works

Addison, W. Innes. *The Snell Exhibitions from the University of Glasgow to Balliol College, Oxford* (Glasgow: James MacLehose and Sons, 1901).
Alexander, Jack. *McCrae's Battalion, the story of the 16th Royal Scots.* (Edinburgh: Mainstream Publishing, 2003).
Allan, Robert. *A Manual of Mineralogy, Comprehending the More Recent Discoveries in the Mineral Kingdom* (Edinburgh: Longman, 1834).
Anderson, RD. *Education and Opportunity in Victorian Scotland. Schools and Universities* (Oxford: Clarendon Press, 1983).
Burnett, John. *Riot, Revelry and Rout: Sport in Lowland Scotland before 1860.* (East Linton: Tuckwell Press, 2000)
Burnett, John. *Sporting Scotland* (Edinburgh, National Museums of Scotland, 1995)
Christison, Robert. *The Life of Sir Robert Christison, Bart, Edited by his Sons.* Vol 1 (Edinburgh: William Blackwood and Sons, 1885).
Cockburn, Henry. *Memorials of His Time* (Edinburgh: A&C Black, 1856).
The Edinburgh Academical Football Club. *Centenary History* (Edinburgh: the club, 1958).
The Edinburgh Academical Club. *100 Years at Raeburn Place* (Edinburgh: the club, 1954)
The Edinburgh Academical Club. *The Edinburgh Academy Register 1824-1914* (Edinburgh: the club, 1914).

Fergusson, Alexander. *Chronicles of the Cumming Club* (Edinburgh: the club, 1887)

Glover, Julian. *Man of Iron. Thomas Telford and the Building of Britain* (London: Bloomsbury, 2017).

Grange Cricket Club. *Centenary of Ground* (Edinburgh: the club, 1972)

Grant, Sir Francis J. *The Faculty of Advocates in Scotland, 1532-1943, with genealogical notes.* (Edinburgh: Scottish Record Society, 1944).

Harvey, Adrian. *Football: The First Hundred Years, the Untold Story.* (Abingdon: Routledge, 2005)

Hutchinson, John. *The Football Industry* (Glasgow: Richard Drew, 1982)

Jamie, Rev. David, B.D. *John Hope, Philanthropist and Reformer* (Edinburgh: Andrew Elliot, 1900).

Jarvie, Grant and Walker, Graham. *Scottish Sport in the Making of the Nation* (Leicester University Press, 1994).

Lugton, Alan. *The Making of Hibernian* (Edinburgh: John Donald, 1995).

Mackenzie, Robert J. *Almond of Loretto: being the life and a selection of the letters of Hely Hutchinson Almond* (London: Archibald Constable and Co Ltd, 1905).

Magoun, Francis Peabody jun. History of Football from the Beginnings to 1871. (Bochum: *Kölner Anglistische Arbeiten, 31*, 1938).

Marshall, Rev. F. *Football, the Rugby Union Game* (London: Cassell and Company, 1892)

Mitchell, Andy. *First Elevens, the birth of international football* (the author, 2012)

Mitchell, Ann. *No More Corncraiks, Lord Moray's Feuars in Edinburgh's New Town* (Edinburgh: Scottish Cultural Press, 1998)

Mitchell, Ann. *The People of Calton Hill* (Edinburgh: Mercat Press, 1993)

Murray, David. *Memories of the Old College of Glasgow* (Glasgow: Jackson, Wylie & Co, 1927)

Old Edinburgh Club. *Book of the Old Edinburgh Club* (published since 1908).

Old Rugbeian Society. *The Origin of Rugby Football; report (with appendices) of the sub-committee of the Old Rugbeian Society appointed in July 1895* (Rugby: AJ Lawrence, 1897).

Paul, James Balfour. *The History of the Royal Company of Archers: the Queen's Bodyguard for Scotland* (Edinburgh: William Blackwood and Sons, 1875).

Robbie, J Cameron. *The Chronicle of the Royal Burgess Golfing Society of Edinburgh 1735-1935* (Edinburgh: Morrison & Gibb, 1936).

Rodger, Richard. *The Transformation of Edinburgh: Land, Property and Trust in the Nineteenth Century* (Cambridge University Press, 2001).

Rogers, Charles. *History of St Andrews* (St Andrews: A&C Black, 1849).

Ross, William C.A. *The Royal High School* (Edinburgh: Oliver and Boyd, 1934).

Scott, Walter. *The Lifting of the Banner*, in Scott, Walter and Hogg, James, *The Ettricke Garland* (Edinburgh: James Ballantyne, 1815).

Shearman, Montague. *Athletics and Football* (London: Longmans, Green & Co, 1887).

Shepherd, Thomas H. *Modern Athens, displayed in a series of views; or, Edinburgh in the Nineteenth Century* (London: Jones & Co, 1829).

Smith, Charles J. *Historic South Edinburgh* (Haddington: Charles Skilton Ltd, 1978).

Society of Writers to Her Majesty's Signet. *A History of the Society* (Edinburgh: T&A Constable, 1890).

Speculative Society. *A History of the Speculative Society 1764-1904* (Edinburgh: the society, 1905).

Stephen, William. *History of the Queen's City of Edinburgh Rifle Volunteer Brigade* (Edinburgh: William Blackwood and Sons, 1881).

Steven, William. *The History of the High School of Edinburgh* (Edinburgh: Maclachlan & Stewart, 1849).

Thorburn, A.M.C. (Sandy). *The Scottish Rugby Union, Official History.* (Edinburgh: William Collins, 1985).

Trotter, James J. *The Royal High School, Edinburgh* (London: Sir Isaac Pitman & Sons, 1911).

3.   Online and digital resources

Many nineteenth century newspapers, periodicals and books have been digitised and can be consulted online, often without cost. The range of resources continues to grow at a great pace, so it would be pointless to try and list them all, but the authors are particularly grateful to the following sites.

The National Library of Scotland (www.nls.uk/digital-resources) has digitised street directories, maps and many other invaluable resources. It also offers access to a large number of 19th century newspapers and periodicals. The rapidly expanding British Newspaper Archive (www.britishnewspaperarchive.com) is an invaluable source of contemporary material. A subscription service, it includes sporting papers such as *Bell's Life in London,* and a range of Edinburgh newspapers including the *Caledonian Mercury* and *The Scotsman.*

We consulted various genealogical websites such as Ancestry (www.ancestry.co.uk), ScotlandsPeople (www.scotlandspeople.gov.uk)

and FindMyPast (www.findmypast.co.uk) which made it possible to follow the lives of individual members, with records including births, deaths, census returns and other databases. Some universities and schools have searchable archives of their students and former pupils, notably Edinburgh University (collections.ed.ac.uk/alumni/).

And finally, there are many superb sporting historical websites which never cease to amaze us with the range and quality of their output, often on a non-commercial basis. A prime example is Athlos (www.athletics-archive.com) which has digitised a number of rare early athletics books, as well as offering a platform for authors to publish original research – such as Peter Radford's study of *The Six-Feet Club*.

4.   Periodicals and manuscripts

Campbell, David, W.S. *Draft Memo of Information respecting the late John Hope Esq WS* (hand-written manuscript, 1894; GD253/14/5).
Finlayson, C.P. 'Illustrations of Games by a Seventeenth Century Edinburgh Student', *Scottish Historical Review*, No 123 (April 1958).
Gordon, Mrs. 'Sortes Scottianae', The *Metropolitan Magazine*, Vols XLV & XLVI (March, May & June 1846).
Hutchinson, John. 'Football in Edinburgh from 1800', *Soccer History*, 15, (Spring 2007), 24-29.
Hutchinson, John. 'Sport, Education and Philanthropy in Nineteenth-century Edinburgh: The Emergence of Modern Forms of Football', *Sport in History*, 28, 4, (December 2008), 547-565.
Hutchinson, John and Mitchell, Andy. 'John Hope, the Foot-Ball Club of 1824 and its sporting legacy', *Soccer & Society*, Vol 19, No 1 (2018), 75-88.
Tranter, Dr Neil. 'The First Football Club?', *International Journal of the History of Sport*, Vol 10, No 1 (April 1993), 104-107.

Index

201

Made in the USA
Lexington, KY
22 April 2018